ALLIANCE
WITHOUT
ALLIES

The Mythology of Progress
in Latin America

Víctor Alba

ALLIANCE
WITHOUT
ALLIES

The Mythology
of Progress
in Latin America

FREDERICK A. PRAEGER, *Publishers*
New York · Washington · London

FREDERICK A. PRAEGER, PUBLISHERS
111 Fourth Avenue, New York 3, N.Y., U.S.A.
77–79 Charlotte Street, London W.1, England

Published in the United States of America in 1965 by
Frederick A. Praeger, Inc., Publishers

First published in Mexico in 1964 under the title
Parásitos, mitos y sordomudos
by Centro de Estudios y Documentatión Sociales

Translated by John Pearson

English translation © 1965 by Frederick A. Praeger, Inc.

Library of Congress Catalog Card Number: 65–18076

Printed in the United States of America

AUTHOR'S NOTE

THIS book is not intended to be a factual report. It is taken for granted that the reader understands the formal meaning of the Alliance for Progress, that he knows how it was born, and that he has some familiarity with the statistics on investments, loans, completed projects, etc.

Nor is it an academic book. It includes, therefore, few footnotes, quotations, or references. The abundance of erudite works on the Alliance relieves the author of the need to accumulate data, cite authorities, or otherwise demonstrate that he knows the subject.

This is a political book, a passionate book—a polemic, if you will. Its purpose, I repeat, is not to rehearse facts; it is to punch and kick the many people who deserve it. Their time has come.

We have become accustomed to studies of Latin America that present a mass of data and statistics (frequently inaccurate—by design or accident), studies that, demonstrating a vast store of technical vocabulary, analyze the composition of Latin American social groups and even produce "Gallup polls" of public opinion. All this can be useful in forming ideas about Latin America, in telling about it, and in proving that one understands sociology and economics. But it has little relevance for political evaluation.

Latin America is not an area to be handled with kid gloves. You have to grab it with your bare hands, feel its texture against your skin, reject tentative pokings and proddings, samplings and statistics, and then live the subject completely. Only then can you understand its total reality, and not just aspects of it, which, because they are only partial, give a distorted view and lead to distorted conclusions.

How can we make a "scientific" or "statistical" study of, for instance, such potent but imponderable factors of life as the ties of friendship and family among leaders of democratic movements and among the oligarchy? How can we measure the amount and extent of ambition, of depth of conviction, and of the sense of inferiority that are involved in the phenomenon of the military *coup d'état?* In the area of student action, how can we properly weigh how much is the result of a sense of mission and how much is attributable to the influence of demagogy and to the time-honored student practice of "raising Cain"? How can we tell to what extent the student groups that are the most vociferous, and the intellectuals who are most ready to sign protest petitions, are representative of the feelings of students and intellectuals as a whole?

Facts have often given the lie to assumptions that once appeared infallible. When President Kennedy visited a number of Latin American nations, the governments marshaled teachers, bureaucrats, union memberships, and students to provide suitably respectful welcoming demonstrations. But everywhere, the governments themselves were astonished at the warmth of his welcome; the streets were filled with hundreds of thousands of people whom no one—not even the United States embassies—had expected to turn out. It may be valid to talk about widespread anti-Yankee sentiment on the basis of what is published in the press, shouted by the students, written by the intellectuals, and discussed by the middle class—in short, as far as articulate public opinion is concerned—but it is not valid in terms of popular feeling.

In this book, many matters will be covered that have nothing at all to do with economic or sociological studies of Latin America, matters that Latin Americans do not discuss through misguided diffidence or extreme nationalism, and from which the students also shy away through fear of being called "anti-Latin Americans," "superior," or "Yankee imperialists." Since I am not victim to these fears, I can and must speak of these matters, precisely because they are disagreeable and because without considering them, one cannot reach any true understanding of Latin America.

I do not eavesdrop under the desks of Latin American generals and government ministers; I know no more about the area than any literate person who reads the newspapers regularly. Why, then, is my view so different from the views of North American experts and Latin American politicians, economists, and intellectuals? Perhaps the answer is that I do not try to make the reader happy, to coddle prejudices, soothe consciences, or justify official policies.

Because I point out these truths and talk about the facts of corruption, inefficiency, and unbridled egotism, it will surely be said that I am slandering Latin America. But let us have done with such evasions. None of the persons or institutions who will be attacked truly represents Latin America. Even if one smothered them with ridicule or buried them in their own cowardice and nastiness, the essence of Latin America would not be changed in the slightest.

Let us keep in mind the old question of which a physician swears to serve, his patient or his hospital. I do not promise to defend the hospital but rather to serve the patient. For me, governments, states, nations, territories, or judicial systems count for very little in comparison with individual citizens. Better the nation serve its citizens than the citizens the nation. My loyalty is not to theoretical forms but to men of flesh and blood.

Mexico City

CONTENTS

ALLIANCE
WITHOUT
ALLIES

1

NOTES FOR A TREATISE ON PARASITOLOGY

Pauperization

EVERYONE talks about progress, economic development, industrialization. But no one says that there is no progress, that Latin America is moving backward—or toward the poorhouse. This fact can be learned more readily from visits to country villages and urban shanty towns than from statistics, but the statistics are clear.

The economic growth of Latin America is stalled because the growth rate of the gross national product, which was close to 6 per cent annually in the period immediately after World War II, fell below 2.5 per cent for the year 1963. At the same time, the annual rate of population growth has reached almost 3 per cent. The result is that the per capita rate of increase in production, which dropped to only 1 per cent in recent years, showed no increase at all in 1963.

Since 1938, the volume of world trade has doubled, but the exports of Latin American countries have increased by barely 70 per cent (by only 40 per cent if we exclude petroleum). Where Latin America once accounted for 7–8 per cent of world trade, it now accounts for only 6.5 per cent. The situation is aggravated by the decline of world prices for Latin American exports over the last decade. If we take the years 1954 and 1955 as a basis, it can be seen that, while the volume of exports increased 38 per cent, export earnings rose only 12 per cent. Declining prices thus canceled out two-thirds of the increase in the volume of exports.

Finally, in the five years from 1955–60, real income per capita rose only an average of 0.8 per cent annually. In 1961, a year in which world prices appeared to achieve some degree of stability, the increase in real income per capita was 2 per cent, but for 1962, the U.N. Economic Commission for Latin America (ECLA) estimated a rise of only 0.3 per cent.[1]

From 1950 to 1961, Latin America received a total of $23.0 billion in public and private capital. Against this figure, $13.4 billion left the area in the form of interest, profits, and dividends (some exported illegally by Latin Americans and some more or less legally by foreign investors). During the same period, the drop in prices for raw materials brought a reduction in income of $10.1 billion.[2] Thus, in eleven years, Latin America had a net loss of $500 million.

This fact, whether expressed in Marxist terms, Keynesian terms, ECLA terms, or theosophical terms, may be reduced to a single, clear point: Latin America is moving backward.

One-fourth of the foreign-aid budget presented by President Johnson for the 1964–65 fiscal year was earmarked for Latin America. This came to $2.59 per Latin American. In 1960, before the beginning of the Alliance for Progress, United States foreign aid amounted to $.59 for each Latin American.[3]

However, neither this assistance nor the figures cited come even close to achieving the objective of the Alliance, which is an annual income growth rate of 2.5 per cent.

With four years now gone by, with many millions spent, with hospitals and schools built by the dozens, with thousands of miles of highways constructed, with credits scattered throughout the continent, the existence of Latin Americans today is worse than it was five or ten or fifteen years ago.

[1] "Panorama de América Latina a través de la Alianza para el Progreso," *Comercio Exterior* (Mexico City), November, 1963.

[2] Raúl Prebisch, as quoted in *The New Leader* (New York), March 30, 1964, p. 6.

[3] *The New Republic* (Washington), April 4, 1964, p. 4.

The Forgotten Ones

It is not evident to the tourist or the visiting expert that the Latin Americans' existence becomes more miserable every day. The people they see in the streets seem prosperous; every time they come, their friends have a new car; the hotels appear more luxurious; the city streets are more modern; the highways to the beaches are wider; the universities admit more and more students. . . .

All this is true. Every year, a larger number of Latin Americans consider themselves members of the middle classes—the small- and medium-sized businessmen, professional people, intellectuals, skilled workers, civil servants. And every year, these middle-class groups live a little better.

But the hard fact remains that the rates of population increase and economic growth are virtually equal, and so balance each other out, and that, therefore, there is no real rise in per capita income.

How then were those $500 million lost, and what is the source of the millions of dollars required each year to permit an ever-increasing middle class to improve its living standards—to spend more.

These dollars could come from only one of two sources: those who have more than the middle class, or those who have less than the middle class.

Very well. Each year, there is an increase in the value of Latin American deposits in banks in Switzerland and other foreign countries. These deposits belong not to the working or peasant classes or even to the middle class. The people who export more and more capital each year are members of the *haute bourgeoisie* and the landowning oligarchy. Then, it is not those who have more than the middle class who provide those $500 million, as well as the millions required to improve the living standards of the inter-mediate groups.

If it is not those who have more, then it must of necessity be those who have less.

Economists can juggle the figures with as many numbers games as they wish and can give complex names to the various aspects of this situation, but the fact is undeniable. The people who pay for the progress of a minority of Latin Americans, and who pay for the losses, whatever their cause, of the Latin American economy, and who provide all the exported capital, are not those who are living better than ever before or those who themselves export the capital. They are the people whose life today is worse than it was ten or fifteen years ago. It is worse because they must pay for a better life for certain small groups.

Luis Buñuel made a widely acclaimed film about the adolescents of Mexico City's slums. He called it *Los Olvidados—The Forgotten Ones—*a title that lost its bite when shown to U.S. audiences as *The Young and the Damned.* A campaign of public vilification was unleashed against the director, who was accused of taking delight in exhibiting the worst side of the city. An international prize saved Buñuel from becoming a victim of nationalists who were disturbed more by the sight of "los olvidados" on the screen than by the fact that the "olvidados" actually existed.

Buñuel's "forgotten ones"—forgotten by the middle classes, by the professional classes, by the students, by the *petite* and *haute bourgeoisie,* by the big landowners, by the professional military saviors of the fatherland, by the no less professional intellectuals who regularly sign manifestoes, by economic planners and militant labor leaders—it is these forgotten ones who are paying for the well-being of the military, the *bourgeoisie,* the landowners, the professionals, the intellectuals, the students, the skilled workers.

And probably that is why they go on being forgotten.

The Middle Classes

"Tell me whom you walk with and I'll tell you who you are," says an old proverb. In social matters, this might be changed to: "Tell me whom you support and I'll tell you how you live."

Later in this work we shall discuss the landholding oligarchy and its near neighbor, Latin American capitalism. First, however, let us try to analyze the ever-growing and ever-prospering middle-class groups.

Latin America has had a middle class for a very long time. It was formed by artisans and merchants during the struggle for independence from Spain. From their ranks came the men who, in the nineteenth century, fought to democratize political structures (without, however, doing anything to alter social structures). These liberals of the last century became the democratic leftists or nationalist revolutionaries of this century. While the middle class has steadily improved its way of life over the last forty or fifty years, this process has been especially rapid since World War II.

It is very difficult to measure the size of this group, but these figures will give an approximate picture:

The middle class constitutes 13 per cent of the total population in Bolivia, 15 per cent in Brazil, 17 per cent in Chile, 40 per cent in Argentina, and 31 per cent in Uruguay. In none of these countries does the upper class make up more than 2 per cent. The rest of the population is categorized as the lower class.[4]

Although there are innumerable subdivisions of the middle class, certain common denominators do exist that permit a general characterization:

1. The middle class is essentially urban, although in certain countries a rural middle class has begun to emerge.

2. It believes that industrialization is the fundamental method of solving great national problems.

3. Although it supports public education, it insists more and more, in practice, on promoting advanced cultural studies and professional education.

4. It is nationalistic, and its nationalism often takes the form of protectionism and, at times, of anti-U.S. attitudes.

5. It not only accepts the existence of labor unions and social legislation, but regards both as beneficial for national development.

6. It supports, in general, the concept of agrarian reform as a means of strengthening the political foundations of democracy and of enlarging internal markets for industry.

7. It looks with greater favor on international investments from public sources than it does on private investment, of which it is customarily suspicious.

8. It is not opposed to nationalization or state operation of large industries, mineral resources, or public services.

9. It supports, in general, economic intervention by the state, and would welcome increased control of the economy; it also supports state investment for industrialization.

10. While it distrusts the army, from which it continually fears

[4] Carlos M. Rama, *Las clases sociales en el Uruguay* (Montevideo, 1960), pp. 36 and 174.

coups d'état, elements of the middle class are now found in the new generation of the military.

11. It shows interest in Soviet methods of development, an interest that sometimes makes it receptive to Communist propaganda, especially in international relations.

12. Politically, it is liberal, democratic, to a large extent Catholic (which is significant in view of the new attitudes adopted by sectors of the Church in some Latin American countries, and socialist in its leanings.

13. It is composed in large measure of immigrants who, soon after their arrival, adopt the most radically nationalistic attitudes.[5]

This description might have fitted the middle class ten years ago. At that time, it was believed to be a potent factor for change and democratization. An indication of how strong this belief was may be found in the following, written by the author in 1955:

> This middle class, hardly born before World War II, remained in its infancy for many years because industrialization was slow and limited. It came to adolescence with the war and as a result of the impetus the war gave to the process of industrialization. Now it is in its young manhood, that time of life when it must make lasting decisions and choose the path it wishes to follow.
>
> It has the ability to make a choice—to become either an ordinary vulgar bourgeoisie or, in time, a creative social class whose interests coincide with those of society in general. . . .
>
> Like any other class, the middle class has its own interests. But it is supremely important that the middle class seize the present opportunity of a period when its interests parallel those of society in general, and when its momentum still imparts a dynamism and idealism, to establish the conditions, limits, and essential directions that will determine Latin America's future development and ensure that the means used to attain this goal always have a direct benefit on the great mass of the continent's inhabitants, and never curtail their liberties or endanger the little that survives of the feeling of community and brotherhood.[6]

[5] For a more detailed study of the intermediate groups, see: John J. Johnson, *Political Change in Latin America* (Stanford, 1958); *Materiales para el estudio de la clase media en la América Latina,* ed. Theo R. Crevenna (Washington, D.C., 1950–51); and Alba, "The Latin American Style and the New Social Forces," in *Latin American Issues: Essays and Comments,* ed. Albert O. Hirschman, New York, 1961.

[6] Reprinted in Alba, *Los subamericanos* (Mexico City, 1964), pp. 23–24.

After ten years, one can no longer harbor such hopes. Day by day, the middle class becomes less and less a factor of social change and more and more a part of the vast parasitology of Latin America.

Public Opinion and the Submerged Masses

In order to understand how this rapid disenchantment is possible, how the middle class abandoned its mission, one must try to understand what Latin American society really is. Neither a Marxist model nor a sociological model—the first divided rigidly into classes, the second wholly divorced from reality—can serve the purpose. Both of them are in large part responsible for the fact that when we speak of Latin America, we refer to a continent which gives no indication of its true nature.

Until now, we have spoken of the working class, the peasants, the middle class as though they were classes in the European sense of the word. Such is not the case. In Latin America, when one says "proletariat," one means a minority of the industrial workers; when one says "peasantry," one means the leaders of peasant organizations or a thin stratum of rural workers who possess a certain consciousness of their own character; when one says "middle class," one refers to groups of professionals, intellectuals, students, civil servants, and certain businessmen, since the rest of the middle class—the less prosperous sector—has no consciousness of belonging to it, or else—as in the case of the more prosperous sector—allies itself or allows itself to be carried along with the landowning oligarchy.

Latin American society, rather than being divided into traditional classes, is split into two great sectors: public opinion and the submerged and sunken masses, the "forgotten ones" whom we mentioned earlier. For the sake of brevity, these submerged masses are referred to generally as *"el pueblo,"* "the people."

These dividing lines were not drawn freehand; they correspond to economic realities. An economist as little given to sociological formulations as Raúl Prebisch, the Director of ECLA when that agency was obsessed with commercial terminology, described those realities in this way:

While 50 per cent of the population accounts for approximately two-tenths of the total consumption, at the other extreme of the distributive scale, 5 per cent of the inhabitants enjoy almost three-tenths of the total, according to estimates.

That upper 5 per cent has an average level of consumption per family 15 times greater than that of the 50 per cent who constitute the lower strata. If that figure were reduced to 11 times, and the consumption saved were channeled into increased investments, the annual growth rate of per capita income could rise from 1 to 3 per cent. And if the figure were reduced to 9 times, the growth rate could rise to 4 per cent or even higher, depending on the political possibilities of this operation and the ability of each country to put it into practice.[7]

Public opinion (to define it in some way) consists of those who are regular readers of the press and amounts to no more than 10, in some countries 15, per cent of the population. These are the more or less informed persons with a certain awareness of national problems and with concrete aims; they are politically active, they discuss issues and vote with an idea of what they are voting for. They keep abreast of world events. These, also, are the people whose economic situation has improved in the last few decades, who feel most keenly the pull of nationalism, who are most impatient for progress, most anti-Yankee, and who, until recently, evidenced the greatest desire for social change.

Of course, a tiny minority of public opinion does not want social change—the oligarchy and its political adherents, the old-line military men and the old-style businessmen. This group amounts to no more than 1–3 per cent of the population.

In spite of differences over aims and methods, all the sectors of public opinion possess certain features in common that bind them together: They are indifferent to the submerged masses; they consider themselves to be representative of the nation as a whole; they live (often unconsciously) at the expense of the masses; and they exist as parasites on the body of the nation so that improvement in their standard of living has been possible, thus far, only through lowering the living standards of the masses, or, at best, by retarding improvement in the masses' condition.

[7] Raúl Prebisch, *Hacia una dinámica del desarrollo latinoamericano* (Mexico City, 1963), pp. 5–6.

To examine this phenomenon more deeply, it is not necessary to immerse ourselves in endless statistics. The simple statistics already presented will suffice to indicate that—except occasionally in a few countries—the increase of population in Latin America is not offset by a corresponding rise in productivity. At the same time, the public-opinion sector becomes more numerous and its standard of living continues to improve; more and more people live better and better. But if the rise in productivity can hardly keep up with the increase of population, what can be the source of the means that enable a growing segment of society to continue to improve its living standards? Any housewife can give the answer: The source must be the masses, whose existence grows worse in exact ratio to the betterment in the living standards of the public-opinion sector.

The popular political movements have been eager to adopt these submerged masses—peasants, small merchants, Indians, unskilled labor, floating urban populations—who together form the 85–90 per cent of the population which reads no newspapers, has no concept of its interests and hardly any of its aspirations, which has resigned itself to its condition, and which is not aware of its exploitation by the privileged public-opinion sector. But since the cultural imperative dictates that the supporters of the popular parties must come from the public-opinion sector and since this group views the masses with indifference—if not with an almost racist contempt—the popular parties have found themselves isolated from the masses. Except in Mexico and Venezuela, where special circumstances apply, the submerged masses continue to be submerged, even where the popular movements have achieved control of the government. Therefore, the middle groups of society have lost their power (or desire) to produce social change.

Had the military not taken power in Bolivia, this country could also be mentioned along with Mexico and Venezuela. But the generals cannot again submerge the Bolivian masses, who were aroused for all time by the revolution of 1952.

By saying this, I do not wish to deify the *pueblo,* as the workers were deified at one point of history. I do not attribute to them virtues they do not have. When the masses achieve the good life, they will be just as much pigs as those who already have achieved it. Indeed, even now, in their misery, the masses have their own share of viciousness and malice. However, if all are pigs equally, that is less unjust than if some are very rich pigs and some very poor pigs. Less unjust and less explosive.

In any event, it is well to recall here something that Unamuno wrote: "Those who make a noise in the course of history are rained up from the immense mass of silent humanity. The intra-historical, silent, and continuous life, like the very bottom of the ocean, is the nourishment of progress."[8]

What determines the existence of those submerged masses is not their cultural level or their ethnic composition. It is rather, the existence of the oligarchy, which, in order to govern, creates a society (not, certainly, by conscious effort, but rather by spontaneous evolution) in which the opportunity to influence decision-making is restricted to a very small percentage of the population.

There is one important aspect of Latin American society that is hardly ever discussed—not out of modesty, but due to the fact that it seems so obvious that no one stops to consider it. This is the fact that the urban population, which has tripled, and in some cases quintupled, over the last few decades, continues to have its roots in the country. In spite of material differences between the city and the country, especially in the comforts of life, the two worlds are much closer in Latin America than they are in the industrial nations. This close relationship explains certain aspects of the Latin American economy, for instance, the instability of the labor force and its consequent lack of skills, despite the outstanding ability of the Spanish-American worker to adapt himself to any task. It can explain, on the other hand, the parasitism of the metropolitan areas, where only a very small proportion of the population actively contributes to the economy—because the peasant, accustomed to the lowest standard of living, can survive in the city despite the discouraging conditions that confront him. It explains, also, the persistence of personalism in political movements and trade unions. Finally, it explains why economic crises, galloping inflation, unemployment, and other financial disasters have less serious repercussions than they would have elsewhere, because of the ease with which the unemployed worker may return to his village and the calmness with which the merchant or small businessman views the fortunes of his enterprise. He knows

[8] Miguel de Unamuno, *Ensayos* (Madrid, 1945), I, 41–42.

that he has a safe haven in the country, where there are family resources and where he has invested the first profits of his business ventures in the city.

What, then, is Latin American society? It is not feudal in the strict sense, since there is no superior authority—no sovereign—nor do the lower authorities retain local sovereignty. Nevertheless, the systems of land tenure retain many features of feudalism, especially in regard to the living conditions of the peasants.

One might call it a society of enlightened despotism, such as that of the eighteenth century, except that there is no single sovereign from whom all power emanates. But the masses today, like those of the eighteenth century, support a minority group which does not acknowledge that they possess any meaningful rights.

One might also compare Latin American society with that of the Soviets in the sense that power is exercised by a caste (in the U.S.S.R., the bureaucrats; in Latin America, the landholders) that subjects the entire nation to its control. But in the U.S.S.R., the dominant caste controls the means of production collectively, whereas in Latin America, the landholding caste as individuals possesses the fundamental means of production—the land.

In the last analysis, the true Latin American condition may best be described as a landholding oligarchy or oligarchic landholding society (and in some countries a banking-landholding oligarchy).

Therefore, although through habit we may say that this society is feudal, we do not mean to describe the society as a whole in these terms, but merely the peasant's position in it.

In its sum and substance, then, Latin American society is a carryover from the monarchical society of the eighteenth century, adapted to the requirements of the twentieth in order to survive therein. And this adaptation, as we shall see, is truly a work of art.

Half of the Population

Half of these submerged people and probably 33–40 per cent of the public-opinion group consists of young persons—less than fifteen, sixteen, or seventeen years old (depending on the country).

The idea is widely held that Latin American youth is revolutionary, Castroite, Communist, and that it presents a real danger

—although no one can specify what sort of danger it is or whom it threatens. But one cannot speak of "youth" in general. There is the youth of the submerged group and the youth of the public-opinion group. There is the youth that is just beginning to see the world and other people as they are, and there is the youth that is beginning to think about getting married and earning a living.

In many Latin American countries, a boy is thought to be a young man at an age when, in Anglo-Saxon societies, he would be considered barely a teen-ager. This is not true everywhere, however. In rural areas, there is hardly any difference between the young and the old, while in the cities, the difference is most apparent. Latin American society offers very few prospects for the young. It is true that young persons can rise quickly, and especially under the democratic system, they can occupy very responsible positions. Nevertheless, a paradoxical situation exists: Mature individuals are called "unfit" and discarded in the name of youth; but many others, certainly old, are not replaced and do retain managerial positions well beyond their actual capabilities.

As far as the matter of well-being is concerned, as opposed to social betterment, Latin American society is very stingy. The rural youth cannot improve his situation vis-à-vis that of his parents. If he goes to the city, even though he may live in surroundings that appear more interesting to him, he will suffer psychological dislocations, and economically he will have few opportunities to rise, living as he will in one of the shanty towns that surround the great urban centers. The true city youths do not speak the same language as those from the country who live in the poor slum areas. They know that these country boys exist, and they protest about their misery, but they feel no bond of humanity with them. As a result, the two groups are not unified in their struggle.

The young, particularly the young of the urban middle class, make up the most dynamic and, at the same time, the most troublesome segment of Latin American society.

The city youth are young, in the political sense of the word, for only a brief period—from the time they enter the university or preparatory school until the last two years of their academic career. Then, all of them—even those who have gone through the experience of guerrilla and terrorist activity—begin to think about a profession and a job and marriage. At that time, although they do not abandon their convictions, assuming that these represented something more than a sentimental reflex, they do abandon active expression of these convictions.

The societies in which the youth of Latin America live are engulfed in tedium. In cities with millions of inhabitants, where anyone who is anyone knows everyone else who is anyone, there is a closed horizon and a sort of fatuous, defensive nationalism. A U.S. observer has accurately dissected the problem:

The rebellion of Latin American youth begins with a revolt against the vision of their own future as represented by their parents and their home. Will they really end up like their parents? Undoubtedly, one of the greatest intellectual transgressions of Latin American youth is their stubborn refusal to consider that it would be more interesting to take as a subject for their writings, films, pictures, and studies the country people about whom they know nothing, rather than concentrate on the middle class from which they came. One needs the perspective of distance and a sense of irony to study how the marriage ends with the mother, how she turns herself into a fool to please her husband; or how money weighs down the husband without softening him, how hard he fights to be able to flick his cigarette ashes on those beneath him (this is what he calls power), how he never is quite able to rid himself of his sense of inadequacy, which everyone shares, and how he tries to hide his inadequacy under a cloak of bravado, vulgarity, and ostentation.[9]

A novelist has described the surroundings in which urban youth is formed—and deformed:

We had some rich friends—the Gómez family—who used to invite us to visit them in the evening. They lived in a house that had a purple, seigniorial spirit, old, and austere. Everything there was solemn. The head of the family had been a minister of state, and he was a man of dyspeptic mien, dry, assertive, and dogmatic; he must have had the soul of a hangman. Tall, stoop-shouldered, slow of movement, grotesquely fleshy, he devoted himself to the writing of history which no one read, which no one cared about, from which no one could obtain more than a dense, academic, leaden boredom. Every thirty or so of these pages brought him some peculiar distinc-

[9] Keith Botsford, "Masas y mesías," *Panoramas* (Mexico City), November–December, 1964. The youth of Latin America has been studied very little and Botsford's analysis is one of the most acute and just interpretations of that subject. For that reason, with the author's permission, I reproduce it at length.

tion, or foreign decoration, or one more academic degree. In his sons, he stimulated self-pride, vanity, contempt, elementary courage, and xenophobic outrage, which he believed to be patriotism. This man appeared to us to be the representative of something rotten in the national life, and we hated him cordially.[10]

The children of Gómez are educated in an atmosphere of the nineteenth-century provincial *bourgeoisie,* yet without that century's sense of bourgeois ethics.

During this brief period, this atmosphere is a stagnant pool of blessings enhanced by the Church, servants, and a comforting sense of privilege. But at fifteen, the girl enters her mother's world, and immediately all her mother's lies overwhelm her. She discovers that she lives in a world of inadequate men, who must learn to make their sexual superiority felt and that she must adapt herself to this game, abandoning her intelligence while gaining nothing in return, not even the satisfaction of love, since the Latin lover makes love with words while posing before the mirror, not as though his feelings were directed to a creature of flesh and blood. And as his sister protects her virginity, the boy goes to school (private, naturally) and receives strictly classical instruction, which has absolutely nothing to do with the world around him. He is taught the rules of rhetoric, but not how to write a simple sentence. He is taught to deal in abstractions and discussions but never to open his eyes and discover the world around him. In the university, he can adopt a posture of revolt without any effort or discomfort whatsoever; it is a revolt as genuine as that of the spoiled first-grader in the United States. He fights imaginary revolutions in the lecture hall, the film club, or the student fraternity; his professor will usually be willing to lend himself to this game since it is easier than teaching. Today in the university, the young student discovers that not only are learning, political regimes, and currency subject to political fluctuations, but that even the language can lose its meaning. The students are offered two languages, one colloquial, which they speak, the other cultured, in which it is supposed that they must think. . . . The greatest imaginable load for a young man who is eager to explore the new realms of thought of this century is to oblige him to read, think, reason, and write in the manner of the journalists, essayists, and politicians of Latin America, in a voice that is not his and that, moreover, cannot even remotely express the reality which surrounds them all. Nevertheless, after he

[10] Eduardo Mallea, *La bahía del silencio* (Buenos Aires, 1960).

has graduated with honors, defrauded by his professors and his training, the young man's brain is more than equal to the tasks that await it upon being faced with the second of the great Latin American dilemmas: "What shall I do with myself?" Fortunately, he lives in a society in which this decision can be postponed forever. He will always have leisure to devote to revolutions, since, however much society demands of him, it will never absorb all his spirit or all his energy. He can be a lawyer in the morning, a politician at noon, a good bourgeois during luncheon, then take his siesta, devote himself to journalism during the afternoon, teach in the evening, and plan coups at night, without ever changing his rhythm.

The moment he enters the real life of his country, all his actions and thoughts become political. And as he once reacted against his home, so now he reacts energetically against the spectacle called the democratic process. Just as he does not want his future to be like that of his parents, neither does he wish to be represented by the current political leader, with his waving locks and protruding stomach, who wears dark glasses into the darkest night clubs and refuses to see anything that does not enhance his own importance.

This reaction of the young against "democratic" politics is universal and parallels the growth of political consciousness among urban youth.

In the prerevolutionary regimes in Latin America, there are two types of frauds, who constitute the greatest prizes in the game of future revolutions, both sufficient to instill in the young a repugnance for politics: those who have risen through the school of hard knocks, bribing the police and corrupting union officials, and those who are the great liberals of the old school. In general, the young prefer the first type to the second, those who forthrightly steal the people's money to the men who pervert language and thought, but they hate both. Furthermore, given the limited size of Latin American societies, politicians cannot conceal themselves from public view. Every young person quickly comes to understand how political matters are negotiated. Colonel A calls Colonel B and says: "My esteemed colleague, I have 4 tanks, 21 machine guns, and 321 men. You have 1 tank, 4 rifles, and 62 men. Are we going to avoid bloodshed?" In the game of politics, there are advances and retreats, and no one loses anything, except that it is hard to lose, even if just momentarily, the prospect of dipping one's hands into the public treasury.

Along with these revulsions come the failures:

The greatest failing in Latin America is not the lack of economic development, although that is very great, but rather the lack of cultural development. The first affects the whole population equally, while the second is the special problem of the young. As the young become adults, what limits their usefulness is not an absence of capital, but rather the lack of habits of thought, of independence of judgment, and of an understanding of reality. . . .

In the conscience of the young everywhere, there is a secret ambition. In Latin America this ambition, in most cases, is to modify living conditions, not only for the person who has this ambition, but for all the rest, as well. A messianic spirit flows in the depths of those nations which isolate their individual citizens in political, economic, and cultural deserts. On the sand washed by the sea, a single footprint takes on extraordinary form and importance. The same thing occurs with the young: Their contribution, however small it may be, is noticed and their ascent is then so rapid that the individual concerned necessarily exaggerates his own importance. If one single work a notch above mediocrity is enough to mark a young man for his entire life, what incentive is there for him to improve upon his earlier feat? Where there are no true standards of excellence—except those imported from other areas, and it would not be fair to measure the local product by them—who will criticize and dispute what is sanctified by society and by the local need for satisfaction.[11]

This urban youth, all things considered, is still the level of society which finds itself emotionally closest to the great submerged mass, or at least to that level of the submerged mass that it can reach with some effort.

But it is also the level which customarily is in daily contact with the oligarchy and which, by virtue of this daily exposure, forgets that the oligarchy exists, forgets above all that the oligarchy is a distinctive structure—the most uncharacteristic and peculiar social group in Latin American society.

The Oligarchy

The word that will appear most frequently in this work is "oligarchy." It is not merely a rhetorical term. The oligarchy exists.

[11] Botsford, *op. cit.*

Because it is less possible every day in industrialized and more or less democratic countries to speak of abstract concepts, such as class, the *bourgeoisie,* the proletariat, many people believe that, in countries whose structure is anachronistic, when one speaks of oligarchy, one is using a term that has no relation to reality, that is an abstraction. And because the oligarchy has often been a subject for demagogues and Marxists, many think that it has no existence except as a demagogic or Marxist slogan. But in Latin America, the oligarchies are not abstractions, but daily realities that can be discussed in terms of family names and square miles of landholdings.

We Latin Americans like to look for scapegoats. The oligarchy has skillfully encouraged this weakness, by which it distracts attention from the reality of its own existence. When we speak of the oligarchy, we are not attempting here to find a new scapegoat; on the contrary, we want to eliminate the existing ones so that reality can be discovered. And the reality in this case is the existence of the oligarchy.

The oligarchy is something so concrete that in every Latin American city one can point out the building where the oligarchs meet: the Jockey Club, the Club Nacional or the Casino.

What is the oligarchy? It consists of the great landowners—the *"latifundistas"*—their political and military henchmen, and their financial allies (the bankers and the capitalists, in the old sense of the word). In many countries, the oligarchy is supported by foreign investors sufficiently myopic to believe that, because the oligarchy maintains a low wage level, it favors their interests. The oligarchs form a true caste, with aristocratic impulses, racist attitudes, and a profound contempt for their own countries.

In Latin America, 73 per cent of the rural population owns only 3.7 per cent of the arable land, while the *latifundistas,* who amount to less than 15 per cent of the rural population, hold 65 per cent of the land. In Honduras, 70 per cent of the economically active population is engaged in agriculture; in Guatemala, 74 per cent; in Nicaragua, 69 per cent; in the Dominican Republic, 69 per cent; in El Salvador, 64 per cent; in Bolivia, 63 per cent; and in fifteen Latin American countries, more than 40 per cent of the economically active population is engaged in agriculture. Agricultural production accounts for 48 per cent of the national income in

Honduras, 41 per cent in Paraguay, 36 per cent in Colombia, 33 per cent in Bolivia, 27 per cent in Panama, 26 per cent in Brazil, and 23 per cent in Argentina. In comparison, 4 per cent of the U.S. national income is provided by agriculture.

In Paraguay, 93.8 per cent of the cultivated land is in the hands of large landowners; five estates occupy 25 per cent of the national territory. In Argentina, 74.8 per cent of the land is occupied by estates of more than 2,500 acres. In Chile, 73.2 per cent; in Peru, 66.5 per cent; in the Dominican Republic, 53.3 per cent; in Uruguay, 55.8 per cent; and in Brazil, 50.8 per cent. While the countries of Central America have a lower percentage of large landholdings, they are actually in a similar situation, even though one cannot apply the same standard of 2,500 acres to such small nations. And although in these Central American republics, such as Panama, Costa Rica, El Salvador, and Honduras, less than 30 per cent of the area is occupied by farms of 2,500 acres or more, they also show a tremendous concentration. One should not forget that El Salvador belongs to 14 families—the famous 14 families of the coffee oligarchy.

In Peru, according to data prepared by the country's present Vice President, Edgardo Seoane, of a total of 11.5 million inhabitants, the rural population of 7.5 million, comprising 65 per cent of the population, receives 13 per cent of the national income, while the landowners, 15,000 persons, or scarcely .01 per cent of the population, receive 20 per cent. These 15,000 have incomes in excess of $3,700 monthly, whereas the average monthly income for rural workers is a wretched $4.40.[12]

One need not be an economist to understand the consequences of such a system: enormous social inequality, low productivity from the land, malnutrition, and lack of culture.

The oligarchy has followed a Malthusian policy. Those Latin American oligarchs who are not Malthusians on the demographic level (since the more workers there are, the cheaper they will be) are Malthusians when it comes to economics; they work their lands at less than full capacity and thus create the conditions whereby industry cannot operate at full capacity, either.

Much is said about the landowning oligarchy and very little

[12] G. Garcés Contreras, report to a conference at the National School of Political Science, Mexico City, January 29, 1964.

about the financial oligarchy. But the truth is that in Latin America the bankers exert a much greater influence than they could in industrialized nations. This influence is most evident in the opposition of the banking community to all anti-inflationary measures based on restriction of credit; that is to say, they oppose any measure that attempts to hold down inflation at the expense of those who live on profits without distributing them to those who live on salaries.

The financial oligarchy is becoming more and more adaptable in outlook and methods and tends more and more to control and dominate the process of industrialization. When a policy of agrarian reform, or even one of agricultural reform, is launched, the oligarchy succeeds in taking over the reform, in financing it, and in converting it into a mere substitution of one large landowner for another.

This situation is not the result of chance. In the nineteenth century, urban Spanish-American society (of which the bankers are an important feature) was a parasitic society. The national budget was financed by customs duties, to the detriment of exports, which were principally agricultural. The beneficiary of the national budget was almost exclusively the city dweller. The result of this situation was a dearth of savings in the rural sector, and the anemia of small-town life and local democracy, which, with its joint landholdings and town councils, had, in times past, offered bright prospects. Savings were poured into the Central Bank down the pipeline formed by the other banks, and credit was extended almost solely to city dwellers. The towns and small provincial cities lived in isolation; there was no expansion or modernization of their means of production and no investment.

In the United States and Western Europe, production developed before there was a market for it. In Latin America, the same thing is happening, but within a structure in which the only market is the privileged cities. In the United States and Europe, industrialization came after the agrarian reforms of the French Revolution, the westward movement, the homestead acts, etc. In Latin America, we are taking the opposite road. Investment, in our part of the world, precedes consumption and the need for the product in which investment is made. Plainly it should be the reverse. We

put to convince him that I was not interested in receiving women by decree. But he did not understand and was extremely offended that I refused this show of . . . hospitality.

Argentina has a million and a quarter unemployed workers. But the members of the House of Deputies increased their salaries from 50,000 to 70,000 pesos (about $320 to $520) a month in February, 1963, at the very time that workers were striking for a 20 per cent increase in their salaries of 6,000 or 7,000 pesos (about $40 or $50) a month.[14]

In Bolivia, in the year 1940 (before the revolution), the monthly consumption of the fermented fruit drink known as *chicha* was 220,500 quarts; of beer, 165,500 quarts; and of milk, only 150,500 quarts.

In Colombia, the violence rampant during the regimes of Ospina Pérez, Laureano Gómez and Arveláez, from 1946 to 1953, accounted for 240,000 political murders of members of the army, the repressive police forces, the government, and the peasantry. Under Rojas Pinilla, from 1953 to 1957, the figure was 4,800, and during the administration of Lleras Camargo, from 1958 to 1962, another 7,800. The total: 252,600 killed.[15]

Uruguay has an area of 72,000 square miles and a population of 3 million. It lacks minerals, natural fuel, and wood; it exists by raising livestock. It can export only meat and wool. In spite of a superdemocratic legal system, the basic economic structure is semifeudal. Political democracy and antidemocratic economic structures exist side by side in a *modus vivendi* that finds expression in the most luxuriant state bureaucracy in the world. The backwardness of the livestock industry is stupendous. On 34.5 million acres devoted to cattle raising, there are 8 million head, and the annual slaughterable percentage of the stock runs from 13 to 14 per cent. This is the lowest rate in the world.[16]

Ecuador is almost as large as Spain, but only half of its area is under any real administrative control. The eastern jungle regions are Ecuadorian only on the map.

[14] *La Prensa* (Buenos Aires), November 29, 1963.
[15] Garcés Contreras, *op. cit.*
[16] Laureano Riera, "La Alianza y las estructuras caducas," *El mundo en español* (Paris, 1963).

It has about 4.5 million inhabitants. Two-thirds of them live on the land, but only about 25 per cent are economically active. It is not that the others do not work. On the contrary, few peoples have a harder existence, such exhausting work, and such adverse conditions as in Ecuador. But only a little more than a million of them work within a market economy.

Of these 4.5 million, how many are Ecuadorian? How many really participate in the governing of the country, how many live a political, social, cultural existence that is involved with their country? Of course, there are no figures for this. Furthermore, after talking to anthropologists, sociologists, and politicians, one comes to a disquieting conclusion: There are no more than half a million Ecuadorians.

The rest are "those poor Indians." Whether they are Indians or mestizos is not important. The important thing is that they are people who live submerged, whose voice no one hears. For example, in the whole country, there is no official anthropological or ethnographical museum. The only one in existence is a private institution, and the ruling military junta has cut off the meager subsidy it used to receive.

One of the most widely accepted myths of our America is that we are not racists. Officially, there is no legal segregation. No one, because he is Indian or Negro, will be prevented from entering a washroom or sitting where he likes in a bus. But does this mean that there is no racism in Latin America? Perhaps more clearly in Ecuador than in any other country one can see the mechanism by which our racism both manifests and disguises itself at the same time.

While it is true that no Indian will ever be prevented from boarding a bus, entering a luxury restaurant, or buying a movie ticket, it is also true that practically no Indian (nor any mestizo whose way of life is on a par with the Indian's) is in a position to go to the movies, to eat in a restaurant, and no one except Indians ever rides the buses in Ecuador. No, segregation is not evident in daily life. It begins much earlier, far from the view of those non-Indians whose consciences are easy because they are not racists. Segregation is generations old, at the very foundations of life—in work, in the economy.

The Indian (and the mestizo who is often his next-door neighbor on the economic ladder) simply has no opportunity to feel segregated, because he is never in contact with non-Indian life except in his role as a menial worker. Class divisions and race divisions go hand in hand. The Indians are segregated not because they are Indians, but because they are poor, uncultured, and primitive. "Those poor Indians" are, in the last analysis, not merely unfortunate but, usually, starving.

There are countries in Latin America where the landowning oligarchy is never noticed except in the matter of power. In Ecuador, the oligarchy is much broader than the small nucleus of great landowners; the oligarchy there encompasses everyone who is non-Indian.

The extreme right, which still has a certain nostalgia for the nineteenth-century President García Moreno, the sons of the bosses, the young lawyers and the poets who make up the ultra-revolutionary groups that consider themselves leftist, the liberal and anticlerical center—all these make up the oligarchy, of which the bosses are only a part. The bosses do not need to exert political pressure. A sort of unconscious solidarity of the non-Indians (precisely because they are not Indians or mestizos) protects them. Regardless of who holds the reins of government, the government is for the half-million Ecuadorians—while 4 million poor Indians are administered.

There is probably no country in our America where the fact of aristocracy continues to make itself felt so strongly in daily life. The Ecuadorian is—and behaves, reacts, and thinks—like an aristocrat in the face of the rest of the inhabitants of the country. And this attitude is shared by the Communists as well as the semi-fascists, by the demagogues as well as the liberals.

But since this aristocracy lives in the twentieth century, what has happened to the other aristocracies of the world has happened to them: It has lost its sense of mission. It is an aristocracy that considers itself to be without responsibilities. It is, for this reason, a false aristocracy.

Every year a million to a million and a half peasants come down from the Andes to work in the sugar harvest and the other harvests on the coastal plantations. A peon earns 5 sucres a day (barely 30 cents) and from the whole sugar harvest may earn as much as 30 sucres all together. The *huasipunguero* (tenant farmer) earns

2 to 3 sucres a day—but this is only on paper, because he is always in debt to the boss.

The fact is, then, that the highlands provide the work force for the coast, and the coast profits from the labors of the mountain people. Later, the mountains take back the children and the old and tired and sick, who no longer can be used for the hard labor of the plantation.

In this way, to the parasitism of the oligarchies and of all the factions of all the political groups (not excepting the Communists, who have no shortage of millionaires among their number) is added the parasitism of the coast, slowly developing at the expense of the mountains. The Indian, scorned and ignored, supports the whole nation with his toil.

There is no recourse open to the peasants. The traditional Church, itself a great landholder, wants no changes. The political groups of the left neither want them nor impose them when they are in position to do so. There is only one small force, hardly born, still wavering, that is trying to achieve something positive in the rural areas. This force is part—although a small part—of the Church, which, in some areas, is beginning to donate its own lands to the peasants for the organization of cooperatives. I do not believe that it is for the purpose of proselytizing, because Catholicism (more or less adulterated in its external forms) is absolutely dominant in the country. This sector of the Church moreover, tries to combat alcoholism, which is very widespread in Ecuador, and to break the hold of the "puebleros," who lend money and take the crops of the small farms as interest. It tries to organize boarding schools for the young so that they in turn may teach the old.

This part of the Church (for example, in the Department of Bolívar, where there is a young bishop) possesses a curious characteristic. Much of the clergy is Spanish. The priests who came from Spain before the civil war or immediately thereafter are diehard conservatives. But the young priests arriving now are open, tolerant, active in social work, and even radical in the methods they propose. The hierarchies in Spain must consider them dangerous and, therefore, ship them off to Latin America. One of these days, the liberals and self-styled leftists—in order to block the threat of social change these young priests pose—will accuse them of being "foreign."

Of all the forms of servitude that have survived into the twentieth century, the Ecuadorian practice of *huasipunguismo*—compulsory servitude exacted from farm laborers—is without doubt one of the harshest, most brutalizing, most unjust, and most uneconomic. And to this date, no administration, conservative or liberal, socialist or demagogic, has done anything—I repeat, anything—to end *huasipunguismo*. The conscience of the oligarchy—or of the virtually racial aristocracy—has been assuaged by praising a few novels that denounce *huasipunguismo*. And the fact that this institution of servitude has brought fame to an Ecuadorian novelist, Jorge Icaza, seems almost to justify its existence in the eyes of Ecuadorian intellectuals. Only now are serious studies of *huasipunguismo* being launched. And the people who are making them are not the self-styled "leftists," not the Communists or the socialists, but Catholic sociologists.

In the highlands, there are 12–15 million acres of land, of which only 15 per cent is arable. And 90 per cent of this is occupied by large estates and bleak plains. In the coastal region, there are 15–17 million acres, of which 80 per cent is fit for colonization. There, the land is used for banana, cacao, and coffee plantations.

In 1895, President Eloy Alfaro decreed that the nation would take over the lands belonging to the Church, which at that time owned 89 per cent of all the cultivated land. The Department of Justice was given 469,000 acres to administer as "public-welfare lands," so called because the income from leasing them (which comes to very little) is applied to social welfare. After being held for some time by the social-security bureau, 175,000 acres were turned over to the Department of Defense. Now there is talk of organizing a form of agricultural conscription to provide labor to work these military lands.

In 1938, an agreement was made between the Church and the government under which the first 422,500 acres were returned to the Church. But the big landowners still hold 3,000,000 acres. And finally, there are 88,000 families of *huasipungueros* who own or work about 250,000 acres among them.

These are the facts. There is no doubt that this situation represents both an injustice and a drain on the progress of the country.

In 1818, the colonial system of forced Indian labor was abolished and was replaced by the *concertaje* system, which was virtually the same thing. In 1918, *concertaje* was abolished, and what remained was the present system of *huasipunguismo*. There is much talk about abolishing *huasipunguismo,* but no one knows what should be done with the workers. They might be given the lands they are now working, but these lands are insufficient to maintain them and their families, and without credit, technical assistance, tools, and animals, they would never be able to increase the productivity of their miserable fields. Moreover, they are now chained down in the middle of the estates, so that even if they owned these lands, they would be surrounded by the old owner's holdings and remain dependent on him for permission to cross his lands, for irrigation, etc. The *huasipungueros* do not seem very enthusiastic about this prospect. Their traditional lore reminds them that each time the landholding system has changed, the rural workers' lot has grown worse and that, under the pretext of increased freedom, they have become less and less protected.

Agrarian reform? Few nations in Latin America have an agrarian situation that demands more urgent and radical reform than Ecuador's. For the last four years, the Congress has been considering various reform projects, and several government agencies have studied the problem and have prepared plans for reform. In 1962 no less than six agrarian-reform projects were proposed, none of which was approved—precisely because there were six. This is a maneuver widely used in other countries (in Brazil, for example); for the proliferation of plans is a means, effective thus far, of preventing any real agrarian reform. Time is spent in studies, discussions, negotiations, and in the end, there is no law—or, when there is a law, it is so weak that even if it is enforced, it reforms nothing. In the best instances, the magic name of agrarian reform is given to what is, in fact, simply a modest plan for colonizing waste or jungle lands, in which even the Indians decline to live. But such a plan accomplishes its purpose—to obtain international credits.

In Ecuador, finally, the only nationalized industry in existence is the liquor industry.[17]

The social structure of Chile has remained virtually unchanged since the middle of the last century. The country has had two reform Presidents, José M. Balmaceda, who ended up committing sui-

[17] A. Costales Samaniego, "La tierra contra el Ecuador," *Panoramas* (No. 5), September–October, 1963.

cide because the Congress did not allow him to achieve any of his reforms, and Arturo Alessandri, who after having promulgated the country's first labor code, ended up committing political suicide by resorting to dictatorial methods during his second term in office.

In 1946, there were two Communist ministers in the government. One of these was Miguel Concha, Minister of Lands and Colonization. There is no doubt that he could have initiated legislation to reform the rural situation. Chile needs agrarian reform and needs, as well, to reform its laws on labor unions. But the Communists, in order not to alarm their allies of the center and right, did nothing.

Chile had the first socialist deputy in all of Latin America, and it produced several important socialist theoreticians (Francisco Bilbao, Santiago Arcos Arlegui). It had a Democratic Party and later a Radical Party that were powerful, popular, and dynamic. Today the Communist Party of Chile is the only strong Communist Party in Latin America, and the only Socialist Party of any force in Latin America is Chile's. The Christian Democratic movement, still nascent in the rest of the continent, has achieved major victories in Chile's last two elections, sweeping Eduardo Frei Montalva into the Presidency, and giving him a sizable bloc in the Congress.

Nevertheless, in Chile the industrial unions have no legal right to bargain collectively; only the craft unions possess this right. The Communists have never attempted to alter this situation, because it is easier for them to dominate small unions. In order to form a union organization, the members must be over twenty-one years of age and at least five must know how to read. But to form a rural workers' organization, the law requires that the members be twenty-five years old and that at least ten know how to read. The difference is significant, since the cultural level in the country is lower than that of the city. It is a fact that this law was proposed by the Communist Concha, while he was minister.

There is a minimum wage in the rural areas. But the owners rent houses to the tenant workers at city prices, so salaries are always, in fact, far below the minimum.

The Chilean social-security system is considered very advanced. The truth of the matter is that there are thirty-two pension funds and three mutual associations. That is, when the oligarchy's legislators realized that they had no choice but to establish social security, they did it in such a way that it became an instrument for the fragmentation of the working class, setting one trade against another through rivalry among their pension funds. Some trades have high pension rates, others have low rates; and a single uniform system is never agreed on because someone would lose something.

What does all this mean? The answer is clear; it means that Chile can boast of possibly the most able oligarchy on the continent, an oligarchy which has learned how to retain all its power without aid from the military, and which has held onto power with the complicity of the Communists while at the same time maintaining a façade of democracy.

There is no doubt that in Chile elections are clean and are respected. But through laws, cultural media, the press, and the demagoguery of the mislabeled "left," a climate of conformity has been created throughout the country. The politicians say: "Chileans don't fight each other." The truth is that the Chileans ought to be like any other people. But the oligarchy, discreet and distant, but implacable, powerful, and intransigent at heart, has known how to maintain itself in power without eliminating the forms of democracy.

It is not, to outward appearances, a defiant and cynical oligarchy. There are no enormous fortunes, or very few, but there are great landowning interests, tied now to some of the new industrial and banking interests. Since the administration of Carlos Ibáñez del Campo, in the early 1950's, inflation has led to a measure of stagnation in the daily life of the country (the people cannot buy refrigerators, automobiles, television sets, etc., in the quantities they would like), but this does not harm the oligarchy's position.

But if you went to the heart of the matter and asked: "Who pays for the broken dishes in Chile?," the inevitable answer would be: "The poor people, the middle class, the workers, and, above all, the peasants." The landholding oligarchy (and its modern offshoot, the banking oligarchy) has lost none of its power. And the agrarian reform which has been promulgated will not give much good land to the rural workers, although it will gild the coats of arms of the aristocratic German, Basque, Irish, and Andalucian families that form the upper crust of the country. Beneath it, the Chileans will go on voting and believing that they live in an authentic democracy.[18]

Brazil is a baffling country for those who do not examine its reality in the light of one fundamental fact: the existence of an oligarchy of landowners who maintained slavery long after it had been abolished in the United States, who have been successful in avoiding open dictatorships and overt militarism, and who have known both how to raise demagogues when it was convenient and how to discard them, as in the recent case of João Goulart, when their demagoguery led them to make promises that could have been dangerous for the oligarchy.

In this context, it is revealing, for example, that, in spite of the nationalism in which Brazil clothes its political attitudes, the government "never concerned itself with establishing ties with the African countries. In the United Nations, it limited itself to accepting *faits accomplis,* but never opposed Portugal and Portuguese colonial policy." This is logical, if one takes into account that the Brazilian Government is colonial; for this reason, it could not be a party to the liberation of the submerged classes of Africa, if at the same time it was not a party to the liberation of the submerged classes in its own country.

The government of Juscelino Kubitschek did not understand its potential field of action in the U.N. in the course of African liberation; it supported fully the actions of Portugal, it allied itself with the interests of the colonial powers or, at most, limited itself to giving *de jure* recognition to the independent activities of the African states. Nothing more, no message of sympathy, no solidarity, not a gesture, to say nothing of cooperation, as if we felt ashamed of the promise of African power, as if they degraded us in that other soul which we possess, as if we despised our identity, as if it were possible to continue a dichotomy between the people and an international policy, directed by a Europeanized elite, tending to the preservation of the *status quo.*[19]

[18] For more details, see Robert J. Alexander, *Labor Relations in Argentina, Brazil, and Chile* (New York, 1962).
[19] J. H. Rodríguez, "La política internacional del Brasil y Africa," *Foro Internacional* (Mexico City), January–March, 1964.

In fact, at the same time as it was following a policy of respecting the *status quo* in Africa, the Brazilian Government maintained a demagogic Latin American policy, always in opposition (although with verbal subtleties) to any action against totalitarian threats to our continent.

For years, books were written, articles published, and program after program launched on the subject of agrarian reform in Brazil. But when an attempt was made to formulate a plan for the Northeast, even as realistic an economist as Celso Furtado proposed an extraordinarily timid reform which would provide lands to the peasants but not take lands from the owners who were responsible for the erosion and misery, and who even now threaten to welcome with bullets any peasants coming to take the new land. In March, 1964, President Goulart announced what he called an agrarian-reform decree which expropriated uncultivated lands bordering federal highways; we can well imagine the Brazilian peasants farming alongside the highways and setting up little stalls to sell their produce to drivers. This program would neither have increased the productivity of the land nor have reduced the power of the oligarchy. For their part, the owners of these lands, who would have been indemnified, had announced before the promulgation of the law that they would shoot anyone trying to take over these strips along the highways. The thing would have been ridiculous, grotesque, if it had not been such a tragic joke on the Brazilian peasants, a joke that was on the point of bloodshed when Goulart, frightened by the mess his demagoguery had created, provoked the military and thus succeeded in leaving power without having to commit suicide, like Vargas, or to resign, like Quadros. In order to save face, Goulart took to the radio and urged the workers and peasants to fight, even while his family was already in Uruguay and he was preparing to flee.

During this period, the Brazilian deputy Francisco Julião, head of the Peasant Leagues of the Northeast, who had recently proclaimed himself a Castroite, seemed to be terrifying all the newspaper readers of the United States. But he did not frighten the Brazilian oligarchs in the least, as is shown by the fact that they made no move whatsoever toward agrarian reform. The oligarchs knew something the American newspaper correspondents did not know: that the Julião family were *fazandeiros* (great landowners), and that all his political rhetoric was only that—rhetoric. If the U.S. public was better informed, possibly it would not be so afraid of these demagogues and would realize what powerful support such demagoguery gives to the oligarchy. It is as if the bullet had been fired from the breech. The United States wanted to convince the oligarchies of the need of social reforms out of fear of Castroism, and now it is the oligarchies that are convincing the United States to give them money for phony and hypothetical reforms, taking advantage of the U.S. fear of noisy demagogues like Julião.

But demagoguery should not make us forget that the agrarian problem really exists. For example, the Bras Burgos Zacarías de Lira family became beneficiaries of one of the most fabulous legacies within memory when they were granted ownership of an area of 145,000 square miles in northern Brazil. This territory, larger than Holland and Belgium combined, is valued at almost $40 million and contains within its boundaries more than 800 towns and villages.[20]

The politicians, too, are *latifundistas*. João Goulart announced in 1962 that he would give 10 per cent of his holdings to the agrarian-reform program. His brother-in-law Leonel Brizzola, then Governor of Rio Grande do Sul, said that he would also donate one of his estates to be divided up among the peasants. Until Goulart's ouster, which toppled Brizzola in its wake, both owned large cattle ranches.[21]

And is the following not revealing?

The Communist Deputy Gilberto Azevedo admitted in the Recife Legislative Assembly that he is the owner of 46,000 acres of land in Rio Grande do Norte, where he also owns extensive salt mines. Azevedo was accused by several Deputies of increasing the valuation of his lands in order to sell them more advantageously. He apparently plans the sale of his land to avoid the political embarrassment of being called a *latifundista*.[22]

Why should it be so strange that the Communists do not alarm the oligarchy, not even when it uses them to make a coup to get

[20] Agence France-Presse, December 26, 1955.
[21] United Press International, February 6, 1962.
[22] *Boletín of the SOCI* (Caracas), July 7, 1963.

rid of the demagogues? I am not exaggerating. Read another report:

> In view of the coming Presidential elections, former President Juscelino Kubitschek, who is a possible candidate, has conferred with the Brazilian Communist leader Luiz Carlos Prestes. When Kubitschek was elected in 1955, he received the Communist vote.[23]

It is common to hear Latin American intellectuals complain that the United States does not understand Latin America and that U.S. studies of our institutions suffer from this lack of understanding. This is sometimes true and sometimes not. No one should forget, for example, that Frank Tannenbaum was the first—before any Latin American—to point out the importance of the indigenous masses in the life and economy of Latin America. But the people who complain of this lack of comprehension forget to add that these uncomprehending studies are made thanks to the existence of hundreds of U.S. foundations that supply funds for travel, books, time, etc., for this purpose. There could be many studies made by Latin Americans—presumably less uncomprehending studies—if the wealthy of Latin America, instead of sending their capital to Switzerland, used a part of it to support educational foundations. But there are no Latin American foundations. Private charitable institutions can be counted on the fingers of one hand, and private cultural or educational institutions on the fingers of the other. The wealthy Latin Americans cannot even support symphony orchestras whose concerts would give their wives an opportunity to show off their bosoms and their jewels; they prefer these diversions to be paid for by the peons of their ranches. There are very few (no more than a hundred) collectors of rare books, of paintings or prints. The Latin American oligarchs possess an egotism as ferocious as it is ignorant, a lack of taste as firmly rooted as their cheapness and provincialism. They prefer to boast about the number of bastards they produce in a year or of drinks they consume in a night than about the scholarships they give or the books they buy. This in itself, even if there were no other reasons, would be enough to condemn our oligarchy.

[23] *Informations Politiques et Sociales* (Paris), December 10, 1963.

Catalogue of Incredible Things

The oligarchy wants power—either directly or, preferably, through political, military, or demogogic go-betweens—because, through power, they can perpetuate their systems of exploitation. The results of this can be seen in a few facts and figures.

Agricultural landholdings of more than 2,500 acres represent 15.0 per cent of the total number of holdings and account for 64.9 per cent of all cultivated land. In comparison, landholdings of up to 250 acres make up 90.6 per cent of the total number and account for 12.1 per cent of all cultivated land. For landholdings of more than 250,000 acres, the respective figures are 7.9 per cent and 23.0 per cent.

But with all this land and all this power, the oligarchy has not demonstrated great efficiency in terms of productivity. The continent of Latin America is effectively chained to agriculture. In Bolivia, with its great mineral wealth, out of a population of 4,000,000 people, only about 40,000 work the mines, and the value of agricultural exports from Latin America far exceeds that of minerals. The proportion of the population engaged in agriculture varies from 25 per cent in Argentina to 70 per cent in Honduras. Close to 6 out of every 10 people in Mexico and Brazil live on the land. In Argentina, about three-fourths of the gross national product is derived from agriculture. Nonetheless, in many countries, the importation of foodstuffs constitutes a large portion of their trade, not only with neighboring countries—such as Brazil and Argentina, who exchange coffee and wheat—but with Europe as well. In addition, there is a substantial importation of luxury food items.[24]

How, then, can it be worthwhile to belong to an oligarchy with such uneconomic characteristics? It is because of exploitation. The exploitation of the peasant in Latin America is unbelievable. There are very few frank, documented studies of the methods of this exploitation. It is referred to obliquely, it is condemned on paper, but practically nothing has been done to wipe it out. We have already seen, for example, that in Ecuador all the public-opinion groups,

[24] William L. Schurz, *Latin America: A Descriptive Survey* (rev. ed.; New York, 1963).

while protesting their revolutionary character, live on the proceeds of *huasipunguismo*.

The exploitation of the peasants is carried on through systems of servitude and feudal relationships between peasant and land-owner. Although the forms I shall describe do not exist everywhere in Latin America, they are found in most of the countries with an Indian population (and affect not merely the Indians); in the other countries they exist to a lesser degree, but are no less un-believable for that reason. Let us look at the catalogue, relying heavily on what has been said by the few specialists on the subject who dare to write about it.[25]

Systems of forced labor occur principally in those countries where the Indians make up a high percentage of the population. In other countries, where the mestizo sector is dominant, the problem is less severe. However, even the farm worker who is not com-mitted to an employer, but is treated as a free day laborer, often falls into a feudal relationship because of the social and economic conditions in which this sort of farm-labor system operates. The most widespread means of feudalizing him is *"aparcería."* Nor-mally, *aparcería* consists of an obligation on the part of the peasant to give the owner a share of his crops in return for the use of a bit of land, seeds, tools, and a cash advance. In many areas of Latin America, however, the peasant is also obliged to perform personal services or to deliver instead an additional share of his produce. Under these circumstances, *aparcería* becomes a form of agrarian servitude.

The condition of the Indians who are subjected to such servi-tude is appalling. Many times they bear the family name of the master of the house, and often when a farm is sold, it is transferred together with its cattle and its Indian families. The Indian servant has lost much of the dignity and pride of the Indian living in an autonomous, joint-landholding community. He is without any

[25] Principally, I shall draw in this section on the work of Miguel Mejía Fernández, *El problema del trabajo forzado en América Latina* (Mexico City, 1950). This is the most recent work. In any event, the situation has not changed, except in Bolivia, where the revolution of 1952 and the agrarian reform that followed it altered the status of the Indian and abolished forced servitude. In Venezuela, the agrarian reform of 1960 has also changed the situation. See also International Labour Office, *Indigenous Peoples* (Geneva, 1953); Roberto MacLean y Estenós, *Indios de América* (Mexico City, 1962); and Costales Samaniego, *loc. cit.*

rights, a blind instrument of the boss, who encourages his vices in order to exploit him the more.

The forms of exploitation can be classified into three groups:

1. A system of service dating from the colonial *encomienda,* by which the beneficiary, although having no rights to Indian lands, had the power to exact tribute—part of the crop or personal services—from the Indians in exchange for the supposed obligation to protect and convert them. This practice resembles, for example, the present systems of *pongueaje, colonato, huasicamia,* and assorted other systems of domestic and agrarian servitude, based on the extralegal seigniory the landowner exerts over the peasant.

2. Forced labor arising out of the monopoly of land ownership and in general out of the means of production, whether or not seigniory exists. The original form, out of which several varieties (*concertaje, yanaconazgo, mita, shirongaje, marronaje, acasillaje,* etc.) have grown, is the system of *peonaje* (peonage), which also originated in colonial times, although it persists in modern capitalistic societies engaged in the exploitation of agricultural or mineral resources.

3. Compulsory labor in the public sector (*tequio, faena, corvea, minga, chunca,* etc.), corresponding to the obligation of the individual to provide free labor for public and communal works.

I have mentioned briefly the most common forms of servitude. The fact that the majority of city-dwelling Latin Americans is ignorant of them only proves their indifference and indicates that, consciously or unconsciously, they feel themselves part of the exploiting group.

In the area of the Andes, the name *pongueaje* has been given to the obligation imposed on the Indian to work five days of the week without pay in the owner's fields, with only the remaining two days available to him for work in the small parcel of land that has been lent to him. The *pongo* belongs to the owner by virtue of seigniory; he receives no salary and cannot leave the owner's service without permission. The owner, on the other hand, can compel him to perform domestic service in the farmhouse and in his town house, in return for which the *pongo* receives only his meals.

A similar institution is that of *huasicamia* (a Quechua word meaning "housekeeping work"), which combines work in the fields with domestic service. The peasant must give personal services and must settle with his family on the farm, from which he receives the use of a lot (the *huasipungo*) in payment for the farm work he performs. His children care for the farm animals or do the housework, although the seigniory the owner exerts over the Indian families is disguised by the "formality" of adoption. In Peru, Bolivia and Ecuador, these children become servants in wealthy homes in the capitals.

The *porambia* is common in the sugar-growing areas of Colombia. A worker receives 10 fanegadas (about 16 acres) of land, and must work for the owner 144 days per year for the right to cultivate it. Sometimes an outside lessee will rent an entire farm and then parcel it out to the peasants, who must pay him half their crop, with all costs and risks charged up to them. Since only rarely do they own animals and tools, they must rent them at high rates that after two or three years exceed their entire original cost.

In Guatemala, the *mozo-colono* is a tenant farmer who must also perform personal services for the owner. The peasant receives the poorest land on the farm, and the value of the crops he produces almost never covers even the amount of his debts (since it is the owner who arbitrarily fixes the value of the crops the peasant must deliver to him, it is the peasant who must absorb any deficit from the over-all operation of the farm). The result is that a chain of feudal existence binds the worker to the farm, and, because of his debts, there he must remain. The owner, on the other hand, obtains his crops at low cost and without risk, and without having to feed this sort of tenant farmer as he would have to feed a peon or contract worker.

The *conuco* is a Venezuelan institution, under which a tenant farmer receives the lands located at the borders of the owner's holding or on the steep hillsides where erosion has depleted the soil. Because he is exposed to arbitrary eviction, he has no interest in building a permanent house, planting trees, or conditioning the soil; he vegetates there with his family in the greatest misery imaginable, which permits the owner to exploit his labor at low prices, whenever the farm's own needs so require. There is no seigniory, but this economic dependency produces the same consequences.

Ecuador's *concertaje* consists of an agreement, the *concierto,* by which an owner advances money to a peasant, who must pay it off in work. What it amounts to is the day laborer's sale of his own person, and in this manner the Indian, supposedly a citizen, granted by law full civil and political rights, is no more than a slave in disguise, at the mercy of the landowner. This system, as well as that of detaining a free day laborer on the land for debt, was abolished by law some time ago, but the practice persists.

The *yanaconazgo* is a collective version of the *concertaje:* The *yanacones* are Indians dragged from their own communities in the highlands and carried in groups to work on the large farms of the coastal areas. The work contract contains only the obligations of the worker, none on the part of the owner. It fixes no type of work to be performed, nor the amount of salary to be paid, nor the duration of the contract. But it can be perpetuated from father to son.[26]

The cultivation of sugar, cotton, and rice in the coastal farms of Colombia, Ecuador, and Peru, is carried out under the *yanaconazgo* system. The highlands provide the Indian labor force; the system of peonage has been nourished by the labor force of the semi-enslaved peasants.

The *shirongaje* is found in the rubber and oil-seed plantations of Peru, Ecuador, Colombia, Venezuela, and Brazil. It is a plain and simple form of peonage that is extended to cover all classes; whites, blacks, natives, and foreign immigrants. Since the end of the last century, local or, more often, foreign companies have obtained vast concessions in the rubber zones. Through hiring agents, they make an agreement with the worker (*shiringero*), who receives two or three lots, generally having 150 trees each. These the *shiringero* must work on his own, delivering the production of rubber to the owner's agent periodically at a price fixed by the company. The company provides the worker with some of his food and a rudimentary dwelling, but sells him the rest of his food along with his furniture, clothing, tools, and medicines. At the end of the contract period, a settlement of accounts is made, and if the *shiringero* comes out on the short end, he must continue working until his debt has been paid off. Since the price for the latex is very low, this is what most frequently happens. The worker cannot leave because a clause of the contract provides that if he does, he may be pursued and arrested. And so it is that he remains all his

[26] Garcés Contreras, *op. cit.*

life in the jungle until death or premature illness claims him. And the company has stipulated that in such an event, the oldest son must fulfill the contract for his father.

The *acasillaje* is found in the yerba maté plantations of Paraguay, where British and Argentine companies maintain the classic system of the *peón acasillado*. The worker never receives his entire salary since his indebtedness is always deducted from it. In addition, he must buy his food, clothing, and tools from the company store (of course, at higher-than-market prices). The owners employ special police who guard the roads to intercept a worker who tries to flee or who does not have the owner's authorization to leave. This system is also used in the lumbering regions of northern Argentina and in Paraguay itself.

In certain cases, the tenancy agreement (*aparcería*) takes on the aspects of a collective tribute. This occurs with groups of families and even entire communities who have been robbed of their communal lands by the great landholders and then find themselves caught within the borders of a latifundium. These peasants not only must hand over a share of their crops in return for the right to cultivate land that used to be their own, but are also subject to the economic, social, and political power the owner exercises throughout the district, since its authorities also are subordinate to his bidding.

But the oligarchs are not content with exploitation for their direct benefit. They also exact labor for the national or municipal governments, and thus make a saving on their taxes.

Although there is no longer a community obligation to provide a labor contingent for a specified length of time to work the mines, nevertheless, by coercive labor enlistment, the companies are assured of a work force that has many of the characteristics of peonage, and is, in fact, a continuation of the colonial *mita* (enforced servitude of the Indians).

Exploitation of the worker is most acute in those mining areas that are largely populated by Indians, and in such areas, the old systems of servitude survive most strongly. Not without reason does the old refrain say: "The Indian serving his *mita* is a dead Indian."

The words *tequio, faena, chunca,* and *minga* are all names for the obligation of an individual to work without pay for a fixed period on highway construction or maintenance, water storage, fences and irrigation, construction of schools and government buildings, and the cultivation of public lands to produce crops that will be sold to obtain public revenue.

All these exist today. None of them exist officially, although they did when these systems were abolished, because the law had to admit their existence in order to abolish them. Although today they are illegal, no one prosecutes the landowner who makes use of forced labor.

In Peru, the law of October 16, 1916, (which was not put into effect until May, 1923) decreed that personal work must be paid for in cash. The law of May 15, 1947, established rules governing contracts for *yanaconazgo* and declared null and void any clauses in such contracts relative to the obligation of the tenant to perform work without payment.

In Bolivia, the decree of May 15, 1945, prohibited civil and Church authorities from forcing the Indians to perform free public services, such as the *minga, faena,* or *corvea.* The revolution of 1952 effectively abolished all these systems.

The Bolivian law of 1945, by explicitly abolishing the *mita,* obliged the farm worker to bring his produce to a town market or shipping point. It thus legalized one of the most grievous of all the seigniorial services that have weighed on the Indian, that of acting as a beast of burden for the landholders.

In Ecuador, Article 252 of the Labor Code provides that "when a peon performs domestic services as a *huasicama* or similarly gives his services, he shall be entitled to be paid the costs of moving, food, and lodging." The same article prohibits the owner from compelling the *huasipunguero* to perform any additional work without pay. The salary of the *huasipunguero* may not be less than one-half of the minimum salary paid in the area to free day laborers, and the *huasipunguero* may not be forced to work more than four days per week. The owner must allow him to cut wood on the land and to draw water from the farm's wells.

What the Ecuadorian law actually did was to legalize abuses by property owners, because it also established measures against "vagrancy," which were nothing less than a legal method for the labor contractors to secure a work force. In effect, laborers without a job or peasants who have been evicted from their small plots can be jailed as vagrants. They are then immediately offered to hiring agents to work off their sentence on farms or in the mines. Mass arrests for "vagrancy" naturally coincide with those periods when the farms and agents urgently need workers.

In Guatemala, the Labor Code provides that owners must allow rural workers "to enjoy the fruits and produce of the land let to them (in tenancy) and to draw out of the reservoirs, ponds, and wells of the farms the water required for their domestic use and their animals." The owners are also prohibited from "inducing or compelling their workers to purchase their living requirements from specified establishments or persons."

Argentina has also provided legislation on this subject. A law passed in 1942 requires the labor contractor to make contracts in writing, to pay the worker's round-trip travel costs, and to provide clean vehicles for travel. He must also guarantee the worker and his family adequate food, clean housing, and medical attention and drugs. The worker must be paid in cash at the salary originally stipulated.

All these prohibitions show what went on in the past, and still goes on, because there is no way to enforce the prohibitions as long as organizing the peasants is also prohibited. How can the Indian *pongo* or *huasicama,* who for centuries has been ground down by moral and physical repression, be expected to rid himself at once of the obligation to supply free personal services to the owner, when the latter, as master of the land, has complete control over the peasant's livelihood? Will the tenant be able to sell his crops in the free market in competition with the owner when it is the owner who provides him with a home? And clearly, nothing has been done legally to suppress either the supply of alcohol in the coastal plantations or of coca in the mines and the Andean plateaus.[27]

[27] There has never been any real interest in limiting the consumption of coca. When he was dictator of Peru, General Manuel Odría—a veritable model democrat—issued a decree establishing a state monopoly on the sale of coca and directing that the proceeds of this sale be used to improve the living standards of the armed services. That the person capable of thinking up this decree seized political power by force or that he should be a candidate sworn to uphold the constitution is of only relative importance. The

On the other hand, how can such a system be abolished when there are such large numbers of rural workers without land? In Ecuador, they represent 58.3 per cent of the agricultural population; in the Dominican Republic, 69.8 per cent; in Nicaragua, 71.1 per cent; in Chile, 74.4 per cent; in Venezuela, 71.9 per cent; in Argentina, 74.4 per cent; in Uruguay, 78.5 per cent; in Colombia, 79.1 per cent; in Guatemala, 80.3 per cent; in Peru, 86.3 per cent; and in Panama, 94.4 per cent. In Bolivia, before 1952, the figure was 95.1 per cent. In Mexico, in 1910, it was 96 per cent; today, it is 35 per cent.

Let us remember, in order to soothe the conscience of the reader, that, according to the definition adopted by the League of Nations Slavery Convention of 1929, slavery is "the status or condition of any person over whom all or any of the powers attached to the rights of ownership are exercised."

Now we can sleep peacefully. The constitutions of all our countries prohibit slavery. Therefore, slavery or servitude *cannot* exist.

After reading all of this, it is easy to understand why reports of the Stalinist system of forced labor never created much of an impression in Latin America. At the doors of our homes, we had systems just as bad and we tolerated them—and we go on tolerating them. A bad conscience (or its ally, indifference) left us no room for indignation over what was happening so far away. And if we were indignant, we were not indignant enough to do anything about it.

Catalogue of Corruption

The exercise, by one means or another, of political power in order to preserve a situation of privilege characterized by what we have just seen is impossible without the existence of a high degree of corruption.

Corruption always exists in the upper echelons of power, even in those very exceptional cases where those who administer the power are honorable persons. But by osmosis, by imitation, by

---

sad fact is that such a decree could be signed and executed and that no one ever criticized Odría for sponsoring this legalized poisoning of the Peruvian Indian masses for the benefit of the military.

contagion, by infiltration, corruption penetrates the other strata of society—those that constitute public opinion—which participate, however little, in the privileges of the oligarchy and which, consequently, are parasites on the submerged masses.

The least important aspect of this corruption is the side that at first appears most spectacular: *"la mordida"* (the "bite"), *"la botella"* (the "bagman"), the bribe, the kickback, the influence peddler—the classic forms of corruption, which are found in all political and administrative machinery. What is peculiar to the Latin American oligarchy is another sort of corruption, which we might call social corruption. It consists of performing acts prejudicial to the interests of the mass of society and, at the same time, avoiding any social condemnation or, at worst, anything more than rhetorical condemnation. In this category belong the embezzlement of national wealth represented by depositing abroad, the theft of raw materials, and the use of classic corruption for political ends.

During World War II, the Latin American nations accumulated large dollar reserves because they had nowhere to spend the dollars they received for sales to the Allies, who could supply only a minute part of the Latin American demand. When the war ended and industries reconverted to peacetime production in the United States, and later in Europe, the monetary reserves accumulated during the war plummeted within four or five years. This outflow of reserves did not go for the purchase of capital goods, but rather to buy luxury goods, that is, to satisfy the needs and caprices of the oligarchy and their pals. From 1946 to 1950, only 1.2 per cent of Latin American purchases from the United States went for the tractors that are indispensable for the agricultural progress of the continent.[28]

The reserves accumulated by the labor of all the Latin Americans during World War II were spent on expensive automobiles, gadgets, expensive fabrics, and similar luxury items—not for all the Latin Americans but only for the comfort of the oligarchy.

The volume of these purchases of luxury items was such that, from January to May, 1948, Latin American reserves fell by an estimated $2.6 billion. Here are the expenditures of the countries that dared to give the figures:

[28] Mejía Fernández, *op. cit.,* p. 36.

EXPENDITURES OF DOLLAR RESERVES
JANUARY–MAY, 1948

Millions of Dollars

Argentina	430
Bolivia	9
Brazil	280
Chile	27
Colombia	27
Costa Rica	14
Ecuador	32
Mexico	404
Panama	125
Paraguay	6
Peru	66
Uruguay	67
Venezuela	258

SOURCE: *Excélsior* (Mexico City), September 5, 1948.

Constantly, one hears cabinet ministers, economists, business-men, commentators, Communist propagandists, and even union officials talk about the price of raw materials. They complain of the fact that Latin America must purchase manufactured goods at progressively higher prices, while the prices of the raw materials it sells continue to drop. In broad terms, this is true. It is true also that what is lost each year through the drop in prices is equaled by what is received in foreign aid—if one agrees that a lack of earnings can be termed a loss. For example, in 1958, the fall in coffee prices meant a drop of $250 million in income for Latin America, (or more accurately, for the big coffee growers). That year, U.S. aid amounted to $500 million. (A fluctuation of 10 cents a pound in the price of coffee means a variation of $400 million in income for Latin America—or for the coffee growers.) What is overlooked in the statistics is that in the years when there is a decline in raw-material prices, there is also a decline in sales by the United States to Latin America. For example, in 1958, when lower prices for coffee and sugar meant a loss of earnings to Latin America of $450 million, U.S. sales to Latin America dropped by $500 million. In the same year, United States investors plowed $7.4 billion into Latin America, which produced earnings of $1.1 billion. The following year, these investments had increased to $8.2 billion, but earnings fell to $774.0 million. This means that the U.S. economy gains nothing from a drop in raw-material prices, although some individual companies do profit from it.[29] These figures indicate that the fall in prices is not dictated by a group of big capitalists sitting around a table but results from fluctuations in supply and demand, following the classic canons of a free economy. Prices fall because of an excess of supply or a lack of demand.

It should be remembered that the demand for many of these raw materials is shrinking because they are being replaced by synthetic products. Cotton will not be marketable within a few years. The same is true of coffee, certain metals, and other textile fibers. It would be logical for the producers of these commodities to investigate market trends and technical innovations, and to revamp their production accordingly. But this would require money, gray matter, and some effort. The oligarchs prefer to cry, invoke cheap nationalism, and demand higher prices rather than take the trouble to change their crops and support studies of the potential new uses for the raw materials that are becoming less and less essential.

An impartial economist, Víctor Urquidi of Mexico, has made an acute analysis of the impact of price fluctuations:

It is evident that anything that can be done to avoid or moderate fluctuations [in the prices of raw materials] will in the long run benefit Latin America. The practice of calculating what Latin America "loses" every time prices fall does not seem to be a very useful analytical method, since what is "no longer earned" is not always "lost"; an economic analysis would also have to estimate the effect that continued high prices would have had on the volume of output and exports. A sharp rise in export prices can be as harmful as a decline, because it may lead to inflationary disturbances and create incentives for production on a scale that is subsequently not justified. But it cannot be denied that the Latin American economy would be strengthened if prices were less erratic and if suitable international agreements were adopted to this end.[30]

[29] "Task Facing Alliance for Progress," *Foreign Commerce Weekly* (Washington), August 28, 1961.

[30] Víctor L. Urquidi, *The Challenge of Development in Latin America* (New York, 1964), pp. 26–27.

The future that awaits us is clear to those who are to think without clichés and prejudices:

Although the general effect of scientific advances will be to bring about a general expansion of world trade, with a resultant increase in production and income, there will be cases in which such advances will have disastrous effects on certain products and their producers. Countries that depend on one or a few raw materials for their foreign-exchange earnings are particularly vulnerable to the possible development of synthetics and substitutes.

In recent decades, trade between the industrially developed countries and those in the process of development has been characterized by a rapid increase in the import requirements of the developing nations, an increase that has not been equaled by the need for importations on the part of the industrialized countries. For example, during the period from 1928 to 1957, imports of the nonindustrialized nations increased approximately 400 per cent, whereas their exports increased only 300 per cent. Likewise, in 1928, the nonindustrialized countries had a foreign-trade surplus of about $1.7 billion, whereas in 1957, they had a foreign-trade deficit of $3.4 billion.

Recent studies indicate that in the future the trade in raw materials will increase at a slower rate than will the need of the developing countries for foreign-exchange earnings.

A nation that is attempting to raise its annual rate of growth by 2 per cent will have to increase its imports by at least 10 per cent.[31]

But our oligarchs have done nothing, absolutely nothing, in any respect, to try to increase exports in order to be able to pay for the 10 per cent increase in imports necessary to maintain a 2 per cent annual growth rate, a rate less than what is required in Latin America simply to keep pace with population growth.

In 1960, when the United States entered into an agreement to fix the price of coffee, this marked a departure from its traditional trade policy—a departure that Washington was willing to make in the belief that it would aid Latin America. The truth of the matter is that it hurt the Latin American people, because the support of coffee prices only delayed the time when the oligarchs must make up their minds to modernize their methods of production and to switch to the cultivation of more marketable products.

[31] "Las materias primas no tendrán comprador," *Panoramas* (No. 2), March–April, 1963.

When the prices of raw materials rise, the masses live no better than before, but when they fall, the oligarchs contrive to have the cost of the drop, or most of it, paid for by the masses, through taxes, subsidies (which the masses pay for), or inflation.

When the Korean War caused raw-material prices to rise (and these inflated prices are now taken as the base point against which present prices are compared, which of course falsifies the entire picture), the Latin Americans lived no better than they do today in a period of low prices. In Bolivia, tin was selling at an inflated price, but the *"rosca"* (the political allies of the mining oligarchy) refused to make any improvements, thus paving the way for the election victory of the Movimiento Nacional Revolucionario (MNR, or National Revolutionary Movement) in 1952 and the violent takeover of power by the MNR when the *rosca* juggled the vote to come out the victors. In Chile, the high price of copper did not prevent runaway inflation. In Brazil and other coffee-producing countries, there was no change in the living standards of the people; the only change was the increase in the coffee barons' bank deposits in the United States and Switzerland.

In 1963–64, prices of most raw materials began to rise, and they exceeded the 1958 level.[32] None of Latin America's share of this increase ever reached the people in the form of lower prices, or a reduction in indirect taxation, or more schools and hospitals. The public did not even hear about it. When the U.N. Conference on Trade and Development convened, nothing was said of this increase in prices. Instead, a demand was again made for stabilization, which, if achieved, would represent a new means by which the industrialized nations would subsidize the landholding oligarchies.

It is worthwhile to underline the fact that those who call most insistently for international agreements to maintain raw-material price levels, that is, for government intervention (especially by the United States) to raise prices, are the same ones who cry the loudest for free enterprise in their own countries. And they feel that "free" enterprise must be protected by high tariffs, which increase the cost of living for the masses. Protectionism may be justified during the birth of an industry, but there cannot be any justification after an industry achieves a degree of development

[32] *The Economist* (London), April 11, 1964, p. 167.

and a normal market. In Latin America, all domestic industries enjoy a high level of tariff protection, as a result of which the financing of the industry is paid for, in the final analysis, by the home market—the mass of the urban population and small rural groups.

The oligarchy never invests in its own country the proceeds from the exploitation of raw-material resources, or of its own country-men. There are always foreign investors willing to put money into the country, those foreign investors who are systematically called plunderers, while the oligarchs with one hand sign checks to finance nationalistic and chauvinistic "movements" and with the other sign remittance orders to foreign banks for the money earned by their exploitation.

The flight of capital has been going on for decades, but in recent years, it has assumed catastrophic proportions. And no Latin American government has ever adopted measures to control it. The laws and regulations promulgated for this purpose hamper the small capitalists but not the big ones, who never let the capital they are going to export get back into the country. If there is any act that would clearly justify expropriation without indemnifica-tion, it is the failure to return to the producing country the entire proceeds of sale of raw materials. But never—I repeat, never—has any government, however radical it may claim to be, ordered the expropriation of assets from persons who exploit the people and then send the proceeds abroad.

These flights of capital are by no means negligible, nor have they been restricted to a few cases. The Trujillo family, in the course of thirty-one years, succeeded in remitting abroad more than $700 million. The big coffee growers and other Brazilian millionaires have salted away an estimated $4 billion in foreign banks—$1 billion more than the total gold reserves of all twenty Latin American republics. The flight of capital from Venezuela in 1960 totaled more than $500 million and, between 1957 and 1960, reached $1.5 billion, according to the Central Bank.[33]

A World Bank study on the Nicaraguan economy estimates that if 1 per cent of the population—the wealthy 1 per cent—were to invest only 10 per cent of their annual income in domestic enter-

[33] National Foreign Trade Council, *Noticias: Weekly Digest of Hemi-sphere Reports* (Washington), December 19, 1961.

prises, the rate of productive investment would climb by 50 per cent; but they prefer to send their profits abroad. In Chile in the past fifteen years (all years of inflation and rising prices), the wealthy have spent more than 60 per cent of their income on luxury consumer goods.

One observer estimates that "in more than one Latin American country that is reputedly 'short of capital' the sums that have been spent in Paris in the last half century by wealthy natives would have endowed the country with a modern transportation system and a well-equipped industrial plant." A conservative calculation of Latin American flight capital from the end of World War II to 1961 comes up with a figure of about $15 billion, which represents 50 per cent more than the total aid the United States is committed to provide during all ten years of the Alliance for Progress.[34]

A U.S. economic analysis reveals that "State Department studies show that a large proportion of the $5.5 billion which the U.S. provided in military and economic aid since '45 ended up in Swiss bank accounts or in private stock portfolios in New York."[35]

These funds extracted from the local economy—speaking plainly, stolen from the people—are obtained by the oligarchs from various sources: from the labor of the submerged masses, from the sale of raw materials, and from the peculiar methods developed by bankers and politicians for administering foreign aid. (It is, of course, common knowledge that the very dignified and honorable President of one southern republic does not accept foreign aid unless it is channeled through several banks of which he was, and probably still is, the attorney.) And a part of these funds comes also out of what the oligarchs steal from the public treasury.

The robbery is managed in two ways: on the one hand, legally, through a fiscal system based on indirect taxation (a high sales tax on consumer goods and high import duties, with low levies on income). And, of course, under this system, it is the poor who pay. The following table shows clearly what the wealthy pay (the taxes in the left-hand column) and what the poor pay (the taxes in the four columns at right):

[34] William H. MacLeish, *More from Those Who Have Most . . . Tax Reform in Latin America* (A *Visión* Report; New York, June, 1962), p. 5.
[35] National Foreign Trade Council, *op. cit.*, p. 2.

Source of National Revenues
(*In Percentages*)

	Income Taxes	Sales Taxes	Customs Duties	Monopoly Taxes	Others
Argentina	29.3	32.7	32.1	—	5.9
Bolivia	14.2	23.4	50.6	1.8	8.0
Brazil	31.6	43.3	11.8	—	13.9
Chile	32.3	41.6	21.8	—	4.3
Colombia	51.7	9.8	33.8	0.7	4.0
Costa Rica	16.9	13.6	57.6	6.8	5.1
Dominican Republic	17.7	22.6	43.6	—	16.1
Ecuador	16.5	10.6	41.2	17.6	14.1
El Salvador	11.4	19.7	60.7	—	8.2
Guatemala	7.1	21.4	53.6	—	17.9
Haiti	9.1	15.1	65.2	—	10.6
Honduras	14.7	29.4	55.9	—	—
Mexico	36.8	29.2	27.5	—	6.5
Nicaragua	9.1	18.2	60.6	3.0	9.1
Panama	18.6	18.6	44.2	11.6	7.0
Paraguay	12.5	25.0	20.8	—	41.7
Peru	47.1	22.5	21.1	4.2	5.1
Uruguay	7.3	25.6	37.2	—	29.9
Venezuela	38.4	39.8	11.0	9.0	1.8

Source: MacLeish, *op. cit.*, p. 5.

In the United States, the tax rate goes up to 90 per cent in the highest income brackets; in Latin America, on the average, the highest income-tax rate is 40 per cent. The oligarchy in Chile pays no more than 15 per cent in income tax.

Another revealing point, and one that helps in understanding certain attitudes of the so-called left: Countries with extractive industries permit their wealthy citizens to pay infinitesimal taxes because these industries (oil in Venezuela, copper in Chile, etc.) finance a great share of the budget. The oligarchs, the Communists, and the so-called left all join in demanding that these industries pay more. This is right. What is not right is that the oligarchs should be spared from paying more also, since the people could well benefit from more schools, more highways, and lower indirect taxes.

Another way of robbing the country and making a joke of the public treasury is by evasion of taxes. The Inter-American Development Bank has stated that there are nations that lose up to 50 per cent of their potential public revenue through tax evasion.

Evasion is particularly severe in the case of direct taxes levied on the oligarchs and industrialists.

Another variety of corruption promoted by the oligarchy is to blame foreign investors for all the evils and resentments engendered by its own exploitative practices. In Latin America, foreign capitalists have been brutal, exploitative, and politically interventionist. They still exert an influence on United States diplomacy and, at times, on the local armed forces, and still try to extract as much profit as possible from the countries where they have invested. But the attitudes of foreign investors have changed, not out of kindheartedness but rather out of the realization that they must adapt themselves, while at the same time, the oligarchy's attitudes have not altered in the slightest. And it must be remembered that it was the oligarchs who opened the doors to foreign capital; it was they who granted it concessions and have always supported and protected it.

To understand the mechanism of this corruption of public information, it is well to look at the structure of capital in Latin America. One can then comprehend the actual importance of foreign capital (public and private) in the Latin American economy.[36]

The truth—although to say so contradicts the propaganda on the subject—is that foreign capital often treats the workers better than local capital. This is clear to any visitor to the plants of even the most justifiably hated foreign enterprises in Latin America. I say justifiably because, although these foreign enterprises treat their workers better than does local capital, they often (more so in the past than now, but even now) become involved in internal politics and create a climate that causes them to be hated. On the other hand, these same enterprises tend to have better relations with the Communist-run trade unions than with the democratic unions, because the Communist unions, in return for this recognition, are less demanding. Thus if foreign capital did not quite frequently show this preference for the Communist unions, the condition of its workers would be even better and the difference between them and the rest of the local labor force would be even greater.

[36] William I. Abraham, "Fuentes y tendencias del ahorro en América Latina," *Suplemento al Boletín quincenal* (CEMLA, Mexico City), August, 1963, p. 238.

The truth is that the hatred that clearly exists toward foreign capital has two causes: One is the constant interference by the large foreign concerns in local politics, always in support of reactionary elements—namely, the oligarchs and the Communists. The other is the constant underhand propaganda the local business interests grind out against foreign capital, and occasioned by the fact that, because foreign capital pays higher wages and grants greater benefits to its workers, its very existence forces local businesses to accede to union demands. The foreign enterprises repatriate most of their earnings and often attempt to evade local laws covering special privileges and exemptions; this, naturally, promotes antipathy toward them and is, furthermore, legally indefensible and politically intolerable. The exportation of profits is harmful to an economy in the process of development, although it would be logical and normal in the case of mature economy. But the campaigns against foreign capital have not sought to compel the reinvestment of its earnings in the local economy or to limit the amount of capital it may remit abroad; they have, rather, been directed against the very existence of foreign capital. In effect, what annoys the local capitalists is not that foreign businesses repatriate their earnings, since the local tycoons do the same when they can, but that this exportation of capital means that the nation has lower foreign-exchange reserves and that, as a result, the local capitalists and oligarchs can import fewer automobiles, bottles of perfume, jewels, and mink coats. This is no mere insinuation; it is a statement of fact. Remember that the importation of capital goods in most Latin American countries is paid for not out of exchange earned by the importing nation but out of foreign credits, generally from international organizations, and that the exchange earnings are either sent to bank accounts or else used to import consumer products for the oligarchy.

What measures do the people who rant about foreign capital want? That it should be subject to local laws? No one disagrees with this, and in some countries it has been done. That the supply of foreign capital be stopped? Then how will the country finance capital outlays? By still greater exploitation of the workers and peasants, for there is no other alternative. And who are the people who object to foreign capital? Those who ship their funds abroad and would never, in any event, be the victims of exploitation.

It would not be necessary, or even possible, to fear foreign capital if there were a supply of local funds, and there could be, were it not for their illicit exportation. Who is responsible for this exportation? The supernationalistic capitalists and the landholding oligarchs. So it turns out that foreign investors, against whom there is so much railing, display more confidence in the countries of Latin America than their own local capitalists and are willing to take a greater risk.

To say all this is to state facts, not to justify the actions of foreign capital (and local capital, its partner in crime) in certain countries at certain times—and even today. But to want to outlaw alcohol because a few people get drunk does not seem to be the best way of fighting alcoholism. On the contrary, it is the best way to encourage bootleggers, which is exactly what those local capitalists are who send their capital abroad.

In this same area of corruption of public information is a belief, promoted by the intellectuals of the oligarchy and accepted by all because it flatters the basic nationalism that these people also promote—the belief that in social legislation, Latin America is virtually utopian.

For example, in the United States, the demand for what is called the "right to work" is considered essentially reactionary; only in certain states was it ever established by law, and in 1965, the U.S. Congress prepared to repeal the legislation under which it had been valid.

In Latin America, on the other hand, without any recourse to the electorate, the "right to work" concept exists in every country. Their social legislation, which the Latin Americans pompously proclaim to be "the most advanced in the world," is, in fact, anti-union legislation, because what the mislabeled "right to work" laws do is weaken the unions and enable employers to block the organization of the vast majority of the workers. The percentage of unionized workers is sharply lower in Latin America than in the United States, and this is due in great part to the "right to work."[37]

Latin America's electoral systems are equally corrupt. On the one hand, it is hard to believe that the peasants can vote freely,

[37] Alba, *Historia del movimiento obrero en América Latina* (Mexico City, 1964). An English-language translation of this work will be published by Stanford University Press in 1966.

subjected as they are to the systems described previously. On the other hand, in many countries, only those who can read and write have the vote. In Brazil, for this very reason, only 13 million people vote; another 20 million adult Brazilians are illiterate and, therefore, have rights to defend but may not vote. In Peru, as well, the vote is denied to illiterates, also on the pretext that whoever cannot read or write cannot be qualified to vote. This would lead one to conclude that those who read and write are qualified. But logic forces us to recall that the Germans, all of them literate, voted Hitler into power in 1933. And we must further remember that the political systems of the United States, Great Britain, and France were established when most of their populations were illiterate.

Under these conditions, to talk about democracy (even representative democracy, which is only a caricature of true democracy) is a joke. In Latin America, elections are held and the people vote. But rarely are the masses governed by those they would have chosen had they been able to participate. This, of course, is not to mention the times when duly elected governments cannot assume power because the army (that is, the oligarchy) prevents them.

These systems of corruption would not be possible, nor would the government belong to the oligarchy, except for the existence of a tradition peculiar to Latin America that created a climate propitious to these situations. I mean, of course, the long tradition of state paternalism. Before the coming of the Spaniards, the Indian nations were theocratic or warrior states, whose rulers exercised aristocratic paternalism. The colony, with its laws to protect the Indians, its *encomiendas,* its trade monopoly, and its control of immigration, was also paternalistic. With independence and during the nineteenth century, state intervention decreased, although the *caudillos* generally maintained a paternalistic attitude on the part of the state, especially evident in the spread of protectionism—in an era when most of the public revenues came from tariffs—and in the fact that no national budgets were prepared until well into the nineteenth century. Today this tradition still continues of always relying on the state, of considering the state responsible for the economic well-being, if not of the country, at least of the pressure groups, and of believing the state to be charged with the task of supporting and assisting the interests of these groups. Both the new classes rising in opposition to the oligarchy and the submerged masses have learned the oligarchy's lesson. The state must protect them.

And perhaps this, which did not happen consciously or deliberately, represents the worst form of corruption, a sort of corruption by history.

From the catalogue just recited, there would appear to be many meaty areas of study for the sociologists and economists of Latin America. Tax evasion alone presents a thousand opportunities, as does the flight of capital. One can imagine the psychoanalytic interpretations that might be constructed about the flood of official, officious, and semiofficial (as well as opposition) statements on the subject of foreign investments, and about the criticism of their presence and the criticism, no less sharp, of their absence, often from the lips of a single person or in the publications of a single institution. One could well imagine that the specialists, psychologists, and economists would dance for joy at such an abundance of subject matter. Nowhere can one find a systematic analysis of the failure to apply the law, or of the distortion of the spirit of the law through insistence on obeying its letter, or of the difference between legislation and fact. And no one can say that potential authors have been discouraged by a lack of cases.

But these subjects remain untreated. No one has studied these aspects of the Latin American reality.

Latin Americans seem to feel a peculiar hostility to these matters that are basic in their lives. For example, there is no good modern study of militarism. Nor is there any on another aspect of Latin American life that is extremely important—corruption in the literal sense.

It is a phenomenon of considerable importance. In some countries, corruption on a large scale has been responsible for the primitive accumulation of capital, which has made it possible to start the process of industrialization. However, this sort of corruption has, in most cases, been only a means of enrichment for the politicians in the service of the oligarchy, only an instrument of political control. Although in a few countries it is found only on the highest political levels, in most it has spread throughout all the administrative levels and even beyond the limits of government. This means that the bureaucrats can augment their meager salaries, and it helps the administrative machinery to function. In this sense, corruption is not economically bad, as long as it permits red tape to be cut and problems to be resolved that, under any other conditions and given the administrative inefficiency of almost all Latin American governments, would perpetuate themselves without hope of solution.

But the important fact is the use of corruption by the oligarchy as a tool for political domination. *Caciquismo,* the old strong-man system of government based on the use of violence, persists only in the rural areas of a few countries; it has been replaced in the rest of the continent by a new version of the same thing, the corruption of political supporters. It is easier for the oligarchy to corrupt than to win over or convince, since the oligarchy has no program, but hands out money, influence, and concessions to those who assist or tolerate it. Naturally, the existence of this corruption nullifies most of the effects of foreign aid, since a percentage of any aid received is filtered down, by unaccountable means, through the channels of corruption. Moreover, corruption employed as a political device permits the oligarchs to sleep peacefully, because they know that a large segment of the leaders who call themselves "revolutionaries" (Castroites or Communists) are as corrupt as the oligarchs themselves, collect salaries from the state, often without working for them, and at the very least acquire sinecures. For this reason, although these "revolutionaries" indulge in a whole gamut of extreme declarations, they almost never get themselves involved in action and almost never, in periods of crisis, take any clear-cut or effective stand. The oligarchy silences or disables them merely by the threat to cut off their salaries or sinecures. However, the oligarchy has never yet used this means to prevent the "revolutionaries" from adopting a pro-Soviet position in foreign-policy matters—because the oligarchy utilizes such positions to exert greater pressure on United States policy and (given the ingenuousness of that policy) to extract more foreign-aid funds. Despite substantial leakage at every stage, these funds increase corruption and even finance the buying-up of the selfsame "revolutionary" leaders. What is astounding is that the United States has not realized all this; it still believes that its aid is helping the people of Latin America.

There are two ways these swindlers may use their payoff: They may reinvest it (use it as national capital to assist the process of industrialization), or they may export it to foreign bank accounts. The first type of theft implies confidence in the people who are being robbed, while the second does not. The first sort of corruption usually occurs only in countries in which revolution has done away with the landholding oligarchy. Here the corruptors born of the people are no less immoral than the oligarchs, but they know their people better and know that there can be progress. Where the oligarchy is still dominant, the corruptors are the oligarchs themselves, who neither know the people, nor trust them. They fear the people, and so they export what they steal. The first brand of corruption is positive—in the terminology of capitalist economics, without ethical trappings—the second is negative.[38]

Naturally, corruption finds fertile ground among politicians. It may be, however, that the politician's greatest sin is not venality but a more insidious and subtle type of corruption; a sort of glorification of inefficiency, an inflating of the personality, a delight in uselessness itself, which makes Latin American politicians of whatever leaning truly despots in a minor key, satraps of the pocketbook (the pocketbook of the oligarchs, of course). This specimen of humanity is well illustrated in an article in the Mexican newspaper *Excélsior*.

> After discourses lasting hours and even whole days, after inflamed debates that at times approached physical violence, and after discussion of dozens of subjects on a scale in which the trivial is raised to unimaginable heights, the problems of America have not varied by so much as a millimeter.
>
> This took place in Washington a week ago. It was a noisy meeting, composed of a crowd of legislators from the whole continent. The delegations were very large: 15, 20, even 30 representatives from each country. They came, in the words of one Demosthenes of the south, to examine the problems of America "under the glass of intelligence and democracy."
>
> Senator Antonio Mena Brito, leader of the Mexican delegation, was interviewed on his return from Washington.
>
> "Was anything achieved at this conference?" he was asked. "Was

---

[38] It would be worthwhile to consult Mark Twain's *The Gilded Age,* a novel about corruption in Washington around 1870. The same words could be used to describe the capitals of Latin America today, the only difference being that the corrupt politicians of present-day Latin America would have to pay much less attention to its readers than did the American politicians of a century ago. It is revealing that there are almost no novels dealing with corruption in Latin America.

any progress made in solving the problems which have prevented efficient operation of the Alliance for Progress?"

"Nothing was achieved and no agreement of any kind was reached. The delegates did not even succeed in understanding each other. For example, the Chileans argued among themselves. They went to the rostrum, as if they were in their parliament at home, to attack one of their own colleagues who had defended the Cuban revolution. They carried on about whether the Chilean Government is competent. The other delegations found themselves plunged into a discussion about the internal affairs of one country."

"The meeting must have been useful in establishing personal contacts to improve relations between the Latin American legislators and those from the United States. . . ."

"Not at all. The delegates ended up furious at their hosts, the U.S. Congressmen. They complained that they didn't have the necessary equipment to do their work."

"What sort of equipment?"

"Typewriters, interpreters, secretaries . . ."

"Was this true?"

"Well, what happened was that everything was disorganized. It was impossible to satisfy so many tastes, so many chiefs; there were a lot of people giving orders, everyone wanted to present a report, everyone wanted to have an interview with the big celebrities in Washington. Then, our Latin American brothers complained that the United States Congressmen were not interested in the meeting. There were 20 people in the U.S. delegation; only 2 came to the final meetings."

"The meeting really wasn't interesting?"

"At the beginning, it was. For example, there was a Spanish observer. He talked at great length about religion, atheists, and bad Catholics. There was a lot of high-sounding language, and so many eulogies to our American heroes that they became exasperating. Poetic phrases and pompous hogwash were the characteristics of the meeting, not analysis or any political position.

"As far as the Alliance was concerned, the delegates displayed total ignorance. Their contributions focused on two subjects: Fidel Castro, the villain, and Kennedy, the hero. Practical suggestions, objective criticism, and documented opinions just did not appear. They seem to think of the Alliance for Progress as a huge strongbox raining money. That is what it means to them."[39]

[39] Julio Manuel Ramírez, "Imperiosa necesidad . . . ," *Excélsior* (Mexico City), February 19, 1964.

The people who attend meetings such as this, if they read what I write, will say that in taking the lid off this garbage can, I am betraying the interests of Latin America. So what!

I damage the interests, I fervently hope, of the oligarchy and its vociferous fellow travelers, who serve it and Moscow simultaneously, but I defend the interests of the people, which are incompatible with those of the oligarchy. The people are not helped at all by the existence of this garbage can and it is better for them if it is revealed. As long as Latins and North Americans do not know (or do not dare to know) that the can is full of garbage, everything they do, including what they think they are doing for the people's benefit, will benefit only the oligarchy, will reinforce it, and give it greater opportunities to oppress, deceive, and manipulate the people. Only when the United States is convinced that there is garbage in the can will there be hope that it will alter its policy to do such things and grant such assistance as will truly benefit the people.

Of course, the oligarchy is not one monolithic entity that holds meetings and decides by majority vote what policy to follow. Within it (often without realizing that they belong to it) are groups that differ in interests and ideology. For instance, during the nineteenth century, there were the liberals and the conservatives: the first, anticlerical; and the second, "mochos" (tonsured like monks). The principal difference between them, the saying went, was that the liberals went to mass at ten and the conservatives at noon. Then there were the radicals, more democratic, more popular. And the demagogues like Perón, who talked a lot about the oligarchy but were careful not to harm it, and even Goulart, who was thrown out of office lest he really find himself forced to move against the oligarchy.

There are refined and cultured oligarchies, like the Chilean, which succeeds in perpetuating itself in power democratically and even dares to take part in the Popular Front. And there are divided oligarchies, like the Peruvian, which is split between the ruffians of the highlands and the gentlemen of the coast, who mechanize their plantations and organize banks. There are brutal, barbarous oligarchies, like the Venezuelan, and degenerate, cheap, alcoholic oligarchies, like those of El Salvador and Panama.

The great strength of the oligarchy—due more to circumstances than to its insight—is that education, habits of thought, ways of life, and culture all combine to make it impossible for the people to conceive of any system that is not oligarchic. The politicians of the left, who often would like to alter the situation, cannot imagine what would follow if they did succeed in destroying the oligarchy. The truth is that no one talked about the oligarchy until Perón made the word fashionable in 1946. And he was thinking in terms of a political more than of a social revolution.

Ultimately, the closest parallel to the Latin American oligarchy may well be the Soviet bureaucracy, which, despite the unceasing struggle for power at its core, presents a united exterior that has created a mentality and a state of mind that prevents the Russians from conceiving of any regime essentially different from the oligarchy that exploits and oppresses them.

Catalogue of Scapegoats

What Unamuno wrote twenty years ago is still true in Latin America today: "The nationalism, the patriotism of the great communities of history . . . is generally a result of the coercive culture of the great landowners, the landlords, the feudal seigniors, and the masters of latifundia."[40]

But in the middle of the twentieth century, when the landlords want to maintain an eighteenth-century society (and in certain respects, it is even more anachronistic), then that nationalism which once was natural must now be created artificially in order to shift attention, calm anger, draw off hatreds, and deflect to other targets blows that logically—in accordance with twentieth-century logic—should be aimed at the oligarchy. For this purpose, the oligarchy has proved very adept at promoting scapegoats. Of course, the oligarchy has found valuable allies in social groups that have also sought scapegoats to reconcile their consciences, which demand change, with their comfort, which demands immobility. The scapegoat makes it possible to justify immobility by reasons other than the real one—the desire not to run risks.

In the search for scapegoats, good use is made of the obvious errors, the bad faith, and the objectionable attitudes of various countries in the past. For some, it is the United States that is to

[40] Unamuno, *op. cit.,* p. 286.

blame for everything; for others, it is the U.S.S.R. or Castro's Cuba; for still others, it is colonial Spain.

A good part of what is imputed to these countries is true. Imperial Spain bequeathed many of its vices and its problems to Latin America. The U.S.S.R. and Castro's Cuba, in the role of bogeymen, reinforced immobility on the one hand, and on the other conditioned the masses to accept all sorts of demagoguery. By its support of the private interests of large North American companies and by the arrogance of some of its diplomatic overseers, the United States helped to paralyze Latin America and to create well-founded resentment within the ranks of Latin America's democratic forces.

But all this is not enough to justify passivity in the face of the oligarchs. To attribute *all* the blame to one of these scapegoats is to exonerate the oligarchy and to disguise the fact that the principal and fundamental source of all the blame is the oligarchy.

For this very reason, the oligarchy seizes gratefully on "anti-imperialism" and, through its press, radio, and television, echoes the propaganda campaigns against the United States (now that it is fashionable to blame everything on the United States). In the encouragement of anti-Yankee sentiment, the oligarchy is just as efficient as the Communists—if not more so. That is why the oligarchy never really harasses the Communists (although this does not mean that I believe that they should be harassed just because they are Communists). That is also why the oligarchy today pursues a policy of "nationalism," which is another way of saying an anti-Yankee policy (as in the cases of Goulart and the revocations of oil contracts in Argentina and Peru).

A recent example is significant (and at the same time reflects how timid or un-imaginative are the people in charge of United States propaganda). During the Panama crisis, the Latin American press was full of photographs (from U.S. news services) of the houses of the residents of the Canal Zone, those horrible suburban houses with their patch of lawn and the automobile in front of the door. Naturally, photographs were included of the miserable hovels in Panama City (also taken by U.S. services). A magazine editor I know wanted to publish photographs of the homes of the wealthy Panamanians, much more luxurious, infuriating, and objectionable (and in much poorer taste) than the houses in the Canal Zone. No news service in the United States had pictures of them. The photographers had not thought that they would interest anyone, and no one can blame them. For of the hundreds of reports on the Canal crisis published in the United States and in Latin America, I cannot recall a single one that pointed out the fact that the difference between the houses in Panama and the Canal Zone would not be so extreme if the Panamanian oligarchs—only twenty families—were not parasites on their countrymen. And no one mentioned that it was these same families who granted the United States a lease on the Zone in perpetuity, just as it is the fabulously wealthy families throughout Latin America who gave or sold concessions to the business interests of North America, Germany, Britain, France, Belgium, and Canada. For there must be quislings within a country in order to open the doors to imperialism. And now it is the quislings of Latin America who have become the most nationalistic and the readiest to nationalize everything—everything except their own lands. So you see how a lack of political common sense on the part of United States journalists serves anti-Yankee sentiment and the oligarchy, since it makes it easier for the people to forget the existence of the oligarchy hiding behind the smokescreen of anti-Yankee propaganda.

The Communists and Castroites would not enjoy the support they do were it not for the benevolent generosity of the oligarchy. The most rabid anti-Yankees hold posts in universities, write for newspapers, speak on the radio, appear on television, and discourse in centers of "high" culture. All this is paid for directly or indirectly out of the state budget. The oligarchy itself does not pay, since there are no patrons or foundations in Latin America. But the oligarchy does administer the budget through its politicians and high government officials. What we find in Latin America are not parlor Communists, but budget Communists. Suddenly, in the matter of people who rant and rave against the United States, the oligarchy discovers an extraordinary libertarian sensibility and decides that to prevent the use of public funds by these people would be to infringe their liberty. But this sensibility disappears when, by chance, someone arises who really attacks the oligarchy and might pose a danger to it. A glance at publishers' catalogues—especially those publishers connected with universities or otherwise supported by the state—would reveal an abundance of anti-imperialist works with a single target (never, however, against Soviet imperialism) and a complete absence of books attacking the oligarchy.

The matter of "anti-imperialism" is most curious. It is, at times, obsessive, although there are sufficient grounds for its existence, considering the number of times that the North Americans themselves have felt it necessary to criticize their own government for its myopic, absurd, and incoherent policy toward Latin America and the fervor with which their government conferred medals on Latin American dictators. But who can explain why it is that two of the countries where anti-Yankeeism is most acute and most virulent are Uruguay, where there are almost no U.S. investments, and Bolivia, where the mining oligarchy is made up partly of Bolivians and partly of capitalists from Chile and other Latin American countries? Why is there no attack on British capital in Argentina and Uruguay, or on German capital in Brazil? Granted that there are psychological motives, but there is also an indisputable fact: The United States is the nation that at the moment, albeit weakly and uncertainly, is pushing for structural changes, and so it suits the oligarchy to impair the prestige of the United States. Moreover, it is Washington, not Bonn or London, that is challenging Moscow, and the Communists would not put their "anti-imperialist" propaganda at the service of the oligarchy if it were not directed at Washington. And, by the way, who can show me even a half-dozen books or serious studies by Communists or fellow travelers on the Latin American oligarchy? In the few that exist, the oligarchy appears as the scullery maid, the mere instrument of U.S. capital and Washington's policy, when the fact of the matter—which the United States still does not see—is that the oligarchy has used U.S. investors and the State Department as its own instrument, often against the best interests of the United States. Naturally, this would not have been possible except for the mental fog that afflicts U.S. diplomats, who are often more preoccupied with the threat of expropriation (or propaganda about it) than with trying to bring the democratic and antitotalitarian aspects of U.S. policy into a genuine collaboration with Latin America.

To say all this is not to defend or attack any country. It is simply a statement of fact. And, above all, to render to the oligarchs what is theirs is to apply the proverb: *"Que cada palo aguante su vela"* ("Let every mast carry its own sail").

Apart from this, the truth is that if the United States did not exist, the oligarchy would have to invent it. In a sense that is what has happened. What I have heard about the United States in Latin America is not much different from what I have heard in the U.S.S.R., and neither has any relation to reality. The criticisms that could legitimately be made about the United States are never made, because they could be applied to a much greater degree to the oligarchy; instead, faults and attitudes are invented which the United States does not have. And this is done, almost always, with public funds provided by the people, administered by the oligarchy, and siphoned off by the Communists. And do not forget, where there is an oligarchy, the old rule applies that the one who pays is the one who rules.

Here is an example. The Communists effectively use the racial problem in the United States to picture it as a racist nation. But they forget to add (because the oligarchy would not allow it) that in Latin America there is racism as well, racism in other forms, but racism none the less. It is a clever paternalistic racism in which violence is replaced by exploitation and the theory of white superiority appears only as a grimace of scorn. In the last analysis, Negroes and Indians are treated not only as economic inferiors but as racial and cultural inferiors, as well. To pretend otherwise is to play the game of the oligarchy, which profits from this silent racism.

Protest against racism in the United States? Of course! And in South Africa and the U.S.S.R. (neither of which is mentioned in Latin America). But if racism is so repugnant to us, why not, above all, protest and fight against racism in Latin America? Many of the most vehement anti-Yankees have Indian or Negro servants in their homes. If one pins these people down in a discussion of the subject, they always come up with this reply: "They are better off here than in their own village." But how many of these Indian or Negro servants have a shower in their room? Do they eat the same food as their employers? But we do not ask these questions because we know beforehand what the answer will be, and we prefer to avoid having to tell our friend to go to hell or else tolerating his concealed racism.[41]

In the field of international politics, the manipulation of scape-

[41] It is easy to prove that throughout Latin America servants prefer North American employers most, Europeans second, and their own countrymen last. There must be a reason—and not only salary, although that would be reason enough.

goats reaches heights of true magic. It should be pointed out that the same armies who so heroically occupy the countries which support them have never contributed troops to the United Nations forces in Korea, Israel, Cyprus, or the Congo (except in the case of Korea, where the Colombian Army, in political control at the time, sent a minuscule symbolic force). This alone should be enough to indicate how devoid the oligarchy is of any sense of international brotherhood and how even in the diplomatic area they pursue a policy of leaving the United States the job of pulling the chestnuts out of the fire.

How is it possible that those oligarchic states, which should fear Cuba and Communism, are so loath to take effective countermeasures against Castro and the Communists (and that when they had dictators they even allied themselves with the Communists)? The answer is twofold but obvious.

1. The oligarchies know very well that the Communists are not trying to seize power but only to create difficulties for the United States. If the oligarchic governments themselves create some of these difficulties, the Communists will not prove intractable in internal affairs. From this derives the axiom that the more reactionary a country's internal policy, the more leftist-oriented is its foreign policy.

2. If the threat from the Castroites and Communists, seen in this perspective, is directed toward the United States, why should Latin American governments get involved and provoke problems internally with the Communists by assisting the policy of the United States—especially when the United States, because of its investment in the countries concerned, will fight the danger for them?

From the point of view of the oligarch—who feels secure in the ability of his military and police forces to prevent any dangerous Communist activity in the country—this position is exactly right. What threatens the oligarchies is not the Communists but the pressure for change exerted from Washington. The people are threatened by the Communists, the technocrats, and the oligarchs, who exploit the people and keep them submerged. The interests of the Communists and of the oligarchs coincide; the interests of the people and of the United States coincide. And the oligarchs are immensely pleased when they see that in spite of this, Washington seeks to tie itself to oligarchic governments.

When one of these governments expropriates, or threatens to

expropriate, a foreign-owned industry, it does so not for the good of the people, but solely for the benefit of the oligarchy, whose interests it administers. When it adopts positions that appear very radical (but always only verbally and never translating them into fact), it does so, again, to protect the interests of the oligarchy. Similarly, it is a common error to think of João Goulart as an extremist or a leftist, when in fact, his whole political biography shows him to be an able oligarchic politico.

But there are at present in Latin America (or at least in most of the countries there) pressures that are mistakenly viewed in the United States as leftist (and by this reasoning, the foreign policy of the United States is automatically considered rightist). These pressures are verbal and only rarely become hardened into facts. Almost always they relate to international policy: The young expansionist businessmen want to do business with the countries of the Soviet bloc and with Communist China. The intellectuals and students, the habitual signers of manifestoes, want to "protect" Castro and win trips for themselves to Moscow or Peking.

The oligarchic governments display a willingness to follow a foreign policy that, in order to hide their true purposes, they call nationalistic. This is the reason why one finds governments which one would expect to be as determined to "block Castro" as the most intransigent groups in the United States (especially since the Venezuelan experience) but which, in fact, line up in opposition to the United States' Cuban policy. Why? Because by doing so, they satisfy the most vociferous "leftists" within their countries, they soothe them and thus buy the passivity and even the complicity of this "left" toward their internal policies, which always defend the interest of the oligarchy.

These governments experience pressure from other sectors of public opinion, as well: from the most conservative and hidebound of the oligarchy, who see Communists behind every bush, and, above all, from democratic elements, the authentic left, who believe that Castroism and Communism are forces of political and social reaction and who see in the present-day United States a force for political and social progress (although frequently they do not dare to say so, for fear of being labeled "servants of imperialism").

Thus it happens, on occasion, that a military man or an oligarchic political group will feel obliged to pull the rug out from under a demagogue who is no longer useful or who, it is thought, has gone too far and could become dangerous, or who, as in the case of Goulart, has acquired such a love of power that he is capable of betraying his masters, the oligarchs. Then there is a lot of talk about anti-Communism and a coup takes place. In the end, the local Communists escape because they are trained to do so and protected (very often they belong to the families of the oligarchy), and those who are persecuted and accused of being Communists are the few elements who really want social change.

In spite of many spectacular gestures, the dictators do not change their foreign policy. Do not forget that the Chilean and Brazilian oligarchs broke relations with the Communist bloc in 1949–50 and outlawed the Communist parties of their countries. The consequences of this action were zero.

Apparently, United States diplomacy has never understood that the more socially reactionary a Latin American regime is, the more "leftist" (neutralist or demagogic) its foreign policy will be.

And this brings us to a phenomenon which sums up all the corruption, all the scapegoats, all that is incredible and deplorable in the oligarchy: that is, political concubinage.

Catalogue of Concubinage

The oligarchy protests that it is anti-Communist. So it is, most assuredly, in the sense that it does not want to be replaced by the Communists in its position of political control and of *de facto* monopoly of land ownership. But the oligarchy has faith in its ability to corrupt and maneuver, and does not fear the Communists. Its anti-Communism is verbal and based on dollars.

Furthermore, every time the Communist movement has achieved any advance in Latin America, it has followed a period when the oligarchy abandoned "democratic" forms and reverted to dictatorship (never, let it be said, to avoid the nonexistent threat of Communism, but always to avoid current or future attempts at social reform). All the Latin American dictatorships of the last thirty years have relied on the cooperation of local Communists. This is an unquestionable fact, one which has been pointed out by the few existing experts on the subject, but which neither the diplomats nor the businessmen of the United States, nor the middle classes nor the intellectuals of Latin America, believe or realize or want to realize. Nevertheless, a simple review of history will prove it.[42]

In Argentina, Perón always depended on the advice of the Communist Rodolfo Puiggrós and the support of the Communist League and its youth group. It was the Communists who worked most intimately with the Peronist labor leaders to remove the socialists and anarchosyndicalists from their positions in the unions. No Communists were attacked on the night Perón unleashed his followers against the Jockey Club and the socialist Casa del Pueblo. The opposition of the Ghioldi-Codovilla Communist group did not turn out to be very aggressive, and few Communists went to jail; on the contrary, Perón never withheld passports or visas to Communists wishing to travel to international congresses. Two months before Perón's fall in September, 1955, the first Soviet industrial exposition ever held in Spanish America opened in Buenos Aires. Since the dictator's flight, the Peronists and Communists have cooperated closely in constant sabotage against the democratic regime.

In Colombia, the Partido Socialista Popular (Popular Socialist Party—the local Communist group) called the Liberal guerrillas' battle against the police—first the police of the extreme Conservatives and later those of Rojas Pinilla—a "reactionary maneuver."

In Cuba, the Partido Socialista Popular (also the local Communists), after having opposed the governments of Ramón Grau San Martín and Carlos Prío Socarrás, contributed several high officials to the regime of General Batista: Julián Sotolongo, Gilberto Galán, Mercedes Chirino, Guillermo Pérez Lamy, and Arsenio González (Under Secretary of Labor). These Communists made up a group, in apparent dissent with the Party, that joined Batista's Acción Progresista (Progressive Action) movement. The official Communist Party, meanwhile, carried on in benevolent secrecy, and when Fidel Castro ordered a general strike in April, 1958, the leadership of the Party, without condemning the move, declared that it had no chance of success. In August, 1958, the Party attempted to break openly with Batista and proposed a union of all opposition groups. This proposal was harshly criticized by Castro's 26th of July Movement.

[42] For further details, consult: Robert J. Alexander, *Communism in Latin America* (New Brunswick, N.J., 1957), and Alba, *Historia del movimiento obrero.*

In Venezuela, the "black" Communists collaborated with the military junta that overthrew Rómulo Gallegos and the Acción Democrática government in 1948; later, they supported Colonel Pérez Jiménez, while their "red" colleagues were working in exile. Both parties, however, joined in fierce attacks on the force that was most active in resisting the dictatorship—Acción Democrática (Democratic Action)—and both had their activists in the forefront of the labor unions, from which, with the dictator's aid, they had ousted the independent and democratic elements. This double game paid off, for when Pérez Jiménez fell, in January, 1958, the Communists were accepted by all the political parties. Nevertheless, they did not succeed in getting the candidate they backed into power.

In Peru, the Communists led by Juan P. Luna (a Senator during the Odría dictatorship) collaborated actively in the government, especially in the removal (with police assistance) of elements of APRA (Alianza Popular Revolucionaria Americana, or American Popular Revolutionary Alliance) from management of the labor unions, some of which, especially those in the south, continued under Communist control after Odría left office. The Communists supported the most reactionary candidate attempting to succeed the dictator, and when Manuel Prado was elected President with the help of APRA, they organized several strikes, which had nothing to do with union demands, but were intended to create an atmosphere conducive to a new military *coup d'état*.

In Brazil, the Communists supported Vargas—who had persecuted them actively—succeeded rather well in infiltrating the army, and maintained their influence among the mass of voters. In October, 1958, for electoral purposes, the Communists allied themselves with two undeniably demogogic parties, the Labor Party of Vargas' son and of Goulart, and the Social Progressive Party of Adhemar de Barros, the mayor of São Paulo (who now is a rabid anti-Communist). The Communist leader, Luiz Carlos Prestes, declared that the alliance was unconditional and permanent; nonetheless, it broke up with a considerable loss of votes for the Communists. In 1964, at the end, the peasants supported Goulart again.

In 1946, the Dominican government of Generalissimo Trujillo permitted the formation of a Partido Socialista Popular. For this purpose, Ramón Marrero Aristy traveled to Cuba, where he convinced exiled Dominican Communist leaders to form the party and to organize new labor unions (in which Trujillo elements cooperated with the Communists), in affiliation with the CTAL (Confederación de Trabajadores de América Latina, or Confederation of Latin American Workers). After the elections were over, Trujillo once again declared the Communist Party illegal. In 1961, however, he allowed the creation of a Castroite party directed by Máximo López Molina.

In 1944, there were numerous demonstrations in Nicaragua demanding that the Somoza family give up its political control. The Communists opposed these demonstrations. One of the Communist leaders was even brought into the government as a vice minister, and at present, the Communists are collaborating with the "anti-Communist" regime put in power by the Somozas.

In the series of dictatorships that ruled Paraguay, the Communists have sometimes been against one dictator and at other times supported another. Moríñigo, for example, permitted the creation of a Workers' Council, directed by the Communists.

In Costa Rica, in 1955, when the democratic José Figueres was in power, the Communists collaborated with their old ally Calderón Guardia and other elements, in an attempted invasion of Costa Rican territory from Nicaragua. In this, they received the active support of Somoza and Pérez Jiménez.

This concubinage is incomprehensible only to those who believe that the Communists belong to the left. The mechanics of this tacit alliance are evident. The Communists are useful to a dictator because they allow him to claim that under his regime there is no political persecution; because they destroy (often with the help of the dictator's police) the democratic leadership of the labor unions, and they turn control over to him, since there are no strikes against dictators; because they often supply advisers of undoubted political ability (a very necessary thing for the military); and because they offer the dictator an instrument of pressure and exploitation against Washington. For the Communists, the purpose of the relationship, in addition to utilizing the dictator's strength to destroy their democratic opponents, is the enjoyment of a clear field to build the political and union organization that one day, when the dictator falls, will serve as a base for other Communists, those in exile.

To make this picture even more colorful, one should remember that dictators have been decorated by the government of the United States, that the White House served as a stage setting for embraces between Presidents and dictators, and also that certain United States business interests have made their own unholy alliances with the Latin American military. But to write about that is just a waste of time and paper because Communist propaganda is already busy reminding us of it (as another means of making us forget the concubinage between the Communists and the dictators). On the other hand, no one recalls the close relations, secret as well as public, of the Communists and the Latin American military. To bring this up does not mean, however, that one can excuse or forget any of the intrigues carried on by the United States, or Great Britain, or even by several Latin American governments.

That the calculations of the Communists in this regard are not mistaken may be seen from what happens when the dictatorships fall from power. The end of the Perón regime, in 1955, signaled the beginning of the end for the other Latin American dictatorships (in Peru, Colombia, Venezuela, and Cuba), although some still persist in the smaller nations. The Communists, in each case, found themselves in the position of being able to participate in the political life of the re-established democracies, thanks to that wing which had operated in exile or in secrecy. In some places, the Communists who had collaborated with the dictator disappeared from the political scene; in others, as in Peru, they continued operating openly, creating difficulties for the democratic regime. In still others, such as Cuba, they capitalized on the political inexperience of the successful democratic opposition to dominate and control it.

Such nonrevolutionary figures as Marshal Henrique Teixeira Lott in Brazil and Rear Admiral Wolfgang Larrazábal in Venezuela enjoyed Communist support for their candidacies. How can this be explained? By the simple fact that inept rulers (and no one is more inept than a military man) who can be manipulated and influenced suit the Communists.

The oligarchy is not squeamish. For more than a decade it repeated over and over that the Bolivian MNR (Movimiento Nacionalista Revolucionario, or Nationalist Revolutionary Movement) was Communist. And once the most demagogic wing of the MNR, supported by the Communists and led by Juan Lechín, split off from the main party, whom did the oligarchic opposition groups that made up the Socialist Falange ally themselves with? With Lechín.[43]

When the oligarchs who bring about or arrange military *coups d'état* claim that they are going after the Communists, one cannot really believe them. A clear example was that of the Dominican coup of 1963. The oligarchs and military accused Juan Bosch of being a Communist or at least favoring Communism. Nevertheless, when the dictatorial triumvirate took power, it harassed democrats, not Communists. One month after the coup, I was in Santo Domingo and wrote as follows:

The coup of September 25 was made on the pretext that Juan Bosch was handing over the government and the country to the Communists. Many of the military and not a few of the merchants, whose shop strike prepared the way for the coup, believed this out of political illiteracy and lack of critical faculty.

From all the elements supporting the coup of whom I requested lists of Communists appointed by Bosch to posts in the government, I received essentially the same answer:

"That is a matter of public record. Everyone knows them."

But up to October 17, some seventy members of the PRD [Bosch's Partido Revolucionario Dominicano, or Dominican Revolutionary Party] had been deported and only six people with Communist leanings.

Even the military—especially the young ones—ask themselves:

"Why aren't the Communists arrested? Where are the arms caches we heard so much about before the coup?"

The police—10,000 of them—have not found any.

The truth is quite different. Anybody who knows the country can guess what it is, because everyone knows everyone else in the Dominican Republic. "Everyone" means, of course, the few thousand people who make policy and appear in the newspapers, their wives, their mothers, and their daughters. And everyone knows that, except for a few well-trained activists drawn from the people, the Dominican Communists and Castroites are *"gente bien"*—well-born—the nephews, cousins, sons, or brothers-in-law of members of the government of the triumvirate. And not one of them has been arrested or deported (or is likely to be).

There are two areas where the sentimental Castroites (more than the disciplined Communists) have a degree of influence: in the

[43] *Libertad* (La Paz), December, 1963.

Fragua [Forge] group in the University (the weakest of the three student groups) and the Agrupación 14 de Junio [The 14th of June Group] (which should not be confused with the Partido 14 de Junio [The 14th of June Party], made up of one-time elements of the Agrupación which broke off due to a reluctance to accept its Castroite sympathies). But neither of these two nuclei, by themselves, can seize power or represent any cause for alarm, although in both there are young elements full of enthusiasm, which under the proper circumstances could be pushed to violence. Precisely for this reason, in order not to drive them to terrorism, Bosch never wanted to harass them.

Dr. J. A. Bonilla Atiles, the triumvirate's Ambassador to the OAS, has made public a list of "Communists." In the Dominican Republic, it has not been widely distributed, but, even so, it is the joke of the day. People on the street greet each other at the top of their lungs (as good Caribbeans, the Dominicans do not know how to speak any other way): "Aren't you on Bonilla's uncle's list?"

The list contains the names of a businessman, Diego Bordas (whose inclusion in the Bosch government displeased many), a couple of Bosch's ministers, two radio and TV owners, a secretary of the Senate, the president of the Chamber of Deputies, a North American, and an ex-leader of the Unión Cívica Nacional, which supported the coup.

This list is for external consumption only. Inside the country, no one can take it seriously. I—who am not, I believe, suspected of having any weakness toward Communists—I can guarantee that at least half of the names on it are those of democratic people who have no tie with either Castroism or Communism.

This cannot be said of the triumvirate. In the first place, because many of the parlor Communists are, as I said, related to ministers of the government. In the second place, because the triumvirate has done nothing to combat the alleged Communist peril. In the third place, because I know at first hand that Juan Bosch found at least twenty-four Castroites and Communists placed in administrative positions by the Council of State (always relatives of Communists), whose spirit still animates the triumvirate.[44]

But this should not surprise us. For the oligarchy, the danger lies not in Moscow or Havana but in Washington, where there are under secretaries who occasionally point a finger directly at the oligarchs themselves as the source on which Communism feeds.

[44] Alba, "Los comunistas bien . . . ," *Excélsior,* October 20, 1963.

If, in politics, we could give proper place to the desire for justice, clearly what Latin America deserves is a terrorist movement like the Russian *Narodniki* or the nihilists, or the French and Spanish anarchists of the early part of this century. The Russian *mujik*, liberated from serfdom by the Czar, was better off than the Latin American peasant. But I doubt that many of the daughters of the Latin American oligarchy know how to plant bombs as did more than a few of the daughters of the Russian aristocracy.

Nonetheless, history has proved the ineffectiveness of those movements, however just their intentions. In Latin America, they would be of no more use than they were in Russia, France, or Spain.

What can be done to emerge from this quagmire in which Latin America is caught by the perpetuation of a system which even a century ago was anachronistic, uneconomic, unesthetic, paralyzing, and inhuman?

The oligarchy keeps Latin America on the edge of history or, at least, by dragging its steps, it forces the continent to advance by a parallel road, laboring in its passage but never reaching its goal. The oligarchy held back the process of industrialization in the last century, when it was natural and could have been spontaneous, and has permitted only a forced and unbalanced industrialization, based in large measure on foreign capital. It has blocked the course of Latin American unification and the trend against nationalism, which would have made possible the solution of many of the area's problems. It has left Latin America disarmed, without defense against foreign attack by diverting armies from their proper mission and by blocking unification, which would have led, logically, to the creation of a Latin American army.

Finally, it is alienating Latin America from its natural place in the Atlantic Community. With its nationalism, its flirtations with Communists and Castroites, with its antiquated militarism, with its uneconomic systems of production, the oligarchy places Latin America not only on the edge of history but also outside of the world. And by doing so, it injures not only Latin America but the world, as well.

II

NOTES FOR A TREATISE ON MYTHOLOGY

Catalogue of False Axioms

A SOCIETY based on an anachronistic and uneconomic system of land ownership can survive only if it succeeds in winning the conformity of groups that would logically be committed to altering the existing social structure.

Such a victory can be accomplished only if reality is masked behind a series of falsehoods or disguises. This masking is certainly not deliberate or conscious, and does not follow an orderly plan. It results from the convergence of the desire of the landowning oligarchy to conceal its power and the desire of the classes that should be reformers to hide their conformism or to make it look like nonconformism. The oligarchy wants material peace, and the middle classes (or the public-opinion group, as we have called them) want an easy conscience. To achieve peace and quiet without altering reality, myths must be created. These myths come not from legends handed down from generation to generation, but rather from imported ideologies, which, when they are adapted to new realities, can generate either reformist theories or intentional myths.

Ideas and doctrines reach Latin America without difficulty. After the Iberian cultural influence came that of the Encyclopedists (and that of the United States in the matter of organization of government), later that of the Positivists. Still later came the Marxist influence, and now Keynesianism. These ideological importations share the fate of the human immigrants—after a few years they become naturalized. Spanish American positivism has little relation to that of Comte, and present-day economists seem to be Keynesian twigs grafted onto a Marxist branch, which is in turn grafted onto a Positivist trunk, and so on *ad infinitum*. This naturalization of ideas and doctrines has a strong flavor of syncretism, which can be perceived most clearly in the area of religion.

Such naturalization is carried out in an intellectual atmosphere in which facts have less importance than desires, and out of this phenomenon, a series of myths accepted by all arises and persists.

Here are some of them:

1. Latin America has great potential riches. Mexico, a poor country, was called the horn of plenty, from its shape on the map.

2. Tropical zones offer infinite possibilities for development, a statement proved false by science and experience.

3. To resolve any problem, either individual or group, it is necessary to have recourse to outside assistance, whether from the state or from foreign nations or investors. This is, without a doubt, a reflection of the paternalistic tradition inherited from colonial times and, above all, from the strong men of the nineteenth century and the long domination of the landowning oligarchy.

These myths—for that is what they are, since each can be disproved by figures or recurrent historical facts—have acquired the force of axioms. Few persons today attempt to dispute them, and they continue to be accepted as unquestionable truths by public opinion.

Neither experts nor presidents, nor diplomats ever talk about one phenomenon that forms a part of their daily life and thought, that frustrates their plans and efforts and destroys their hopes for the future—the demographic explosion.

The Central American nations, for example, today have the world's highest rate of population increase. In those five republics, there are 13 million people, and their rate of population increase is 3.6 per cent. (The world rate is only 1.8 per cent.) Every twenty years, the population of Central America doubles. In 1985, it will total 26 million. Within a century, there will have been five geometric progressions. In the year 2065, there will be 416 million people in Central America, more than now inhabit all of Latin America and as many as inhabited the entire Western Hemisphere, including the United States and Canada, before World War II.

If roads, hospitals, and schools are being built today for 13 million people, where will the money come from to build for a population of 26 million twenty years from now? The rise in production and income is not keeping pace with the increase in population; the annual development rate is less than 3.6 per cent.

Birth control will not solve the problem. It does not solve the problem in India, for example, although it seems to mitigate it somewhat in Japan, an industrial nation. There is no reason to think that it would succeed in Latin America, however much propaganda is turned out, and assuming that the Church would support the propaganda. There is revealing information on this point. Some years ago a survey was taken in Puerto Rico, where the birth rate is enormous. Sociologists questioned thousands of peasants, poor urban residents, and members of the middle class and the *haute bourgeoisie*. These were the results: The well-to-do practice birth control, or do not oppose it. On the other hand, the workers and, above all, the peasants (among whom the birth rate is higher) do not want to have anything to do with it. Because of religious compunctions? No. Why, then? For reasons of prestige. Because to these people, having children is, for a man, a sign of masculinity and for women a sign of family solidity.[1]

Statistics show, then, that birth control is accepted only where it is not necessary from a demographic point of view. But what can be done if it is not possible to make use of birth control in Latin America (where the situation and the people's reactions are similar to those in Puerto Rico)? The economists, who until a few years ago held the wonderful concept that the greater the labor force, the greater the development, finally became uneasy and have now reached the conclusion that the only means of keeping the population increase from nullifying the benefits of development is to increase the rate of development enough so that the rising population will come to enjoy certain living conditions that in themselves will produce the same effect as they have in all industrial societies—a decline in the rate of population increase.

[1] J. Mayone Stycos, *Family and Fertility in Puerto Rico* (New York, 1955), chap. x.

Another widely held myth is that, by and of itself and invariably, industrialization brings democracy. This is not necessarily so. It has been and still is asserted about the U.S.S.R. (the Austrian socialist Otto Bauer promoted this thesis before World War II), but the facts disprove the theory. However much one stretches the meaning of the words, "liberalization" is by no means the equivalent of "democratization" or "social equality," both of which features are entirely missing from the most optimistic picture one might draw of Soviet society. And it would not necessarily be different in Latin America. Industrialization does not inevitably assure even a higher living standard; only in the most fortunate cases does it produce higher national income, and even then it does not assure that this increase will be shared equally. In fact, without agrarian reform, industrialization will not benefit the great submerged mass of peasants who remain without land (or without enough land). On the contrary, industrialization can lead to totalitarian, technocratic forms of government, through a desire for industrial acceleration at the expense of the human factor.

From time to time, these myths generate strange collective superstitions which the economists and politicians of the moment dress up with pseudo-scientific trappings. These are the panaceas. In Latin America, there is always a panacea handy. Yesterday, it was industrialization. Last year, it was foreign investment. Still earlier, it was protectionism, and before that, during colonial times, the ending of state monopolies. Today, it is monetary stabilization in some countries, and agrarian reform in others.

A panacea takes the place of fundamental solutions; it is, in a certain sense, a fundamental solution, but one applied through a single instrument in a single area, with the hope—not always unfounded—that the transformation of one aspect of national life will indirectly transform all the others. The transformation comes, in effect, because it is not possible to alter one single factor without affecting the whole. But it does not always take the desired form.

The Myth of the Call of Liberty

There is one myth that disquietingly can encourage the tendencies, produced by other factors, toward dictatorship. It is the Latin American myth of the call of liberty. It is a pompous expression that may be effective oratory, but it is empty; it has no relation to historical reality or even to common sense. It does not happen that some nations desire liberty while others do not. There are nations which in specific moments of their history (because of social, economic, political, and cultural circumstances) wish for liberty and fight for it, and which at other times resign themselves to not having it, do not feel the need of it, and do not defend the liberty they have.

In Latin America, the people have never felt the need of liberty and would never have known what to do with it if they had had it. Yes, yes, I know—you will cite dozens of phrases by Latin American political leaders, intellectuals, and poets extolling liberty. You will cite cases and more cases of heroes who gave their lives to win liberty or defend it.

But citing names and phrases only proves one thing; that Latin America (that is, the mass of Latin American people) has no call of liberty. Because all the names cited belong to a minority, always the same, of cultured persons possessing a minimum of economic well-being—generally persons of the middle class, but at times of the oligarchy.

For these people, liberty had and has a meaning. They knew and they know what it consists of. For them, to live without liberty means not to live at all.

But are these people Latin America?

No. Let us not go on being hoodwinked into believing that Latin America is composed entirely of the educated, the well-off, the restless, those who make policy, those who vote with a knowledge of the issues, those who know, more or less, what they want. Latin America is much more. It is also the others of whom no one speaks (or only rhetorically), the people who, if they vote (when they vote), do so without knowing for what or for whom, who cannot read or write or who, if they have learned, do not read or write, who live under subhuman conditions, who cling to habits, traditions, ceremonies, and social groups that are stagnant, inefficient, and pathetically anachronistic—because, despite this, they are the only things that truly belong to them.

And these people (the overwhelming majority of Latin Americans living in the country, in villages, and in urban shanty towns), who know nothing of progress, of what is going on in the world, who have no concept of politics, who could not even articulate the meaning of democracy (who probably have never heard the word), these people feel no call of liberty.

They have no reason to feel it, for liberty is a product of a certain minimum of education and well-being, and to these submerged peoples, the question of whether or not they have liberty means nothing; it makes no difference in their way of living, feeling, or thinking. For they have never had real liberty and thus know neither what it is nor what it can mean.

If they were to arrive at an understanding of the concept of liberty, it would appear to them to be the privilege of those who exploit them, scorn them, disregard them, and keep them in servitude. Perhaps they would think that liberty is a tool to keep them as they are and no more. And, in fact, the word "liberty" has been just that in the past.

But even the liberty of the most aware minorities has remained no more than a dream. Real liberty we have never had in Latin America. At times, not always, we have enjoyed political liberty; much less often, cultural liberty, because various myths and fears (for example, the fear of appearing reactionary or revolutionary, as the case may be) have repressed thought. But economic and social liberty—these we have never had in a continent where social legislation that pretends to be so advanced establishes governmental control over the labor unions and often places shameful limitations on union existence, in a continent where 80 per cent or more of the inhabitants never have a chance to make an economic decision for themselves, however modest it may be, because they lack the most elemental but indispensable means of sharing in the economic life of their country.

Latin America knows only the smell of democracy and liberty, but it has not yet had a chance to taste them.

The Myth of the Desire for Progress

Another myth is that of the desire for progress in Latin America.

We are accustomed to hearing and reading all sorts of statements about the spirit of progress in Latin America, about development, about the little local miracles performed in our continent. So it must seem absurd that someone should suddenly come out and say that Latin America has no will for progress.

But is it really so absurd?

Nations, all nations, in specific periods feel the desire to progress; the people experience new needs and exert themselves to satisfy them. At other times, these same nations are comatose; they seek nothing, they resign themselves and accept their situation as inevitable. They cling to the past or to a precarious present.

Precisely because resignation and the desire for progress recur intermittently in the same society, it may be asserted that they are not determined by those supposed racial factors that, for example, make some whites say that the Negroes can never progress and make some *criollos* claim that the Indians are incapable of adapting themselves to modern life. The factors that decide whether a nation, in any given moment, is to be immobile or dynamic are social, cultural, and economic; in short, the society in which the people live. And when a nation tends toward immobility, if it wishes to inject dynamism, the first thing that must be done is to transform the society which has benumbed it or has contributed to its resignation.

Naturally, all the sectors of a society are never dynamic at one time, nor are they ever all immobile. What determines the tone is the character of the decisive forces, those that carry the most weight within the society. What are the dynamic social sectors of Latin American life, the sectors that favor progress? Let us check them off.

The landowning oligarchy wants no changes. Any progress, however minimal it may be, lessens its power and brings the moment of its demise nearer. The oligarchy is the great force for immobility. From time to time, it resigns itself to accepting certain reforms, because they seem inevitable, but it manages to assure that the oligarchy will be the exclusive beneficiary, or at least that the mass of the people will not participate in the benefits. The oligarchy always takes care that the people remain as they are, that no modern influences touch them. This is the basis of its power. For the oligarchy knows that the force for change in Latin American society —the middle class—cannot achieve its objectives if it does not receive aid and support from, and does not work in the interests of, the people.

At the same time, the middle class, as constituted at present, lacks the economic means to extend the desire for progress, because its economic activity is developed within a narrow frame, serving only to satisfy its own needs and those of the oligarchy.

But in a society that is only beginning to industrialize, there can be no real progress if the desire for it (that is, new needs and the effort to satisfy them) is not shared by the majority of the people. And since the landowning oligarchy, at times in partnership with the industrial *bourgeoisie* and the army, opposes this extension of needs, of the will to progress, it is incumbent upon the middle class to discover a means of instilling in the masses the understanding of, and desire for, progress.

Without this—and without the democratic political manifestation of this desire—Latin America will not change.

The Myth of Racial Equality

It is said that there is no racism in Latin America, that there is authentic racial equality. The truth is something else again. There is a subtle racism, disguised at times as difference of class (since often separation of classes and of races coincide). There is anti-Semitism, especially in the countries where the influence of Nazi ideology was extensive. There is religious discrimination; the Protestant minority finds itself virtually beyond the pale socially, even where the law protects it and where there is respect for the law.

One does not need to live more than a short while in Latin America to see that racism is real there. It is not overt racism; it is a disagreeable racism that takes white superiority for granted (and it thus need not be verbalized). It is a racism of attitude more than of principle. It is a racism that is indispensable to the perpetuation of the feudal system of relationships between peasant and landowner.

A UNESCO expert on these matters, the anthropologist Juan Comas, has described Latin American racism in these terms:

> The nonwhite population in Latin America, dominated by the "whites," was from the first subjected to a sort of "racial discrimination" which motivated an "economic discrimination," as a result of which these groups remained, and continue to remain, on a level of dependence and exploitation *sui generis* which is manifested not only in lower salaries and lack of the social-security guarantees of the "white" worker, but also in an obvious resistance to vertical mobility within the social classes. The result of this state of affairs—*de facto,* although not *de jure*—is that large sectors of the population are not "integrated" into their respective nationalities.

The degree to which racism in oligarchic Latin America has a social function is seen in these statements by Comas:

It is evident, then, that the socio-economic inferiority and nonintegration of colored groups in Latin America are due, in part, to a "racial" discrimination that:

1. Exhibits characteristics and features quantitatively and qualitatively different from what can be observed elsewhere in the world.
2. Is a more or less generalized practice, but never institutionalized. On the contrary, the rights of the colored citizen (Amerindian, Negro, mestizo, or yellow) in Latin America are publicly recognized by the fundamental laws of each country.

The "white" sector attempts to avoid class antagonisms by substituting for them antagonism between "racial" groups, and thus a minority tries to continue exploiting the majority group.[2]

The Myth of Representative Democracy

One of the biggest myths, and among the most dangerous, is that there is representative democracy in Latin America, or in most of the countries. The next step, of course, is to conclude from this that real democracy exists there—or will exist soon. Representative democracy is, of course, only one aspect of true democracy, a necessary, but not determining, factor. But in Latin America, we do not even have that. Leaving aside the dictatorships (and every Latin American country has, in the course of the last 150 years, been subjected to dictatorship several times), it may be said that even those nations which have been free of dictatorship for some years do not have democracy, or even representative democracy. Because of the strong-man rule in towns and provinces, economic pressure, limitations on the right to vote (often on the ground of illiteracy), and the indifference of the submerged mass toward political campaigns that they do not begin to understand, because, finally, of the fact that only a small minority reads the newspapers, listens to the radio or watches television, the percentage of Latin Americans who participate in elections is about one-third that of North Americans.

2 Juan Comas, *Relaciones inter-raciales en América Latina, 1940–1960* (Mexico City, 1961), pp. 39 and 40.

Throughout Latin America, the average electoral participation is 20 per cent, which means that of every five citizens, only one registers on the voting rolls. If we add to this the figures for absenteeism on election day, the level drops still further. This percentage holds roughly for all Latin American countries except Argentina (with 53.5 per cent registered), Bolivia (71.4 per cent), and Venezuela (39 per cent). The "normal" rate of participation should exceed 50 per cent; in the United States, it is 57.3 per cent, and in Great Britain, 67.7 per cent.

This means, then, that Latin America does not yet enjoy universal suffrage. The limitation is no longer, as it was in the nineteenth century, fiscal (the poll tax) but rather educational. Today illiteracy is the barrier to democracy that poverty used to be. The electoral process is only partially representative. Political power and political representation are distributed among the 20 per cent of the citizens having the highest economic and educational status.

The degree of electoral participation is a vital element in the economic, social, and cultural evolution of society. It has been observed that, in general, the degree of participation is equivalent to that of educational advance and that these three factors affect political stability. Education, per capita income, electoral participation, and political stability are the terms of an equation in which all these factors interact.

Illiteracy, low degree of electoral participation, low per capita income, and political instability are almost always found together. To prove it, here are some basic data on these three phenomena:

RELATION OF ELECTORAL PARTICIPATION TO EDUCATIONAL
AND INCOME LEVELS

	Percentage of Electoral Participation	Percentage of Literacy	Annual Per Capita Income (In Dollars)
Argentina	53.5	89.8	500–600
Brazil	19.4	42.6	100–200
Chile	20.5	80.0	403
Dominican Republic	24.4	32.0	—
Guatemala	10.0	30.0	100–200
Mexico	21.5	47.0	200–300
Venezuela	37.7	51.3	600–700

SOURCE: *Comentario* (Buenos Aires), January, 1964, p. 4.

History of a Frustration

In the United States, just as there are certain groups who have great admiration and affection for Franklin Roosevelt, there are also those who hate him. The same can be said of Kennedy, although the hatred has been somewhat dissipated since his assassination. Roosevelt produced true social change in the United States, and Kennedy, although he neither achieved such change nor even attempted it, succeeded in bringing about social adaptations to new realities. It is significant that there is not one popular political figure in Latin America—not even among the most radical leftists—so hated or so loved as was Roosevelt in the United States. The only exception is APRA leader Víctor Raúl Haya de la Torre, against whom the military, more than the oligarchs, maintain an irrational hatred growing out of a single incident—the death of army officers in an Aprista uprising in Arequipa more than thirty years ago—and fed by the obsessive propaganda that has been carried on in military circles ever since. But there is neither respect nor hatred toward any of the outstanding personalities of the left in Latin America. Why? Because none of them has ever done anything to jeopardize the oligarchic order.

Forty, twenty, even ten years ago, it was generally believed that the middle class would supplant the oligarchy, either by destroying it or by forcing it to give ground. The leaders of the middle-class movements were certain that they were on their way to power. This was the force of discontent which was coming to the forefront, which hoped to transform Latin America, and which required, for its own development, more freedom, more social justice, more democracy—or, rather, genuine democracy. The middle class and the movements growing out of it constituted the hope of Latin America.

Today they still talk about the middle class as a force for transformation, but they talk without enthusiasm, without faith, simply because there seems to be no alternative force, or none they know of or want to acknowledge.

The truth is that, down deep, we all believe that the middle class has failed as a force for social change in Latin America. This failure can be explained, fundamentally, by a tragically simple fact: When the middle class needed social change, neither the internal situation nor United States diplomacy was favorable to change and neither offered any of the material means to attain it. When the internal situation and United States diplomacy were favorable and did offer the material means, the middle class had already developed vested interests in the oligarchic system and no longer needed change.

To understand this story of frustration, let us begin by discussing just what that middle class was.

First, some essential statistics. In Latin America, even today, industry contributes little to the national income: In Bolivia and Panama, it accounts for 9 per cent; in Honduras, 11 per cent; in Venezuela and Costa Rica, 12 per cent; in Paraguay, 14 per cent; in Peru and Brazil, 17 per cent.

The middle class, then, had a weak industrial basis. And its human basis (not in terms of the middle class as such, but in terms of the elements that could echo its needs and its struggles) was not much stronger. It is enough to glance at the illiteracy figures to guess what that basis must be: 89 per cent in Haiti, 70 per cent in Guatemala, 69 per cent in Bolivia, 68 per cent in the Dominican Republic, 66 per cent in Honduras, 65 per cent in Nicaragua, 57 per cent in Brazil and El Salvador, 55 per cent in Peru, 53 per cent in Colombia and Mexico, 43 per cent in Ecuador, and 20 per cent or less in only a few countries—Argentina with 10 per cent, Uruguay with 18 per cent, and Chile with 20 per cent.

Thus the middle class was, in a sense, an isolated element. Moreover, it came into being in a manner quite different from the circumstances surrounding the growth of the middle class in other continents.

The most important single reason why, up to the time of the second World War, there had not been a strong, anti-aristocratic, bourgeois, capitalist middle class in Latin America is that there had been no industrial expansion great enough to generate such a pressure-group. The growth of cities in Latin America has had very little to do with the growth of industries, and the attitudes, inclinations, and tastes of Latin American city dwellers have little or nothing in common with those of the inhabitants of industrial cities elsewhere.[3]

[3] Claudio Véliz, "Obstacles to Reform in Latin America," *The World Today* (London), January, 1963, p. 23.

All the successful revolutionary movements (those onto which reality has ingrafted social content even when they had none originally), such as the Mexican and Bolivian revolutions, and even the Cuban (if you wish to call it a revolution), have been led by the middle class.

In the period between the World Wars, doctrines and movements appeared which had certain common characteristics better fitted to Latin American reality and needs than the ideologies transplanted from Europe (socialism, anarchism, and which could, more readily than socialism, adapt certain Marxist conceptions to what was feasible in America.

These nationalist revolutionary movements, Aprista or democratic leftist (APRA in Peru, Acción Democrática in Venezuela, Partido Revolucionario Institucional in Mexico, Movimiento Nacionalista Revolucionario in Bolivia, Partido Revolucionario Dominicano in the Dominican Republic, Febrerismo in Paraguay, for a while Liberación Nacional in Costa Rica, and the Partido Popular in Puerto Rico), can truly be called populist movements.[4]

They are parties not of a single class, but of several; and they must be considered as a coalition of the middle class, labor, and the peasants. They are anti-imperialist, supporters of Latin American unity, and of a gradual march, by democratic methods, toward a type of mixed economy in which the state plans investment and orients development.

These movements have been successful in some areas in organizing the peasants; in every country where they exist, they control, fully or partially, the union movement, and enjoy the support of the working class and the antipathy of the Communists, the oligarchy, and the military.

In some countries (Venezuela, Puerto Rico, the Dominican Re-

---

[4] Good summaries of these movements and their ideologies, although very optimistic about their future, are: Harry Kantor, "Los partidos populares de América Latina," *Journal of Inter-American Studies* (Gainesville, Fla.), April, 1964, and Robert J. Alexander, *Prophets of the Revolution* (New York, 1962). A Jacobin critique of these movements is found in Mario Monteforte Toledo, *Partidos políticos de Iberoamérica* (Mexico City, 1961). On the attitude of the intellectuals and professional groups, see Alvaro Mendoza Diez, *La revolución de los profesionales e intelectuales en Latinoamérica*, a schematically Marxist work but rich in documentation. On the relations between the populist and labor movements, see Alba, *Historia del movimiento obrero*.

public), they have taken power by democratic means, while in others they have won it by revolution (Mexico, Bolivia) or have several times been on the point of winning it (Peru). In some countries, after coming to power, they have been dislodged by military coups (Paraguay, the Dominican Republic, Bolivia). Many movements that in reality are a tool of the oligarchy adopt populist slogans and programs, only to abandon them once in power.

It can be said, then, that populism has played a role in Latin American politics similar to that of the socialist and anarchosyndicalist movements in Europe before World War I and that it aspires to achieve, within the Latin American context, the equivalent of what Roosevelt achieved in the United States with his New Deal.

These populist movements have exercised a great influence— perhaps more when in opposition to dictatorship than when in power themselves—as much in the political evolution of Latin America as in reform theory. And they have also had a considerable influence in the United States' change of attitude vis-à-vis Latin America, especially during the three years of the Kennedy administration.

But the social and economic changes in Latin America have put the populist movement in much the same position as that of the European socialist parties. One part of their programs (the nationalist part) is being applied (at least in speeches) by the oligarchies, who use nationalism to disguise their real motives and to divert the attention of public opinion. The part that is not applied has been overtaken by events; it is not operative in the reality of Latin America today, or else it appears faded and weak, in contrast to the people's aspirations.

The traits that characterize the middle class have been described earlier. These traits were reflected in the populist movements and were the source both of their strength, because they represented something authentic, and of their weakness, because they represented it in an anachronistic form.

Populism has found itself in a very curious situation. It has had to adopt an anti-imperialist position, first, because this position answers the needs of their countries and, second, out of fear that it will be overtaken by the left or even by the right—that either the Communists or the oligarchs will appear more anti-imperialistic than the true left. This has undermined the position of the Latin

American left, for while anti-imperialism may have been and may continue to be necessary and advantageous, it is neither necessary nor advantageous to throw all sorts of irrational attitudes and anti-Yankee prejudices into the same anti-imperialist pot and to reject programs that would be beneficial to the people simply because activation of these programs might give the Communists and oligarchs a pretext to call the left agents of imperialism. In some countries, the left seems to be overcoming this fear of ideological blackmail, but this brand of terrorism is still very strong.

It is traditional for the Latin American left to blame the existence of dictatorships on the United States, because the United States automatically gives them diplomatic recognition. However, in the cases of Peru in 1962, and the Dominican Republic and Honduras in 1963, the United States withheld recognition of the military juntas for several months, while in the meantime almost all the Latin American governments recognized them and maintained normal diplomatic relations. The leftists did not devote even one drop of the saliva expended in criticizing the United States to demand that their own governments break off relations with the dictatorships. The fact that breaking diplomatic relations is not enough to topple a dictatorship does not mean that such a regime must be recognized, much less does it mean that governments should not be pressured to break off relations. This only underlines the obsessive and irrational quality of a certain type of anti-Yankee feeling which is nothing more than the desire to evade the responsibilities imposed by national facts of life.

When Kennedy launched the idea of the Alliance for Progress, Costa Rica's José Figueres and Peru's Haya de la Torre wrote to the democratic parties of Latin America asking that they join together "to welcome the new attitude of the United States toward Latin America." Twenty-four democratic parties supported this manifesto. Eight of them either were in power or belonged to governing coalitions. But the idea never went beyond the manifesto stage because the democratic parties did not dare to make the Alliance a part of their electoral platform and their immediate program.

Why did the democratic revolutionary movements fail to do so? Fifteen years ago they would have done so. Not today. They are afraid of being called imperialists if they do, and this fear has made them abandon the masses to the demagogues and made them throw away their great opportunity to transform Latin America. Perhaps, afterward they heaved a sigh of relief, for nothing seems as distasteful to the parties that once were "popular" as the prospect of achieving changes. It could be said that they really do not want political power for fear that power itself will force them to make changes.

To this extent, these movements have failed.

What does this failure mean and how did it come about?

The revolutionary democratic movements were formed in an era when the immediate threat came from dictatorships. They fought them, but they did not know how to eliminate the basic reasons for dictatorship—the social reasons.

Many of the leaders and rank and file of these populist movements came from oligarchic social groups or groups associated with them. They were resolved to destroy these groups, and it is true that with the passage of time, the oligarchies have been weakened somewhat, but they have not been destroyed, and they are now in the process of adapting themselves, of protecting themselves by taking on new shapes that are less incompatible with the general advance of the world. The Latin American oligarchies are like prostitutes who, during a puritanical epoch, put on low-heeled shoes, a long skirt, and a high-necked blouse, but continue to earn their living in the same way. And their new air of modesty may even bring them more customers.

Unfortunately, the oligarchies' new customers include some "democratic" groups, the radical and liberal parties, for example.

Perhaps this failure to destroy the dictatorships was inevitable, because years ago no one in Latin America paid any attention to the masses. Politics were carried on by minorities, especially urban minorities. But now the masses are awakening and beginning to exert some influence, and elements are arising to court them—the false democrats, the Castroites, the Peronists, and other demagogues. And the democratic revolutionary movements (save for a few clear-sighted exceptions, such as Acción Democrática, APRA, and the Dominican PRD) do not know how to speak to the masses and do not approach them. And as the masses begin to be a power factor, a power vacuum is produced, which, naturally, attracts those who dare to approach the people.

As long as the "democratic" movements have as their leaders

big bosses, corporation lawyers, people who profiteer on food provided by foreign aid, coffee barons, landowning organizers of agrarian leagues, and well-heeled, bureaucratic union officials, these movements will not find an audience among the people; in reality, they do not even dare to look for it. Until what could be called incompatibility of interests manifests itself, not only in legislation but also in the conscience of the democrats, the failure of the democratic movements will not be overcome. Nor will it be overcome as long as the democratic ranks do not exorcise the fear of not being the furthest left, the most radical, and substitute for it the desire to be the closest to the people.

The populist movements were useful to consolidate a political democracy and to combat dictatorships. But now, in order to avoid new dictatorships or the coming to power of forces that are latently dictatorial, and also because it is the trend of our era, and because it is right—now the fundamental goal must be to transform political democracy into a genuine social and economic democracy. To provide social content—as it is usually put—the populist movements must examine their positions, revise their programs, analyze reality with new eyes, and arrive at clear, sharp concepts of what they want and how to achieve it. They must distinguish unequivocally between their own and totalitarian methods of development. At the same time, they must free themselves from the easy and sterile habit of throwing all the blame on imperialism, on the oligarchies, on militarism, on clericalism, or on any other scapegoat. In politics, just as there are no panaceas, there are no scapegoats. And just as foreign influence cannot destroy a regime that does not want to give up its power, neither can it impose one if the people really resist.

In the final analysis, the populist movements that have not already done so must come to the people, become one with the people, and take their inspiration from the people. It is not enough to think *about* the people, or offer representation and defense *to* the people. They must *be* the people.

Up to now, in the best instances, democracy has been government by the people. In a few instances, it has been government for the people. In others, government against the people or in place of the people. It is now coming to be government of the people.

These are not just phrases. What have the democratic movements done (with the few exceptions we have noted) to overcome strong-man government, to give the people (not just their own followers, but the mass of the people, the peasants, the shopkeepers, the laborers, and the white-collar workers) a solid political education? The answer rests in one word and decades of inertia and mental sloth: nothing.

The urban middle class has improved its condition to the degree to which industrialization has developed—however little it has. Because it does not know how or is not able to make the revolution, this mass of the urban middle class has become conformist. Its livelihood depends more and more on the oligarchs, since it has been unable to destroy them. And we have already seen that its progress and numerical increase have occurred at the expense of the living standards of the submerged classes, because there has been no real expansion in income.

Probably the middle class is not aware that it has acquired a parasitic quality. But the parasitism is there, and, although it may exist only in the collective unconscious, it does influence the attitudes of the middle class. This whole class—businessmen as well as students and intellectuals—has turned its back on the old democratic movements and has surrendered to the happiest *modus vivendi* with demagoguery, playing the game of the Castroites and Communists as far as verbal attitudes are concerned and of the oligarchs in the area of practical attitudes. The first part of the game serves to excuse the second and leaves the middle class with a clear conscience.

For this reason, the parties of the left lose elections in the big cities and must depend on the peasants and the provincial and rural middle class, which still retains its illusions and which, having improved its living standards less than the urban middle class, feels less closely tied to the oligarchy and, for that reason, less impelled toward the demagoguery of Communist protest.

> Populist left-wing support is today mostly concentrated in rural areas, whereas the old voting pattern gave left-wing coalitions strong support in the cities and not in the countryside. . . . Venezuela's Rómulo Betancourt became President on the strength of the rural vote, while he lost decisively in Caracas. . . .[5]

[5] Véliz, *op. cit.,* pp. 26–27.

While on the political level the myths noted earlier circulate and are accepted, myths that form the spiritual bread of the Latin American left (backed by the right), other myths have developed in the cities. It is said, for example, that Latin American society is open, that it has a high degree of social mobility and even a lowly worker can count on becoming a great captain of industry. In pondering what he will want to defend when this comes to pass, the worker begins to defend it in advance, while he is still nothing more than a member—a compulsory member—of a labor union. Reality gives the lie to this myth, but the fact that it is accepted and believed has considerable political consequences.

In Latin America, there is a phenomenon whose existence tends to be smothered in the technical language of sociologists. The Chilean analyst Claudio Véliz has described it thus:

This unexpectedly conservative attitude on the part of the Latin American urban middle sectors is relatively new. Until the second World War their political leadership had maintained a reformist position and had even become associated with a number of national Communist and Socialist parties. In fact, during the years between the wars, several reformist political movements, broadly based on urban middle-class support, managed to get near the sources of political power in their respective countries. By so doing, they reversed the traditional order in which social classes or groups perform their climbing feats. The well-known sequence of social ascent usually begins with the acquisition of wealth, continues with the achievement of political power, and ends in the long and tedious quest for social prestige. The urban middle sectors of Latin America, however, reached the sources of political power with the support of the popular vote, while they were still economically unimportant. They did not represent growing industrial pressure groups nor were they associated with the traditionally foreign-dominated extractive industries. The land was still held by the old aristocracy and commercial activity was controlled either by foreign business houses or by well-established minor local firms. There was no area of the economy from which the rising urban groups could derive substantial financial support. In fact, before the crisis of 1929, there had been practically no industrial development worth mentioning in Latin America and therefore it is impossible to attribute the rise of these middle sectors to changes in the traditional social structure. They were recruited from the distributive trades, the bureaucracy, the white-collar workers, the professions, and the intelligentsia.

. . . the political leadership of these groups during the 1930s was essentially reformist. Confronted with the mansion of privilege and power, they wanted to demolish it and build a larger one where at least the whole of the urban middle sectors could have a place. A variety of reasons explains the failure to implement these reformist policies. Firstly, the middle groups seldom had absolute political control. Although victorious at the polls, they had to share political power with an established administrative bureaucracy and moderate their policies in order to obtain support from other powerful political parties. Only in Mexico did they manage to become supreme; there they have governed the country through a single-party system up to the present time. Secondly, they did not have a clear-cut programme, apart from the usual platitudes about freedom and prosperity. Once in power, they lost considerable time and also impetus in finding out what to do and how to do it. Finally, the outbreak of the second World War created a new situation which opened unprecedented opportunities for rapid industrial growth.[6]

Basically what happened to the Latin American populist movements is what Engels described with respect to certain political leaders:

The worst thing that can befall a leader of an extreme party is to be compelled to take over a government in an epoch when the movement is not yet ripe for the domination of the class which he represents and for the realisation of the measures which that domination would imply. . . . Thus he necessarily finds himself in a dilemma. What he *can* do is in contrast to all his actions as hitherto practiced, to all his principles, and to the present interests of his party; what he *ought* to do cannot be achieved. In a word, he is compelled to represent not his party or his class, but the class for whom conditions are ripe for domination. In the interests of the movement itself, he is compelled to defend the interests of an alien class, and to feed his own class with phrases and promises, with the assertion that the interests of that alien class are their own interests. Whoever puts himself in this awkward position is irrevocably lost.[7]

[6] *Ibid.*, pp. 24–25.

[7] Friedrich Engels, *The Peasant War in Germany*, trans. Moissaye J. Olgin (New York, 1926), pp. 135–36.

Some will protest that it is not a case of the democratic forces having failed but rather that the oligarchy, with the systematic help of the military establishment, has prevented them from implementing their programs. This is precisely their failure.

A comparison will help to explain this. When Fidel Castro began to accuse the United States of imperialism, and of wanting to murder the Cuban revolution, his duty was to lead his revolution (assuming that it deserves this name) by routes that would foil this imperialism (supposed or real) and would make the "murder of the revolution" impossible. What Castro could not in good logic do, but did do, was to accuse the United States of the responsibility for his own failures and difficulties. If I state that a woman whom I want to marry is of easy virtue, it seems absurd for me to complain later that she put horns on me.

Equally, the *raison d'être* of Latin American populism was to destroy the power of the oligarchy and to neutralize militarism. To complain that it was not able to do so is potently an admission of its failure.

And let it not be said that the oligarchy's power was too great. Politics consists precisely in reducing the strength of one's adversary to the point at which he can be removed from power. Of course, the "outs" are always weaker than the "ins," but history is full of examples of opposition groups that seized power. We have them in Latin America, as well. But we do not have examples of groups who gain control and know how to wrest power from their socially anachronistic, paralyzing, and parasitic opponents. And this also is part of their failure.

What is it in Latin America that causes these repeated failures? My impression is that except in a few cases (Peru, Venezuela, and Mexico at one time), the democratic movements have been called revolutionary, but in fact have represented (and still represent) only simple, more humane derivations from the oligarchy, which they face up to politically, but which they do not want, do not know how, do not dare, or do not intend to oppose in the only area in which they can possibly succeed—in the area of the structure of the society. In this sense, the "revolutionary" democrats of Latin America (with a few exceptions) have fallen victim to the rhetorical autosuggestion to which they subject the masses. They have never gone to the people, they have not lived with them or helped their own leaders to emerge. The only thing they have done is to talk. And to talk to the people is paternalism. Our "revolutionaries" have been, in general, as paternalistic (although with other methods and better intentions) as our dictators. The people have never felt that any of these movements represented them, except in periods of extreme emotional tension, when they are most receptive to suggestion. Basically our "revolutionaries" have felt, as have the Communists and oligarchs, a personal disdain for the people, arising out of fear of what they do not understand. Because they are not the people, they seek only to assist them from without. At best, they are only political Little Sisters of the Poor; at worst, they are like the good ladies of St. Vincent de Paul.

Out of the Lincolnian trinity, our "revolutionaries" have wanted to retain only a single element: government *for* the people. They have never intended that government should be of or by the people. The result of this (and lack of education is an effect and not a cause, in this respect) has been that politics interests only a minority of the population, that public opinion is composed only of a small segment of the urban population, and that the masses, the vast submerged masses, remain submerged, without our "revolutionaries" having done anything (always with some exceptions) to bring them to the surface. They feared that, if they did, the mass would smother them. Between fear of the masses and fear of failure, they have always chosen failure, which placed them in the comfortable position of being the victims and thus able to enjoy the victims' supposed right to recrimination. Success would have forced more difficult responsibilities upon them, responsibilities that neither their origin nor their make-up prepared them to shoulder.

And these "revolutionaries," like the oligarchy, have always had a scapegoat available to justify their failure: the United States.

Although these "intermediate" groups (as the sociologists so tactfully call them) are still committed to social change and have ceased to be revolutionary (in everything but words, of course), people within middle-class groups, in Latin America as well as in the United States, persist in believing that they represent the same force for transformation that they did thirty, twenty, or ten years ago.

This has political consequences, in that the initiative for creating change continues to be entrusted to a social group that does not want it and thus frustrates the change.

It has consequences in other areas, some of them curious and not without danger: for example, in the fields of political information and education and the rougher field of political propaganda.

Let us clarify this. In what groups has Communism up to now exerted a certain degree of influence? Not among the workers or the peasants. When a union or an agrarian league, for example, is run by Communists, it is due not to the ideology of the leaders, but to the fact that they have shown themselves more active, more able (and often, one must recognize, more honorable in the day-to-day matters of bribery and dirty deals) than the non-Communist leaders. In other cases, this domination has occurred thanks to the indifference of democratic factions or the complicity of the dictatorial police, who always prefer a Communist to a democrat.

On the other hand, among elements of the middle class (merchants, businessmen, students, professionals, even the young military), Communism has found an audience.

How is this explained? In part, by the frustrations these groups feel within Latin American society. And in part, also, by the effect of anti-Communist propaganda, which has dwelt upon the privileges enjoyed by intellectuals and technicians in Soviet society. By this method, such propaganda has tried to prove (and has succeeded) that Communist society is not egalitarian and that there is more social injustice in it than in democratic, industrial, capitalist society.

But to the technicians, to the intellectuals, what does equality matter? None of them has evidenced any true feeling for the people. None of them has gone beyond verbal declarations and signing manifestoes. How many extreme Castroites and "leftists" among the technicians and intellectuals spend a few hours a day visiting union halls and talking to workers? How many participate in such activities as organizing the peasants? How many literary or scientific discussion groups for workers have been established by present-day Latin American technicians and intellectuals?

As far as the technicians and intellectuals are concerned, because of the small market in Latin America for their merchandise (which is their knowledge), they depend on the state, which pays them little or, if they are lucky, on business, in which they have a limited field of operation. To tell them that in the U.S.S.R. intellectuals and technicians earn fantastic salaries, that they enjoy special privileges, that their works are published in editions of thousands of copies (while in our case, they run to 1,000 or perhaps 2,000 copies, and often at the author's expense), is to tell them that if Communism were established in their country, they would be better off. Not the people. But as far as the intellectuals are concerned, the people are no more than an aspirin for their conscience. They never concern themselves actively, with any degree of risk or sacrifice, with the people. Why then should they be worried about the mass of society under Communism?

Something similar happens in the case of businessmen. When they are not connected with the oligarchy or foreign business interests, they exhibit a very curious sort of nationalism, which conceives of the nation as an abstract entity at the service of economic progress and of their country's citizens as economic units at the service of development. In consequence, these young nationalistic businessmen (nationalistic although among them are many foreigners and more than a few North Americans) would prefer that economic development be achieved without foreign investment or credits (or only credits managed by them). They see in Soviet methods of development and capitalization, as presented by propaganda, an ideal tool, which they would like to use in their own country. And although they talk of reforms, progress, and social justice, they have no true interest in the people (at least they do not demonstrate it by providing funds for libraries or scholarships or by letting their young workers educate themselves or improve their skills on company time). Whatever regime promised them administrative efficiency (which cannot always be achieved without a certain degree of arbitrariness) and the opportunity of expanding capital through superexploitation (which would, of course, be called emulation, overtime, or piecework, all in the name of patriotism) would be welcome. This is what the Communists do where they are masters. The young businessman would not like Communism in his country, but he would love to use the Communists' methods of development.

And what difference would it make for the people? The difference might be found in the ministries of government, in the international position adopted by the nation, but for the man in the street, who creates capital out of his labor, there would be no difference. This would hold all the more true the more the supporters or leaders of such a regime found themselves unable, after a while, to maintain even token democracy, unable to respect liberties, to uphold the law, to guarantee rights, or to avoid arbitrary acts. And they would be unable to do so for a very simple reason: because it is impossible to capitalize by Soviet methods and at the same time respect the freedom of the people who must be squeezed dry in order to create the capital.

Another example: We speak of Soviet laws and of the fact that in the U.S.S.R. there are no guarantees for the accused, who may be sentenced to death for economic crimes. What could the reaction to this possibly be in Latin American countries where the poor defendant has, in fact, almost no juridical rights and where the rich get off scot-free, where the economic crimes of the oligarchs and politicians almost always go unpunished, and where the bosses and the farm managers recognize no controls and do not hesitate (at least in certain areas of specific countries) personally to inflict violent punishment on thieves, sometimes even killing them.

All this presents a strange problem to the propagandist, because what he says about the U.S.S.R. is true. Well then, should he conceal the truth, in order to avoid arousing sympathy toward the U.S.S.R. among these "revolutionaries" who do not care about the people? To me there is no dilemma. The truth should be spoken. Let the chips fall where they may and let anyone be seduced who wants to be. In the last analysis, these "revolutionaries" will be seduced anyway, if not by the Communists, then by the first demagogue of efficiency yelling on a street corner or rattling his spurs in a bar.

But the propagandist must know that by speaking the truth, as is his duty, he will provoke the backlash that I have predicted. And he should, therefore, take care that his truthful propaganda reaches, above all, those to whom it can serve as a warning; that is, to those who can lose the little that they own if control is won by Communists, demagogues, or other elements who live with their backs to the people and from whose lips the words "the people" are never heard.

History of an Accommodation

If the middle class is no longer a force for change—no longer revolutionary—will the working class then take over this role?

The schematic Marxists (that is, the Communists) maintained so until the era of the Popular Front, when they saw that they were making inroads more readily among intellectuals, shopkeepers, and bureaucrats than among workers and peasants. Others of us believed, with less dogmatism, that the working class, weak because of the weak position of industry and because of the contradiction between its anti-imperialist principles and its dependence for growth upon an increase in foreign investments, could not play a leading role but could serve as a forceful pressure group. We said, ten or twenty years ago, that in Latin America, there was a possibility, unheard of in the world up to then, of planning a capitalistic structure with none of the defects of the capitalisms of Europe or the United States. Clearly this involved planning on a grand scale, and although it would not make these new capitalists into little angels, it would ensure that they would develop with at least a minimum of feeling for the community.

From this stems the paradox which, because it has not been understood, has immobilized the labor movement in the grip of its old formulas: The paradox is that the planning of this new Latin American capitalism ought to have been carried out by the labor movement. None of the objectives of labor can be achieved in a feudal society with a nascent capitalistic structure worse than any already established. Nor is it possible to pass—the facts prove this, even if the theories do not—from feudalism to socialism or the control of power by labor, even if labor's program is very moderate. The logical answer, then, is for the labor movement to devote itself to creating the conditions that make its action effective.

For this, its own efforts are not enough. It must have the active assistance of the middle class, which the labor movement must convert into its instrument of power during this long transitional stage. It must have the assistance of the peasants, whom it must convert into small landowners and into a base on which the middle class can rely for political support.

What is this working class from which we expected what we believed was so little and has turned out to be so much?

Its traits can be summarized as follows:

1. A high percentage of illiteracy among the workers or, an even more dangerous situation, a high percentage of literates with only the most elementary education. This causes them to be uninterested,

in general, in any cultural activity, to be unreceptive to complex explanations, and to be distrustful. Moreover, this low cultural level helps foment differences within the working class, and the creation of castes of more (or less) skilled workers. It increases salary differentials and weakens the feeling of solidarity among union workers.

2. The peasant origins of the great majority of industrial workers, who, in periods of economic crisis or lay-offs, return to their villages, where they can be sure of a roof over their heads and food in their bellies, however meager these may be. It is also not unusual for a worker to leave his job to participate in week-long festivals in his village and to assist with the harvest. This causes a constant fluctuation in the available labor force and in union membership, and makes it more difficult to train workers in the techniques and skills of higher-paid jobs. These semi-migratory workers could, on the other hand, be converted into missionaries of worker education, if one could figure out how to take advantage of this situation, as long as it continues.

3. The persistence of the peasant mentality—isolation, distrust, indifference to social questions and to culture—in the urban worker. A special study should be made of the influence of this fact on the psychology of the Latin American worker, on the job as well as in his home and in his recreation. Undoubtedly, it would be discovered that the widespread alcoholism, consumption of narcotic herbs, and emotional and familial instability are caused principally by the failure of the peasant to adapt to urban life and an urban job.

4. The worker caught in a period of changeover from craft labor in small plants or shops to assembly-line operations. This creates problems of adaptation that affect the worker's attitude toward his union and his conduct in general.

5. The low rate of participation in industry by women. In the case of Mexico, the rate in industry is 1 in 233, i.e., 0.41 per cent (against 1 in 153, or 0.65 per cent, in the professions and 1 in 243, or 0.43 per cent, among university students). This disproportion is the cause, also, of maladjustments at work, in the home, and in emotional life, and it often provokes union injustices.

6. The abundance of child laborers of less than legal age. Although it does not focus on them, worker education should take account of the fact that some of those who would benefit from such

education will have started working in their childhood and thus lack sufficient education and the habit of study.

7. The general lack of interest in almost all Latin American countries in social problems and the lack of information on them (such as is provided elsewhere by magazines, books, conferences, workers' study groups). Worker education, then, must operate in virgin territory in which, at best, it can count on the aid of experience and only in a few cases on a certain curiosity about current problems.

8. The Latin American worker's lack of two components in his social personality that are commonly found in workers in Europe and the United States: He has no appreciable awareness of the ideologies and history of the labor struggles of the nineteenth century and no memories of lay-offs.

In our America, there is no labor tradition as such (the traditions brought from abroad were weak and for this very reason are almost forgotten), and there is no basis of past experience. There is, therefore, no ethical norm specifically applicable to the labor struggle and union operations. Moreover, unemployment and the Depression were never as severe in Latin America as in the United States and Europe, and the worker always had the option of returning to his village in the country, where he could cushion the temporary hardships. Thus, he does not share the memories that would link him with the mass of society.

For better or worse, the absence of these two elements affects the position of worker and union. The Latin American labor movement has left the peasants and Indians to their own devices and has become a parasite on the least fortunate sector of society. In a period such as the present, when in both the Old World and the United States, the worker's condition is the subject of innumerable studies, polemics, laws, and propaganda efforts, not a single person is concerned with this matter in Mexico and almost no one in all Latin America. In its sin, the labor movement has found its penitence. Isolated by a lack of ideology and goals, it has separated itself from the rest of society.[8]

The union movement in Latin America developed because of the influence, first, of the European immigrants who fled the repres-

---

[8] These views are expounded in more detail in Alba, *El líder* (Mexico City, 1957).

sions of 1848 and 1870 and, second, in certain countries, of the Spanish anarchosyndicalists and the U.S. IWW. It was a movement of positive ideological content: Its purpose was to defend the immediate interests of the workers—at that period still in the first stage of transition from craft labor to proletariat, from peasant or rural artisan to urban laborer—but it also had a special vision of what Latin American society should be, and it was obliged, at the same time as it was creating workers' parties and political groups, to assure that society evolved in the direction that the workers wanted it to take.

The period between the World Wars saw a modification in the character of the union movement. The Communist influence—exercised particularly through fronts and alliances—neutralized the political action of the unions, by allying them with interests foreign to those not only of the working class but of Latin America as a whole. When the U.S.S.R. entered World War II, the Communists, who had succeeded in unifying the labor-union movement through the instrument of the CTAL and at the same time killed its reformist spirit, made a concerted effort to emasculate this organization in order "not to harm the Allied war effort." The result was that, once the war had ended, the Latin American proletariat, numerically weak and ideologically weakened, felt profoundly disillusioned and abandoned its political positions to take refuge in a variety of unionism limited exclusively to the defense of immediate interests.

For this reason, the union movement did not play a significant role in any of the movements that fought the dictatorships in 1944–45, nor did it know how to defend the democratic regimes against the wave of military coups in 1948–49, or how to resist the seductive praetorian demagoguery of Peronism. Where there was no change in political stability, as in Mexico, the labor movement was no more than an appendage of the government.

Prior to World War I, the labor movement had not succeeded in synthesizing the ideological influences from Europe and North America with the needs of Latin America. And Communist sectarianism kept the Latin American Marxists (José Carlos Mariátegui, Aníbal Ponce) from achieving such a synthesis.

Since the initial period of effort during its formation, when principles meant more than tactics, the labor movement has been losing its dynamism. The successive continent-wide labor organizations (Confederación de Trabajadores de América Latina, Confederación Interamericana de Trabajadores, and Organización Regional Interamericana de Trabajadores) have not been able to stem the process of deterioration. To a certain degree, the CIT and ORIT managed to keep the labor movement from becoming a tool of the CTAL, which was strongly Communist-influenced, but they did not succeed in providing the movement with any ideological content. The North American concept of apolitical unionism prevailed, even though the North American context is totally different from the Latin American.

The result has been that the labor movement has simply been converted, to a greater or lesser extent, depending on the country, into a lever manipulated by others. When these others are democratic political forces, the result is not negative, although it is far from what one would wish. But when the unions are manipulated by demagogues such as Perón, Vargas, or Goulart, or by dictators such as Batista, the result is clearly negative for the labor class and for the country concerned.

The union bureaucratization that has accompanied this process —in countries where union members are far too few to require a large bureacratic apparatus—has led to dishonesty on the part of many labor leaders, to knuckling under to political power, and to indifference on the part of the union rank and file. Instead of playing an active role in helping the peasant or artisan to adapt to industrial life, the union is becoming more and more a combination of parasitical groups of bureaucrats and militants.

The primary consequence of this abandonment of ideology by the labor movement was that the middle class found itself without its former natural ally in attempts to alter society. This desertion by the union movement has meant that democratic regimes have been without the means of defense against military coups. Under dictatorship, labor has paid for its timidity, for the dictators have systematically helped the Communists to gain control of the unions, and oust democratic union leaders. As a result, when political democracy has been re-established later, the labor movement has found itself divided or, at the least, subject to contradictory influences— on the one hand, the democratic elements, and on the other, the Communist elements supported earlier by the dictator, but now opportunistically shunning him so that they can present themselves as having opposed him all along. In other cases, the corruption of the union movement has permitted the Communists to lead movements which the militants intended to serve as moral forces within the union, but which the Communists used merely for infiltration and disruption.

Thus the absence of ideology has paralyzed the labor movement, and today it is totally lacking in dynamism.

Industrialization in Latin America can be successful, on the economic level, only if it ceases to be an imitation of the capitalism of other countries and breaks its ties to the landowning oligarchy. This will not be possible unless an organized working class, with its own ideology, propels it along this path.

No one can say what the ideology of Latin American labor should be. It will not be, certainly, any of the ideologies that in Europe and the United States have already been overtaken by events. It is most probable that, by the very process itself, new aspirations will arise that will give Latin American syndicalism its own vision of the future and that will inspire it to transform this vision into reality.

With appearance of this ideology, which, I believe, is now taking shape within the very immobility and conformity of the Latin American labor movement, it will become an essential element of Latin American development. Latin American society still finds itself in the midst of change—and now more than ever, although the phenomenon will doubtless be short-lived. In order to make certain that this society, which unquestionably will be capitalistic, leaves the door open to future changes without recourse to new violence, it is essential that the labor movement decide upon and chart the directions it wants the future to take.

But for the moment, the ties between the labor movement and the government are strong. These ties must be credited to the skill of the oligarchy's politicians, who have known enough to give in to the labor movement, through legislation, at the moment its development could no longer be opposed. At the same time, in many countries, this legislation has divided the workers; for example, by setting up separate social-security funds for each industry (as in Chile), or by banning the formation of labor federations (as in Brazil).

In the present Latin American reality, there are many features that are bound up with certain principles first defended by socialism, although today they may already have been adopted in watered-down form by the capitalist systems of the more industrialized nations.

Latin American society has always been a managed society; this was so before the discovery of the continent and during the colonial period. Through its Laws of the Indies, the crown regulated the most minute details of the colonial economy. If independence was won in the name of rationalism and democracy, in the years that have followed (except for a few liberal interludes), the state has been controlled by the oligarchy, which, through its politicians, was able to set the course of the economy throughout the nineteenth century, and even today, without abandoning the façade of economic liberalism popular at the time.

Latin America is, then, historically conditioned to accept a managed economy. Not even businessmen seriously oppose planning and state intervention in economic matters. The Latin American economy is more and more a mixed economy, with private and public investment. Even where there is no planning, public investment controls economic life. Until now, except in a few countries, this control has been exercised for the benefit of the oligarchy. But if the populist or socialist movements (or whatever they are called in the future) obtain power by democratic means, they will find that society has already accepted the mechanisms necessary to control the economy and to direct it to the benefit of the submerged masses, and they will find also the mechanisms for the establishment not only of political democracy, but of its economic and social counterparts, as well.

This is, perhaps, more important than the typically socialistic phrases and claims that figure in almost all the programs of popular movements and of others that are not "popular." The word "socialist" appears in the names of many parties that are actually conservative or rightist. It indicates the point to which the myth (if not the philosophy) of socialism has penetrated political consciousness. But this implicit socialism, the product of a long historical tradition, seems much more far-reaching.

The mission of the labor movement, which used to seem clear to any authentic socialist, has been frustrated. What we could call the "old" labor class (the segment that has experienced one or two generations of urban life) has become specialized, has formed a caste within the proletariat, has become bourgeois in its way of life (although its resources have not improved measurably), and has rounded its existence with the exercise of power within a highly democratized labor movement. This part of the proletariat which is conscious of being proletarian, then, has become conformist; it accepts the present social reality (in fact, if not in words) and, by accepting it, becomes a parasite on the people. Therefore, it is virtually an ally of the oligarchy, no less so than is the middle class.

Celso Furtado noted this phenomenon in his native Brazil, and the same might be said of the proletariat of other nations, if they had economists capable of facing up to reality. Furtado observes that the proletariat of the São Paulo–Rio–Minas Gerais triangle find themselves confronted by the underdeveloped masses of the Northeast in a situation similar to that of the European nations vis-à-vis their old colonies. Experience indicates, Furtado says, that although these sectors of urban society may support the reformist views of the labor unions, they are not willing to risk their livelihoods to impose changes in the existing social structures.[9] I should add that this explains why not a single military coup has been met with a spontaneous and prolonged general strike, which could have spelled the downfall of the military.

The working class has reconciled itself to its role as a parasitic group. This is the pattern followed by every group that comes up from the great submerged masses; after improving its position at the expense of the masses, it succeeds in forgetting them (to keep its conscience clear) and collaborates with the very groups that keep the masses submerged (to preserve its immediate advantages and privileges).

The working class is not, then, per se an element of change, and it is no longer revolutionary, although in certain countries (such as Venezuela), for reasons which we shall see, it acts in support of the forces of social change.

Nonetheless, there is something that separates the working class from the middle class and the oligarchy. This "something" is the fact that it would be the working class that would have to toil ten or twelve hours a day if the oligarchy or the middle class succeeded

[9] Celso Furtado, *A pre-revolução brasileira* (São Paulo, 1960).

in imposing the methods of development it would like to see imposed—methods which it would call nationalistic but which would be, in fact, totalitarian.

Who Pays for Development?

In Latin America, one can find political manifestations corresponding to every imaginable ideological classification: There are reactionaries and conservatives, liberals and radicals, democrats and socialists, anarchists, national revolutionaries, Christian socialists, fascists, and Communists, under different names, all of which leads, at times, to confusion if one is not familiar with the individual antecedents of each movement. For instance, there is no connection between the old Falange Socialcristiana of Chile and the Falange Socialista of Bolivia, nor does either have anything to do with the Spanish Falange. There are parties calling themselves socialist or social democratic that are conservative (in Bolivia and Brazil, for example) and parties calling themselves Christian democratic (Acción Nacional in Mexico) that are, in fact, reactionary. Each party name must be evaluated in the light of its history and its program.

Latin America is in the process of development. This development is the vital question, and it is the basis of all political and social positions. Thus we must classify the political ideologies of Latin America in terms of their position on economic development.

Of course, one can regard economic development from different points of view. In the world today, and concretely in Latin America, these are the major points of view:

1. Classic Capitalism.
2. Soviet-type Capitalism.
3. Experimental and Nationalistic Capitalism.
4. Anticapitalism.

Two factors are fundamental to economic development: the method of capitalization and the character of change the society experiences.

To develop the economy requires capital. Where will it come from? Who will decide the allocations to this or that sector of the economy? Who will determine the distribution of the wealth it will produce? The answers to these questions establish to which of the four ideologies any one position properly belongs.

Let us see what these ideologies are and what answers they give:

1. Classic Capitalism

Capital for development must come from private investment. Given the weakness of local capitalism in the Latin American countries, most of this private investment must come from foreign sources. It may be complemented, but not replaced, by public investment from international and national institutions, especially funds earmarked for social development (communications, sanitation, education, power, irrigation, etc.), that is, investment that produces no immediate return on income but whose benefits have a favorable effect on the productiveness of private investment.

In the case of funds for economic development, the allocation of capital to the various sectors of the economy should be made by the investors themselves. The free play of supply and demand is sufficient to orient investment in such a way that it will both be profitable and have beneficial effects on the economy.

Similarly, the distribution of the wealth produced by this capital can be made freely without the imposition of a budget or other legislative regulation.

The change that is taking place in Latin America is, in the eyes of those who support this classic capitalist position, an evolutionary change, which does not alter the social structure. It must be achieved through collaboration with the oligarchic classes and without affecting their systems of ownership, although occasionally the power of the oligarchy may be limited, especially its power to control private investment so that its interests are not hurt.

Logically, this classic capitalist position should manifest itself in democratic societies (at least, outwardly democratic) and should not constitute any threat to freedom, since such a position is theoretically based on the free play of economic interests.

Experience shows that although this may be so (and there is room for argument) in the industrial societies of Europe and the United States, it is not true in present-day Latin American society.

In Latin America, recent history demonstrates that classic capitalism, because of a desire for immediate benefits and a fear of rapid and fundamental change, has allied itself with the oligarchies and, instead of encouraging development, has retarded it, or at best has supported it only in certain sectors of the economy which benefit the oligarchy and the sources of investment capital.

In Latin America, the application of classic capitalism (which in the political sphere would be called conservatism) has often resulted in dictatorship or, at best, in the mere forms of democracy, lacking popular content and more a ritual than a true opportunity for the society to decide its own destiny.

In the social field, this position has resulted in a superexploitation of the labor force, that is, a higher level of exploitation than would be considered normal in an industrialized capitalist society, high enough to lead predictably to economic misery, cultural isolation, and physical hardship. The subhuman condition of a large percentage of the Latin American peasant and proletarian groups, especially until recent years, must be blamed on the widespread application of the classic capitalist position in conjunction with a respect for the oligarchical survivals.

In summary, the classic capitalist position has not stimulated economic development in Latin America, has not respected the freedoms or improved the living conditions of the mass of the people. Economically, and often politically, it has been a position of dictatorship.

2. *Soviet-type Capitalism*

Capital for development must come from internal sources and only from them.

Allocation of investment to the various sectors of the economy should be made by the state, with primary emphasis on political considerations.

The distribution of wealth should also be controlled by the state, again with primary emphasis on political factors.

The change taking place in Latin America is, in the eyes of those who support the Soviet capitalist position, a popular revolution; it is a matter of creating a "national" front that holds power in the name of "all the people."

The result of this position can be seen on two levels: On the directly human level, it is clear that since the countries of Latin America do not have capital to invest and since the Soviet capitalist position requires that this investment be made exclusively with internal capital, these funds must then come from the citizens of the country involved. How are they to be made to produce capital? By subjecting them to a system of superexploitation. Just as the classic capitalist position uses superexploitation of the masses to increase the profits from their investments, so the Soviet capitalist position exploits the masses to a much greater extent than is normal in an industrial capitalist society, in order to produce capital for investment.

On the political level, the Soviet capitalist position has as its necessary consequence the deprivation of the freedom of the entire population and the establishment of systems of regimentation. This is logical, since only through systematic regimentation is it possible to maintain a regime dedicated to the superexploitation of the masses over several generations. Classic capitalism relies on a number of factors to perpetuate superexploitation: that superexploitation is not equal for all social classes; that the regime is considered to be the product of a historical tradition and of a series of axioms often accepted even by those who are superexploited; that the oligarchy and the army, which supports it, as well as other social forces (the Church at times, the bureaucracy, etc.) sustain and "justify" it.

But the Soviet capitalist regime does not have these forces behind it, and its superexploitation is not limited to strictly economic areas. The regime requires the full allegiance of all the populace. To achieve this, it must submit the people to a systematic "treatment" in all aspects of life: education, culture, entertainment, information, housing, work, family life, sex, in addition, of course, to the purely economic aspects. This cannot be achieved without controlling the life of every citizen and this control is not possible without the elimination of all liberties. Paying lip service to democracy, Soviet capitalism retains democratic ritual (elections, assemblies, etc.), but it suppresses all political activity. The paradox is that in a society without a true political system (without parties, ideologies, or programs that differ from the official forms), the distribution of wealth and the allocation of investment is based on political considerations—in order to benefit the governing class (a bureaucracy of political commissars and technicians) and to serve the political objectives, national and international, of that class.

In Latin America, examples of the application of the classic capitalist position are numerous (actually, all Latin American countries were in this camp until recent years and some still are), but there is only a single example, as yet provisional and incomplete, of an application of the position of Soviet capitalism, and that is Cuba, where the inability to attain social change within the framework of democratic institutions led to the adoption of Soviet capitalist methods.

We must, therefore, look for examples on other continents, in the U.S.S.R., China, and the so-called people's democracies.

It is essential to clarify one question of terminology. Soviet propagandists say that their regime is "socialist" and that it is moving toward "Communism." Many who are not Soviet propagandists have allowed themselves to be infected by this vocabulary and refer to the Soviet bloc as the "socialist world." The facts do not justify these terms. According to Marxism (and in this case, it must serve as our touchstone), capitalism is characterized first by the appropriation by one social class of the surplus value produced by the proletariat, and second by the alienation of the worker in his labor. This appropriation occurs because the means of production are in the hands of the class which is benefited by it and of which the state is a mere board of directors.

But the fact that in the U.S.S.R. the means of production are in the hands of the state rather than of private interests does not alter the fact that in Soviet society there is a proletariat that produces surplus value, that the portion of this surplus value not destined for capital investment is appropriated by a management class, and that the state is the board of directors for that class (the political and technical bureaucracy), nor can it disguise the alienation of the worker, which is much more apparent in the Soviet situation than in classic capitalist societies. Thus, although its forms are different, the basic factors of the Soviet social regime are identical with those of the capitalist social regime—except that the Soviets have less freedom and a much more superficial and ritualistic democracy.

In the U.S.S.R. and its satellites, it is said that the proletariat holds power. In Latin America, where, according to Marxism, there must be a stage of bourgeois revolution before "socialism" is achieved, the methods of Soviet capitalism would strive to accelerate this stage artificially and to the greatest possible degree, a process that would require the adoption of even more coercive methods than are normal in Soviet capitalist societies that have already attained the stage of "socialism."

Just as classic capitalism stimulates development to a limited extent (albeit only in some sectors of the economy), the Soviet capitalist program accelerates the rate of development and achieves spectacular advances at times, but does so by concentrating on limited sectors of the economy (heavy industry, mining), while neglecting other sectors that are indispensable to the general well-being (light industry, food production). In both types of capitalism, development and its immediate results (whether this be the inflation of classic capitalism or the scarcities of Soviet capitalism) react only upon the mass of the people, leaving the privileged managing class unaffected. In short, the poor pay; in the case of classic capitalism, they provide the profits of the capitalists and the oligarchy; in the case of Soviet capitalism, they pay for the greater well-being of the managing class and supply capital for new investment.

3. *Experimental and Nationalistic Capitalism*

Those who support this position believe that capital must come partly from local investment (public investment, for purposes of stimulus and orientation, as well as private investment from existing sources of capital) and partly from international institutions, preferably public. They do not, in any case, support the principle of superexploitation to create capital.

They believe that government and public institutions must determine general priorities for the allocation of investment capital. They also believe that government, principally through the budget and through structural reforms, should achieve more equitable distribution of the national income.

Among those who support this position, there are two viewpoints. Some regard it as a period of transition toward new forms of organization of the state and society, which they wish to reach through evolution and at a time when the proletariat possesses sufficient influence and a strong enough ideological basis, and when the level of industrial development makes it possible to establish a system that could be considered socialistic. The other group desires only the development of a modern capitalism, efficient, respectful of freedoms, and disposed to bring about a fairer distribution of national income, but without aspiring to more advanced forms of social organization. Temporarily, both points of view coexist.

Why have I called this type of capitalism "experimental and nationalistic"? The capitalism that we know in Latin America is the product of imperialism, of foreign private investment and, to a lesser extent, of foreign public investment, as well as local, public and private investment. In its major elements, it appears to be an example of classic capitalism, but it would not hesitate to utilize the methods of Soviet capitalism, if it could so without fear of the political consequences. But in the next few years, economic development will stimulate the formation and rapid growth of a new capitalism (at least, if the supporters of the position which I have just analyzed succeed in implementing their views). This system will be based on capital less greedy than that of classic capitalism; its formulation will occur in a period of political struggle and profound social change. At the same time, the trade-union movement will develop and nationalistic revolutionary movements will grow stronger. Thus, for a relatively brief period, the possibility exists of molding the system of capitalism produced by economic development and of limiting its political and economic ambitions, causing it to accept these limitations as normal conditions of its existence. It is the labor and nationalistic revolutionary movements that can, and should, impose the kind of development that makes possible this kind of capitalism, which I call experimental (because it is really a social experiment), and also imposes limitations on the capitalistic system itself, limitations that will permit, in the less immediate future, its replacement by other social forms.

This sort of capitalism is nationalistic in the positive sense of the word, in that it retains national ownership of the essential sources of wealth (land, subsoil, public services) through either public investment or nationalization and structural reforms.

It is immediately obvious that this type of capitalism must be politically democratic, must encourage respect for and exercise of freedom, and must reject superexploitation as a method of capitalization.

4. Anticapitalism

Actually, we should use this term in the plural. It would be reasonable to include under this heading many supporters of Soviet capitalism who are not conscious Communists and also those supporters of experimental capitalism who believe this to be only a temporary stage in Latin American development. There are movements (socialist, anarchosyndicalist) that are by definition anticapitalist, although they accept the fact that current development leads to the formation of a nationalistic capitalism, and therefore, they try to oppose development in all its manifestations. These movements, which had some strength and influence in the past, have been on the decline precisely because they could not understand that, in the Latin American context, the best method of being anticapitalist is to accelerate the formation of capitalism, to place controls upon it, and to create the proper conditions for replacing it.

Naturally, those who claim to be anticapitalist and who reject the capitalist stage, even as a transitional period, must accept fully the Soviet capitalist method of development, a method of development by national means at all costs, without the participation of private capital (neither local nor international), which would be possible only if its supporters seized political power; but in this case, they would find themselves compelled by the pressure of reality to apply methods that would not differ from those of Soviet capitalism in either the economic or the political area. Although ideologically, the strict anticapitalist position is the most just (since capitalism, by definition and in even the most controlled and limited form, is always a source of injustice and the erosion of freedom), for Latin America it is equivalent to complete passivity or de facto acceptance of Soviet methods of development.

The only effective sort of anticapitalism, the only sort with any possibility of success, in Latin America, is that which realizes (in accordance with the teachings of Marxism) that it is not possible to skip stages of development and that a semifeudal regime, such as predominates in Latin America, can be followed only by a capitalistic regime. But beyond this, it must be prepared to accelerate the replacement of the nascent capitalism and seek ways of minimizing for the mass of society the greedy, unjust, and harmful characteristics of this capitalism. This is the position advanced by the supporters of experimental and nationalistic capitalism as a transitional system.

Thus we find ourselves with two types of ideology about development, both of which produce varying degrees of superexploitation and a loss of individual freedoms. One of them (classic capitalism) has not proved itself very effective in stimulating development. The other (Soviet capitalism), although it may have been successful in promoting development in a few countries, has done so at great cost in human suffering, indignity, and coercion. A third type of ideology, anticapitalism, although it may in principle be capable of accelerating development and although it proclaims itself a supporter of personal freedom, would, in the Latin American context, lead inevitably to a totalitarian system, a system as pernicious as any of the two capitalistic systems.

One ideology remains—experimental capitalism, which to date has been the only one that has shown itself effective in promoting development, and which has had only occasional and temporary recourse to methods of superexploitation and deprivation of freedom.

Nonetheless, many of the supporters of experimental capitalism have become impatient. They believe that the acceleration of development by democratic methods is not enough and they would prefer to apply certain of the methods not only of classic capitalism, but especially of Soviet capitalism. They believe in good faith that they could avoid in their own country the unfortunate consequences that could not be avoided in others.

Certain of these elements, which we might call mixed, contend that development cannot be accelerated without a degree of superexploitation, although they maintain that this would be only temporary and not very oppressive. Facts show, however, that where there is superexploitation, totalitarianism and loss of freedoms invariably follow.

Others, exasperated by the procrastination of the democratic system and by endless discussions of methods that to them seem to be of obvious urgency, would like to organize society in such a way as to achieve efficiency not by superexploitation but rather by a suspension of freedoms. But experience also shows that where freedoms are suspended, they eventually disappear.

Superexploitation and destruction of liberty are inseparable. When one is established, the other follows. This is unavoidable. And even if it were not, one of these features would be enough to disqualify any economic system from the point of view of both economic development and, it goes without saying, human dignity.

Therefore, we must emphasize that the four ideological systems are mutually incompatible. They cannot be mixed; it is impossible to take something from one and something else from another.

Actually, the totalitarian systems of development may adopt some of the forms of experimental capitalism—and discard them when the disguise is no longer needed or when the circumstances that required the compromise disappear. But the experimental capitalist system cannot compromise by one iota; it cannot adopt any facet of the other systems without discrediting itself and ceasing to be what it is.

It might be thought that capitalism, in its various forms, offers the only possibility for development in Latin America. Many avoid this conclusion by putting a different label on what I have called Soviet capitalism. They call it socialism or Communism. Others regard it as merely a progressive form of nationalism. In the last analysis, whatever the label, it leads to the use of methods employed in the U.S.S.R. and its satellites. And these methods do not differ in their fundamentals from those of capitalism.

If Soviet capitalism or anticapitalism were the only alternatives to classic capitalism, it might be thought that Latin American economic development could never get out of the capitalistic rut. In the present situation, not only in Latin America but in the rest of the world as well, experimental capitalism is the least of the possible evils. What we call revolutions in African and Asian nations are actually only the seizure of power by the local *bourgeoisie,* often in concert with certain feudal groups or interests that were in the colonialist camp until very recently. The installation of a capitalist system constitutes a classic bourgeois revolution. It is this revolution that is taking place in Latin America.

However, our level of development is more advanced than that of Asia and Africa, we have a longer political tradition, and our cultural roots are basically Western; this creates possibilities for replacing capitalism that have not yet appeared in African and Asian countries.

But this replacement presupposes three lines of action which can —and should—be followed without waiting for political control:

1. To strengthen unceasingly the obstacles to the capitalist tendency toward exploitation, that is, to look for democratic measures within the labor scene, to reinforce the labor unions, and to control the impatience of the young elements of the army and the techno-

crats that may lead them to apply Soviet capitalist methods, or if they attempt to apply them, to oppose them as energetically as possible. That is, more than anything else, the protection of the individual in his work and in his political and cultural life.

2. To study the current reality of Latin America and the world to see what things can be useful, what can be improved, and what must be rejected or destroyed, in the existing systems, including experimental capitalism. To know not only the aspirations of the people but their needs as well and what can satisfy these needs without endangering freedoms and without requiring superexploitation. Such a study will lead us to answer the question: "What do we want Latin America to become?"

3. To immunize men and movements, social groups and certain government sectors (the military and the technicians) against the temptation to mixing methods. To show them there can be no superexploitation without destruction of freedoms, nor any destruction of freedoms that does not lead to superexploitation. This immunization cannot be achieved by pronouncements alone, but has to be produced by actions, these for example: solution of such problems as agrarian reform, industrialization, and militarism on the continental level through democratic methods, and the demonstration, by this solution, of the fact that these methods are more effective, less costly, and demand fewer sacrifices than the methods of classic capitalism or Soviet capitalism. Finally, a requirement of fundamental importance is the creation or strengthening of powerful popular movements which desire to achieve development by democratic means, in an atmosphere of complete freedom, and which, at the same time, are dedicated to working for the replacement of the capitalism that this development creates; that is, movements derived from the people, which will bring the submerged masses up to the surface.

In summary, the political and social ideologies of present-day Latin America are concerned primarily with the choice of methods for development. Rather than use the method of classic capitalism, which has proved a failure, or the inhuman method of Soviet capitalism, we can encourage and direct development in such a way that the capitalistic system that results will be less of an evil and less damaging than either classic or Soviet capitalism, and can be replaced in the future.

In order that we do not succumb to the temptation of supposing that the Soviet method is the most efficient or that the classic method is the easiest, it is necessary that the democratic, libertarian methods of development be proved easier and more efficient. With oligarchies in power, and in the face of conformist middle classes and contented working classes, this appears to be almost impossible. This is the source of the danger that haunts Latin America today—worse than the military dictatorship or the Communist dictatorship, because it embraces both.

The Punishment for Failure

For permitting itself to become divided, the labor movement was finally punished—with fascism. Equally, the failure of populism and, more generally, of the Latin American middle class (the failure to destroy the oligarchy) may receive its punishment in the near future in technocratic militarism.

We all know that in Latin America, there is a long militaristic tradition, which differs little in its causes and effects from the militarism that still afflicts Spain, and which, as in the Spanish case, paradoxically, has a liberal origin. Each time that two or three dictators fall, it is said that democracy is entering a period of stabilization. What happens is that militarism changes its pattern. Following the garrison militarism of Melgarejo and Gómez came the "hacienda" militarism of Somoza and Trujillo, and still later the demagogic militarism of Perón and Pérez Jiménez. This in turn gave way to the paternalistic militarism of the juntas, in Ecuador, and to the "guided" systems of the military in Argentina and Brazil. And now technocratic militarism is appearing, a strange mixture of young officers and anti-Communist businessmen, together with Castroite intellectuals and Communist organizers.[10]

We must not forget, in the light of what I am here attempting to point out, Plato's observation that the man who knows how to free the people also knows how to enslave them. For there is no tyranny worse than the paternalism which makes "revolutions" from above.

[10] For a better understanding of militarism, see: Edwin Lieuwen, *Arms and Politics in Latin America* (rev. ed.; New York, 1961); John J. Johnson (ed.), *The Role of the Military in Underdeveloped Countries* (Princeton, 1962); and Alba, *El militarismo* (Mexico City, 1959), and *El ascenso del militarismo tecnocrático* (Mexico City, 1964). See also the speech of Senator Ernest Gruening in the U.S. Senate, *Congressional Record,* August 2, 1962.

This technocratic militarism of the near future has ideological roots that are, to say the least, somewhat curious.

Every two or three generations certain discoveries within the realm of ideas repeat themselves. Today Latin America is rediscovering Marxism (or perhaps one should say "Marxism," for what circulates under that label is a strange mixture of defeated Stalinism, nostalgia for the Popular Front, and malevolent digests of the works of a few Marxists). It is a curious discovery, in the sense that it does not derive from the reading of the fundamental Marxist works, nor even the works of the Marxist-Leninists. Rather, it is acquired from conversation, popular articles, and résumés of Lukacs' books; it is a "quicky Marxism," taken out of its historical context because this new type of "Marxist" knows absolutely nothing of the polemics between Marxists and nothing of the history of the labor movement. Our Marxists today are Marxists by osmosis.

They become Marxists for the same reason that others become addicted to alcohol, drugs, eroticism, or jazz—as an escape. Except that those who escape by other means are hardly concerned about a clear conscience. Those who escape through Marxism, however, indulge their consciences by so doing and, thanks to their new "Marxist" label, feel that their consciences are calm and contented.

The phenomenon of escape through the medium of "Marxism" is characteristic of men under forty, especially among intellectuals, students, the middle class. The workers—and even less the peasants —do not achieve such subtlety of thinking, and their consciences, although they may be more conventional, are generally more demanding and are not content with rhetorical games.

Most of these "Marxists" are concerned about the situation in Latin America, but decline to become involved in it. They defend Castro, who is at a distance (and whose regime they would not wish for themselves), and thus soothe their consciences and find an excuse not to become caught up in what is happening in their own countries. Defending Castro gives them prestige (at least, it did until a few years ago) and imposes no hardship on them. To be involved in their own country's situation entails running certain risks, creating enemies and fighting. In the past, Castro has been the "tranquillizer" for these "Marxists." But precisely because he no longer serves this purpose (especially since the Cuban missile crisis of October, 1962), they now require different ideological aspirins. From this follows the rediscovery of Marxism and its transformation into "Marxism," into a theory that requires as few sacrifices and risks as did the defense of Castro.

Castro has created a crisis among Latin American Castroites. The "Marxism" that we have been talking about is the result of this crisis. In manner of speaking, this "Marxism" alienates them from Castro and supplies them with the rationalizations (for example, the dialectical argument that it is impossible to skip stages of development) that permit them to cease being Castroites while still thinking of themselves as "revolutionaries." Because this "Marxism" customarily offers all sorts of very "revolutionary" reasons for inaction, allows one to adopt "all or nothing" attitudes (and since it is impossible to achieve "all," one does "nothing") and to amuse oneself with Byzantine polemics (which recall the best periods of Trotskyism) instead of going to the people, educating them, organizing them, and helping to create in them the conditions out of which their new leaders will arise.

This is the third time that Marxism has been discovered by Latin Americans, but it is the first time that it has been used as a pretext for inaction and self-deception. Marxism was first discovered at the end of the last century, among European immigrants, and it served as a basis for the formation of several of the socialist parties (especially the Argentine). The second discovery occurred after World War I, with the formation of the Communist parties. Later came the systematic Stalinist adulteration. And just as the Communists are abandoning the Marxist lexicon (all that they retained of Marxism), Marxism reappears, emasculated, however, by the desire to be "revolutionary" without risk or sacrifice. This "Marxism" weans away from Castroism and Communism many who until now could be considered fellow travelers. At a time when being a fellow traveler is no longer profitable, when it becomes obvious that Moscow missed the boat in Latin America by at least a generation, Marxism now offers the means of continuing to be thought of as revolutionary without having to climb on a bandwagon that is going nowhere. Although in a way this is useful for Latin America, it also offers certain dangers, because it deprives the movement for social change of elements who might be useful if they could only face facts. In reality, this road of pseudo Marxism offers the way for yesterday's Communist fellow travelers to be the fellow travelers of tomorrow's technocratic dictators. And these dictators have also discovered Marxism.

Almost at the same time that the young men of the middle class were discovering Marxism, the Latin American military began to do likewise. This tardy discovery was influenced by two factors: the doctrine of psychological warfare picked up by certain French military groups in Indochina during the war against the Vietnamese Communists, and Castroite propaganda.

The military are not attracted to the political and social concepts of Marxism, or to its philosophic basis. Among the young Latin American military men who read Marxist books and manuals, there are few who can give a definition of the dialectic or supply examples of historical materialism. Fewer yet have a clear notion of the theory of surplus value. But, on the other hand, what has come to be called Marxist strategy and tactics (actually Leninist and Stalinist), especially that with the Chinese seasoning cooked up by the chefs of the French Secret Army Organization, is the specialty on the intellectual menu of all these young military men. And they continually circulate among themselves reports and commentaries on Soviet industrial development, the methods by which it has been achieved, and the repercussions it has had on Russian military strength.

Naturally, what others consider a condemnation of the Communist regime and its procedures is, for the military, a defense for these methods. The strong hand, efficiency above liberty, regimentation of the masses, military systems of social discipline, these are methods that would be repugnant to any one of us. But to the military, accustomed to barracks discipline and to rule by force of arms, without recourse to reason or consideration of popular reactions, these Communist procedures present a most seductive image.

In a manner of speaking, the young Latin American military feel that they can no longer appear to be dictatorial oligarchic militarists without an ideological justification. Marxism—what they assimilate out of it and accept as methodology while officially rejecting it as ideology—offers them this justification.

To use these Marxist methods, the conviction that the ends justify the means, and to put these methods to the service of popular ends to which everyone aspires (agrarian reform, industrialization, destruction of the oligarchies, real participation by the masses in national life), this is what the young military of Latin America find more and more tempting.

All this is no exaggeration. Marxism is on the curriculum of the

Center for Advanced Military Studies in Peru, as well as in certain
Nasserist circles in Argentina. Almost every army has these courses
in Marxism, organized for the purpose of "knowing the enemy,"
but whose results are boomeranging: They make Stalinists (or Le-
ninists, at best) out of many of the young military. They will fight
Communism, but they will use Communist weapons to do it. And
the consequence will be that the Latin American people will find
themselves subjected to "revolutionary" and demagogic dictatorships which will carry out some reforms, but although they were
thought in the beginning to be anti-Communist, these dictatorships
will end up being directed by local or imported Communists.

These young military men, and the technicians and certain ultra-
modern businessmen who join them, will not be able to effect the
reforms they genuinely desire without damaging vested interests.
Moreover, they will have to promote enterprises producing a high
return and low level of consumption. To overcome the resistance of
wounded interests and exploited workers, they will have to seek the
support of the masses. But the masses, by then skeptical and tired
of militarism, will support them only if mobilized, given a mystique,
and an organization. And later on, when the inevitable disillusionment of the masses takes place in the face of reforms that are
destined to fail (because they are paternalistic and lack the real
participation of the people) and when sacrifices are demanded in the
name of capitalization, then the new technocratic dictators will
have to alter their methods of organizing the masses—not to maintain their enthusiasm, but rather to check their protest and to control them. Finally, the strong man will appear. But to arrive at this
point, the impatient military and technocrats will have had to
request the help of the only group in Latin America capable of
organizing the masses and establishing the necessary systems of regimentation and collective brutalization—the Communists.

The battle Moscow lost in Europe in 1945–48, and lost again in
Cuba in 1962, it may be able to win in Latin America sometime in
the 1960's through the new breed of militarists. If so, it will be because of the knowledgeable imbecility of the oligarchies and the
timidity of the democratic left.

In Latin America, the uniformed technocrats and their cronies
are as remote from the people as are their counterparts in the
Nasserist countries. They are inspired by good intentions (those
good intentions that in politics always lead to dictatorship), which

are attuned neither to the goals nor to the needs of the people, but which can momentarily attract and reflect the people's disillusion and frustration. And the experiment will of necessity result in the failure of these good intentions, to an even greater inefficiency than that which they meant to correct (greater because there will be no freedom to criticize it and overcome it), and thus to the continuation of social injustice, with fewer possibilities of fighting it.

These efficiency experts will end up leading us to well-planned chaos and the impatient reformers will end up teaching us patience with a club. Perhaps then the U.S.S.R. will feel that this time the situation warrants risking more than it did for Cuba, and will try to fish some profit out of the marvelous *mare magnum* that will result from the pedantic inexperience of the military technocrats and their cohorts.

Stalinism, Castroism, and the dictatorship of the impatient technicians stem from situations that may seem different, but have something in common: a revolution that has been adulterated, betrayed, and unsuccessful. In every society, there are minority groups that lose confidence in the masses, because the masses are less energetic, less efficient, and less enthusiastic than these groups would like. Once confidence in the masses has been lost, there is no longer any reason to resort to democratic forms (although a façade of democracy is retained for purposes of propaganda). At this point, an almost unpremeditated drift toward paternalistic methods begins, and an attempt to force the people into what the leaders of the moment conceive to be happiness. This process concludes by giving the name of happiness to misfortune, liberty to dictatorship, brotherhood to distrust and accusation. This technique is not solely a Stalinist discovery, but under Stalin, it reached heights never before imagined. It is merely what Stalinism has in common with other postrevolutionary regimes in which at least one of the aspirations of every revolutionary movement becomes frustrated, i.e., the transformation of society, or at least of a large social group, in order to give each of its members greater freedom to be himself (within the term "greater freedom" is included economic freedom, that is, the material possibility of enjoying all the other types of freedom). Occasionally, as in the case of the French Revolution, the libertarian aspect is thwarted. In other cases, due to special circumstances, both the libertarian and social aspects are frustrated.

In still others, such as the Latin American revolution, the social aspect is completely thwarted while the libertarian remains only half-realized (or else it, too, is thwarted, as in the case of Cuba). It is this frustration (and not economic misery, as many say) that creates fertile ground for Communist propaganda and for the dictatorial paternalism of the technocrats—for the dictatorship of efficiency.

And indirectly, the dictatorship of efficiency not only attracts the Communists (who are attracted to any regime in which they can wield influence) but also, as I have explained, makes them indispensable components of the regime.

All these elements that have become frustrated, impatient, disillusioned, incapable of sacrifice themselves but entirely capable of demanding sacrifice from others, have a common war cry: "Democracy has failed. We must try other ways to develop Latin America." What is bad about this cry is that many voice it in good faith, in the belief that Latin America has experienced democracy, and since we are still what we are, then we have proof that democracy does not work.

But if one looks at the history of Latin America without the distorting spectacles of privilege, one sees immediately that Latin America has *never* experienced democracy, that at the most we have had (and not always or everywhere) an imitation of representative democracy.

Everything has been tried: efficient dictatorship and corrupt dictatorship, the militarism of animals in uniform and the militarism of intelligent men, anticlerical and exploitative liberalism, clerical and paternalistic conservatism, false revolution and authentic revolution. All have failed (except the authentic revolution in a few countries). The masses remain submerged, power remains in the hands of the landowning oligarchy, the standard of living of the masses sinks while a minority's existence improves. None of the systems that have been tried has been able to bring progress to Latin America. The only thing that has not been tried is democracy, real democracy, democracy that is at once political, social, and economic, that is government *of, by,* and *for* the people.

So then, forgetting the myths and the privileges of social parasitism, the logical question should be: "Suppose we try democracy?"

This is what the Alliance for Progress wanted to attempt.

III

DIALOGUE OF THE DEAF AND THE DUMB

A Revolution on Easy Terms

IN 1959, Castro began to make Washington nervous. Nixon's spittle-spattered trip to Latin America gave the diplomats goose pimples and the politicians a theme. No one seemed to understand that those who spat at Nixon represented, not the revolutionary, but the reactionary forces of Latin America. Even the ones who spat did not know it.

Washington then began to listen to what the Latin Americans of the left had been saying all along. In this sense, Castro and the Caracas rioters were useful, perhaps more for U.S. diplomacy than for the people of Latin America. In the United States, people began to think that possibly there was something to the position of those in Latin America and in their own country (of whom there were many) who saw a need to create the conditions for authentic and stable Latin American democracy.

Many economists and intellectuals, and a few politicians, began to see that, even discounting the danger of Communism, the national interests of the United States had something in common with the social interests of the Latin American people. And it was believed (at that time, we all believed it) that the middle class, represented by the populist movements, was the element that could speak, and wanted to speak, in the name of the Latin American people.

Even before his election, President Kennedy proposed the Alliance for Progress, to which he tried to give official form once he was in the White House.

No one—not Kennedy, not his advisers on Latin American affairs, not the populist leaders, not the political commentators, not even the most violently pessimistic persons, such as myself—could see then that the Alliance could not be a governmental project, at least as far as Latin America was concerned.

We were all convinced that, under the combined pressure of the menace of Castro and North American loans, the oligarchy would be reconciled to conceding at least some of its privileges. We believed in a revolution on easy terms—payable by the United States. Events quickly proved us wrong.

Today we can view the Alliance with a certain perspective, we can strike a balance and suggest alterations, not in the concept, but rather in terms of strategy, structure, and even tactics of what should have been from the start an offensive rather than a series of maneuvers.

The history of the Alliance reads like a monumental joke. It is the story of a mute who wanted a deaf man to listen to him; of a bureaucracy which did not know how to convince the people to lend it their voice and which tried to convince the oligarchy, always deaf, to listen to the voice it did not have.

President Kennedy expressed the motives of the Alliance very clearly. He asserted that there was agreement on the need for a revolution in Latin America, peaceful or bloody. But he maintained that a peaceful revolution was possible.

But how was this to be achieved? How could we assure the victory of the revolution that Kennedy, and everyone else, believed could be peaceful? For this, Kennedy looked beyond the outworn concepts of the "Good Neighbor" Policy and dollar diplomacy, as he did beyond a narrowly anti-Communist crusade. What he envisioned was a flexible, "bold" vocabulary of approaches and techniques—"a vast effort, unparalleled in magnitude and nobility of purpose, to satisfy the basic needs of the American people."

How far-reaching this effort should be Kennedy himself indicated: "Political freedom must be accompanied by social change. For unless necessary social reforms, including land and tax reforms, are freely made—unless we broaden the opportunity of all our people—unless the great mass of Americans share in increasing prosperity—then our alliance, our revolution, and our dream will have failed."[1]

But the fact that the Alliance had been proposed by the United States did not allay all fears. Until recently, the United States was neither interested in Latin America nor disposed to assist the Latin American people to achieve their aspirations.

How was it then that suddenly the idea of the Alliance was brought forth? I say suddenly because an evolution in the mechanism of a government over a period of two or three years (since Nixon's trip and the fall of Batista) is virtually instantaneous, as evolutions in government mechanisms go (although certainly the process was much more rapid than it would have been in the case of Latin American governments). There can be no doubt that Nixon's trip and the Castro phenomenon were important factors in this evolution; but they were not the only factors. The principal one, and one that escaped the notice of almost all observers in Latin America, is that the United States became aware of what is called the revolution of the third world—the Latin American revolution, the revolution of the new peoples, the revolution of the proletarian nations. This was nothing but a bourgeois revolution, simply and purely a revolution whose aim was to change semifeudal social structures into capitalist structures.

And this is one of the things that had to be made clear. The good faith of the United States in proposing the Alliance for Progress could be accepted on the grounds that it was an instrument to achieve, not a socialist revolution, but a capitalist revolution, of the sort that in Africa will have certain given characteristics determined by the tribal character of the society it is attempting to alter, that in Asia will be molded along lines dictated by the tradition of satrapy, and that in Latin America will have other characteristics, determined by the semifeudal character of the present society and by the long tradition—inherited from the colonial era—of state direction. This direction (which in the United States is called creeping socialism) is simply one of the many forms a capitalist society may adopt.

This was a fact that had to be understood and accepted by all,

[1] The two preceding quotations are from President Kennedy's speech of March 13, 1961, at the White House, in which he presented the idea of the Alliance to the governments of Latin America.

especially those who did not think that the capitalist form of society was ideal or that it was the objective of their struggle. Without this capitalist society, there is no chance to go further; it is impossible to pass from feudalism to any social form proceeding out of capitalism without falling into totalitarianism. Marx has said so.

For decades, the most progressive forces in Latin America had complained that the United States was not giving the area enough assistance, that it thought of Latin America only in terms of its private investments. For the first time, the United States was offering Latin America a program of aid greater than that offered any other continent. And it was offering it, not to promote United States business enterprises, but to resolve the problems that keep Latin America tied to the apron strings of the oligarchy.

Who in Latin America wanted this peaceful revolution? The middle class, above all. Because the small *haute bourgeoisie* (probably because it was so small) had preferred to ingratiate itself with the landowning oligarchy. The middle class, which was growing in size and influence, needed the support of the working class and the peasants to oust the oligarchy from power and achieve this revolution. The workers and peasants could not bring the revolution about by themselves (even in Cuba, the revolution was started by the middle class and only later taken over, not by a class, but by a party intent on dominating both the middle class—which it wants to erase from the social map—and the workers and peasants). But the union of these three forces could make a peaceful revolution, which would logically benefit the middle class in particular and, indirectly, the *haute bourgeoisie,* which, in addition, would find itself free of its not always comfortable alliance of convenience with the oligarchy, a situation which limits its freedom of choice. The workers and peasants would also, logically, benefit from this revolution, if only because industrialization would increase the specific weight of the working class and agrarian reform would convert the peasants into a rural middle class.

Very well then. Neither the oligarchic governments, nor the bureaucratic and technical organizations in charge of implementing the Alliance (and these groups had to be utilized, since at present, there is no other instrument to carry out an economic and social plan), nor the political parties that saw the Alliance only as a means of fighting Communism and not as something that had to be done whether Communism existed or not—none of these groups could support the Alliance.

To ask the bureaucrats to act like revolutionaries, the technicians to view things in political terms, the oligarchs to renounce their privileges, the reactionaries to accept the democratic revolution, is to ask for miracles that could come to pass only in a political dream world.

The United States had concluded that what so many Latin Americans had been saying for decades was true; that industrialization produces instability and disequilibrium if it is not accompanied (or preferably preceded) by agrarian reform; that without agrarian reform, the benefits of development cannot be distributed equitably; and that industrialization makes the rich richer and does very little to lighten the poverty of the poor. The paradox is that at the very moment when the United States was becoming persuaded of the validity of this concept, it was being forgotten by the very people in Latin America who had been propounding it for so many years.

Any agrarian reform, however well planned it may be, produces at least a temporary drop in agricultural production. In Latin America, where the rate of population increase exceeds the rate of production increase, any drop is especially dangerous. The Alliance must, therefore, supply the means, technicians, and material to shorten the period of lower production.

But at the same time, a democratic agrarian reform presupposes that property owners will be indemnified for the lands expropriated from them and that the peasants who become the new owners of the land will be furnished with the means of profitable cultivation: tools, seed, tractors, cattle, roads, technical instruction, as well as housing, schools for their children, and hospitals. All this costs money. It would not be fair for the United States to have to pay for this also, and one would suppose that the countries involved would feel their national pride hurt if this were even suggested. The countries themselves must pay.

But how? The answer is obvious: with the money of those who earn it. That is to say, by equitable taxation. The Latin American fiscal system is one of astonishing injustice. Knowing the details, one wonders why this fiscal injustice has not produced outright insurrections. The only explanation is that the injustice is hidden by a tangle of technical phraseology.

To pay for agrarian reform, then, it would be necessary to reform the fiscal system. But this would surely provoke protests, taking the form of exportation of capital and a drop in reinvestment. These protests could be counteracted in two ways: on the one hand, by paying indemnifications to the owners of expropriated latifundia in such a way that they would be forced to invest these funds in the national economy, and on the other, by repatriating flight capital through indirect methods. And it is this that ought to be the principal function of the Inter-American Development Bank.

In summary, every social change creates problems that, unless they are resolved, will lead the very persons who brought the changes about to adopt antidemocratic and coercive methods, which in turn will lead to totalitarianism. But if a mechanism exists to support those creating reforms, so that the problems arising out of the reforms can be resolved without resort to coercion and totalitarian processes, then reform can triumph. The Alliance ought to be that mechanism.

And that is what it was, at least in the minds of those who conceived and proposed it. It never was that in the minds of the majority of Latin Americans, both the leaders and the led.

No one made the man in the street understand the opportunities the Alliance offered, no one made him see that with the Alliance, there was no longer any valid excuse for not carrying out agrarian reforms, not altering the fiscal systems, and not integrating the economies of Latin America.

And if some groups kept the man in the street in ignorance about all this because it suited their interests, others did so out of fear that they would be accused of being pro-Yankee if they spread the facts about the Alliance.

The attitude of the United States is critical for the Latin American economy and will be for a long time to come. This attitude had been traditionally characterized by fear of changes in the social structure, rejection of investment in any kind of social improvement, and by stinginess in economic assistance. The Alliance represented a complete about-face in attitude.

As early as 1960, by the Act of Bogotá, international public investments were placed at the service of social goals. Furthermore, public loans began to be offered to governmental enterprises.

The United States had always been opposed to any long-range

plan and cold toward attempts at economic integration. This also changed. Kennedy asked his Congress for a general plan for foreign aid and suggested that social and economic development should be planned for Latin America, as well as methods of integration.

There was even more: Washington had never intervened in Latin American attempts to stabilize export prices of raw materials. But in 1960, the United States Government realized that without stabilization, steady and solid economic development was impossible, and Kennedy himself proposed that a common study be made of this problem.

To a certain extent, we could say that Washington moved away from the policy of bilateral approaches that it had followed for so long and began to look for multilateral solutions on a continent-wide scale. This step had incalculable consequences and offered Latin America the opportunity of deciding its own destiny.

In short, Kennedy invited Latin America to analyze all its problems, leaving nothing out and concealing nothing. Even the Marshall Plan never went this far, for in 1947, U.S. specialists drew up their own plan, which was then presented to the nations of Europe. But now the Latin American specialists and ministers themselves were given the responsibility of laying out the general lines of the plan for Latin America. Perhaps this was the initial reason for the failure of the Alliance.

In addition to eliminating the taboos that had retarded Latin American development and had channeled the benefits of whatever development was achieved into the pockets of a privileged minority (the taboos of integration, loans to government enterprises, and investment in the area of social improvement), Washington destroyed another taboo, under the pressure of events and because of a new political comprehension of world realities—the taboo of the immutable social structure.

This change of outlook was tremendously important. It can be summed up in the statement that Washington hoped that Latin America could achieve a revolution from above with the collaboration of the base of society. Washington hoped that the governments of Latin America, with financial assistance from the United States and Western Europe, would adopt methods that would transform the social structure and that would make the man in the street a participant in their implementation, so that he would finally enjoy the benefits of economic progress.

This was in itself a revolution in the Latin American policy of the United States. The Punta del Este Conference of 1962 was to offer an opportunity of observing whether there had been a parallel revolution in the spirit and the minds of Latin American political leaders, if they had finally realized the urgency and importance of social change.

The Internal Enemies of the Alliance

The danger was that in Latin America there were governments or powerful social groups who clung to the taboos which Washington was in the process of weeding out of its Latin American policy.

The Organization of American States planned the Punta del Este meeting under the impression that this danger would not assert itself. It engaged groups of experts (not as representatives of their respective governments, but in their personal professional capacity) to draw up plans on which the ministers and their advisers would work.

There was another danger, no less serious—that of overoptimism, with the concomitant danger of disillusionment, which in Latin America would be conducive to demagogic adventures and in the United States to a reversion to its former policy It was essential to make the United States understand that the Punta del Este Conference would not overnight dispel the Latin Americans' deep-rooted mistrust of Washington.

But none of these dangers was as important as the fear that in some cases governments would go on sleeping, while in others they would limit themselves to Potemkin reforms.

At the Punta del Este meeting, the Latin American governments were divided into two groups: the big nations and the small. The latter proposed that a multilateral agency be established within the Alliance to make multilateral decisions in regard to loans and money management as well as to planning. There is no doubt that planning on the national level is not enough; problems such as agriculture, the Indians, population, raw-material markets, and militarism can be solved only on a continent-wide basis. It was not the United States that opposed the multilateral and continental character the small nations wanted to give the Alliance. It was the large nations that, hoping to get a bigger slice of the Alliance funds, created in effect a system of bilateral negotiations and agreements, relying on the greater pressure they could exert by virtue of their size and greater economic importance. As we have seen, nationalism in Latin America does not yet mean a Latin American nationalism; it is very much narrower in its manifestations.

By eliminating the supranational, continental, or multinational elements, these governments failed to make the Alliance become what it should have become—a means for making the voice of the people heard—and turned it over to the diplomats.

The Charter signed by all the Latin American governments at Punta del Este was called a "declaration *to* the peoples of America" and not a "declaration *of* America." It was the governments that paternalistically made promises to the people; it was not the people themselves who assumed the responsibility. Under these conditions, the Alliance was from birth condemned to be an instrument of the governments. If the governments are oligarchic, then the Alliance must of necessity serve the oligarchies.

The military and landowning oligarchies, the feudal and Castro-Communist reactionaries have turned out to be less dangerous than the enemies the Alliance has harbored within itself.

These internal enemies are the bureaucrat, the technician, the "fireman," and the supernationalist—those who have managed to turn the Alliance into an Alliance for the Progress of the International Bureaucrat, of the Expert, of the *status quo* disguised behind each nation's reforms. For this reason, the problems of Latin America persist, aggravated by the loss of time, effort, and money, and by the frustration built up because of this loss. In the face of this conspiracy, the United States has become impatient and has decided to do the whole job itself. The Alliance has now become an Alliance for the Progress of Good Relations Between the United States and Latin America, which lessens its scope and provokes added frustration, since it does not achieve even this end.

The Alliance was a totally new concept for which, on the practical level, not even the Marshall Plan could serve as a precedent; thus it required totally new organs. But the Inter-American system was encumbered by a weighty inheritance of bureaucrats accustomed to other problems and another rhythm of activity. The danger existed that the old bureaucrats would tend to drag the Alliance down to their level of achievement, and thus paralyze it. There was also a danger that the new staff member would become bogged down through the irresistible administrative temptation of studies, paperwork, and red tape. And both things have happened to an even greater extent than had been feared.

It is an unpleasant but undeniable fact that experts and technicians are also bureaucrats. In addition, this class of bureaucrats is obsessed with efficiency, and efficiency is not exactly the distinctive characteristic of reform. Reform presupposes a certain degree of waste, error, disorganization, inefficiency, and amateurism. The technician may tend to put efficiency above social results, to sacrifice the fundamental elements of reform on the altar of the aesthetics of organization, graphs, and statistics. And if he cannot do this, he will most probably become a submissive bureaucrat, spending his time unenthusiastically making reports and studies. This danger is compounded, moreover, because the young Latin American technicians tend to have a hygienic obsession with efficiency, while those of the United States cannot conceive of waste that has not been planned in advance and never leave room for improvisation by amateurs (who often have a better nose for what they are doing than the specialist). This worship of efficiency has had very serious consequences. For example, to decide whether the plans presented by the various countries really merit the assistance of the Alliance, technicians have been appointed who are so narrowly technical, so apolitical, so lacking in vision, that it is doubtful if they are capable of putting their foot down and facing up to governments that try to sell them a bill of goods. And, in fact, these renowned experts wind up accepting imitation reform programs as the real thing. Certainly, reforms based on studies are preferable, but in the final analysis, it is better to have reforms without studies than studies without reforms.

The technician who tries not to rock the boat, not to muddy still waters, can also be dangerous. In order to avoid creating minor problems, he may sacrifice the solution of greater problems. The Alliance ought to ignite enthusiasm, and the "firemen" who put out the candles while the house is burning constitute another element of possible frustration.

And let us not even talk about the supernationalists, the ones

who saw in the Alliance the opportunity of doing in their own countries something that their neighbors were not doing, of exerting
national one-upmanship, of maneuvering to satisfy their political
backers, and who always have been willing to conceal the fact that
some particular achievement is due to the Alliance in order to post
it on the asset side of their meager governmental or personal balance sheet. It is all very well for international agencies to supply
millions of dollars, automobiles, technicians, and equipment; it is
much better to make the voters think that all this comes from their
own government. Naturally, as long as this attitude persists, the
Alliance remains a confidential matter, never reaching the man in
the street, and one of its collateral objectives remains frustrated:
that of inspiring the continental solution of continental problems,
rather than dealing with them on a fractional, stop-gap basis.

When a man suffering from dyspepsia goes to a doctor who
begins to tell him not to eat highly seasoned food, the man has a
right to complain: "I didn't come here to be told not to eat spicy
food. I wanted you to tell me how I can keep on eating it without
getting a stomach-ache." Unfortunately for the dyspeptic, science
cannot yet give him this answer. But what a person can be forced
to accept on the individual level cannot necessarily be accepted on
the collective level. Technicians do not exist for the purpose of
saying: "This is necessary, but it cannot be done yet, or it is
absolutely impossible, or it can be accomplished only in part."
They are here to say, rather: "This is necessary, it is difficult, but
it can be done in such and such a way." If they don't give this
answer, technicians negate their own purpose. Because when something is necessary on the collective level (that is, when it is politically necessary), if it cannot be achieved according to the
technicians' method, then it will be achieved by other methods,
however brutal, harsh, incorrect, or inexpert they may be. The
technicians should, properly, supply the manner, the method—the
technique, in short—of achieving what is necessary without recourse to brutality, without risking error, without displaying
inexperience, without employing harshness. And if not, they are
not technicians, whatever the titles that decorate their expensive
uselessness.

In the case of the Alliance, the technicians do not say: "It cannot be done," but neither do they say what is possible within the

required area—the political area; they merely tell us what can be done in the area in which such action does not matter—in the strictly economic or, more pompously, in the technical area. The oligarchs have been operating in this area for generations. Thus, because of a lack of political intuition, timidity in the face of facts, and a belief that they are more secure if they constantly keep washing their hands, these technical Pilates, these Pontiuses of official wisdom, have become the oligarchy's accomplices—often without knowing it and occasionally against their own consciences. They have depoliticized the Alliance and, by so doing, have pushed it toward failure and, therefore, have risked their own position, the very security for which they sacrificed their boldness, intelligence, and conscience.

Naturally the worst enemy of the Alliance has been the oligarchy. That is to say, the governments. And this fact not even the oligarchic politicians themselves have been able to hide:

Perhaps the best explanation is to be found in a paradox which can be, and has been, stated in various ways, one of which can be quite elegantly summarized as follows: As the creation, in part, of governments in the need of reform, the Alliance has turned out to be, in the last instance and from the Latin American point of view, an instrument forged by these governments to exert pressure on themselves. It is as if they had been given the job of urging something, just enough to be able to say that the will to do it was not lacking, but not enough so that there would be no recourse but to do it. This would be a typical instance of strategic diversion designed to divert attention from fundamentals. This is not true in all cases, but it is in many.[2]

What could be devised to remedy this situation? A new organism, the CIAP (Comité Interamericano de la Alianza para el Progreso, or Inter-American Committee on the Alliance for Progress).

Ex-Presidents Juscelino Kubitschek of Brazil and Alberto Lleras Camargo of Colombia and the Alliance's economic advisers, the Council of Nine, proposed, although in different terminology, that the CIAP decide on the distribution of Alliance funds. The Council of Nine, with unassailable logic, added that the distribution should be made in accordance with the recommendations of the *ad hoc* committees responsible for evaluating development plans. Further-

[2] *Visión* (Panama), March 6, 1964, p. 17.

more, they wished to see the CIAP use the reports on progress made by the Council of Nine itself to revise the terms of foreign aid, especially where the nations involved were not meeting their commitments. The multilateral approach to decisions on administration and distribution of resources and the fiscal controls of the CIAP were wrecked at the meeting of the Inter-American Economic and Social Council in São Paulo, at which this emasculated CIAP was created.[3]

In another area, the bureaucratization of the Alliance obstructed every drastic attempt at reorganization:

The Inter-American Development Bank insisted that the CIAP should not be given too great a voice in the disbursement of funds. This was logical if one takes into account that the Bank did not want the new organization to duplicate its own functions.

The OAS made a long legal study of the recommendations of Lleras and Kubitschek, in which, reading between the lines, one could discern a fear on the part of the Secretariat that the CIAP would usurp a part of its authority.

The United States publicly supported the cause of a vigorous CIAP, but within the Kennedy administration, there existed a strong current of opinion against this proposal. The various departments and offices of the United States Government realized the advantages of Latinizing the Alliance and leaving it to the Latin Americans to take charge of policing their internal reforms, but many of these departments feared that, with a strong and independent CIAP, they would lose ground to the Latin American governments and have trouble with Congress over the lessening of control over United States assistance funds.

And now they can see the results of all this meditation, maneuvering, lobbying, and hot air:

In connection with the creation of the CIAP, it was necessary to consider the distinct and at times contradictory ideas which had been suggested, and as a result, some believe that the powers of the Committee are somewhat vague. Concretely, the recommendations were:

To study the problems that might arise in connection with the

---

[3] "El mecanismo de la Alianza para el Progreso," *Comercio Exterior* (Mexico City), December, 1963.

functioning of the Alliance and to resolve them or suggest solutions to the competent authorities.

To continue trying to strengthen the multilateral character of the Alliance.

To make an annual computation of the sums actually required for Latin American development, as well as a calculation of the funds available from both internal and external sources.

To submit to constant study and revision national and regional plans, the methods adopted, and the actions taken within the framework of the Alliance, and to formulate specific recommendations to the members of the Alliance and to the regional hemispheric organizations on these plans, methods, and actions.

Moreover, the CIAP was made responsible for revising the programs and budgets of the Alliance, accelerating regional integration, coordinating its activities with those of existing agencies, and, in short, assuring the achievement of many other desirable ends.

As far as its own position was concerned, the CIAP remained within the framework of the OAS, but with considerable autonomy in the management of its own affairs, depending, above all, on the attitude of its president. The CIAP is coming to be the executive arm of the Inter-American Economic and Social Council, with an independent president elected for a three-year term and eligible for re-election for another three-year term. In addition to the president, who is not the representative of any country, the CIAP is composed of seven other national delegates representing regional blocs; they are elected for two-year terms, with the exception of the United States representative, who has permanent tenure.[4]

Who could dare to talk, in good conscience, about *this* Alliance to the Indians of Ecuador, to Brazilian peasants, or to the workers in Santiago?

The technicians and bureaucrats have sterilized, emasculated, and mummified the Alliance. There was little left for the oligarchic governments and the Communists to do to destroy it.

The External Enemies of the Alliance

Perhaps if the Alliance had not been paralyzed by its internal enemies—actually bureaucratic and technical fifth columns—it might have found itself some allies. They could and should be

---

[4] *Visión, loc. cit.*

found within the ranks of the people. Everything that we have said about Latin America thus far proves that only the people can be interested in modernizing society and in creating the conditions for modern capitalism and a democratic political and social system. But neither the bureaucrats nor the technicians are capable of realizing this, much less of going to the people, capturing their imagination, and mobilizing them. The ones who do not fear the people, scorn them or, at best, ignore them.

Precisely because the Alliance, upon passing into the hands of these fifth columnists, isolated itself from its potential allies, it was easy for it to fall into the power of its born enemies, the very ones it should have destroyed—the oligarchy and the Communists.

There was no open opposition to the Alliance. No one denied its virtues (just as no one denies the virtues of an ugly, stupid woman). No one publicly rejected its goals. Who was going to reject a concept backed by so many hundreds and thousands of millions of dollars? The thing to do was to get hold of the idea and squeeze all the juice out of it. There was no opposition, only a series of apparently innocuous "buts."

Those who said "but" offered nothing better. They did not even suggest methods that could replace the Alliance and be guaranteed better. Some merely said that if you start making reforms, however modest they may be, no one knows where it will end or how you can avoid more radical reforms later on (which luckily is true). Others said that the Alliance was a trick to increase United States influence in Latin America.

Nevertheless . . .

On March 13, 1961, President Kennedy said: "Our unfulfilled task is to demonstrate to the entire world that man's unsatisfied aspiration for economic progress and social justice can best be achieved by free men working within a framework of democratic institutions."

The concept was correct. But it did not relate to Latin American reality. Except that at the time we all seemed willing, in good faith, to forget the stubbornness of the facts. There never were, nor are there today in Latin America—with a few exceptions—any "structures of democratic institutions."

Only if this fact had been understood would it have been possible to avoid the initial error of the Alliance, which scarred it for all time and which Kennedy himself committed when he spoke of the Alliance as "an Alliance of free governments." The governments of Latin America are not free. They are slaves of the oligarchy, even those that are the products of revolutions or elections that bring populist movements to power, because these governments exist in a continental context dominated by the oligarchies and, at best, can only partially protect their citizens, never daring to be explosive. The explosive solutions are acceptable in Latin America only when they are found on the extreme right: Trujillo, Somoza, Juan Vicente Gómez, Perón, Castro; but what hostility there was toward the Mexican revolution, what indifference toward the Bolivian revolution as soon as the United States did not refuse it aid, what intentional misunderstanding toward Betancourt's struggle in Venezuela!

At times, a question of semantics has political consequences. This has happened with the Alliance. The North Americans call their government the "administration." They say, "the Kennedy administration," when we would say, "the Kennedy government." And they have always thought, automatically, of Latin American governments as administrations. They have wished the Latin American administrations to be good administrations. Occasionally they have helped them to be so. But a good administration is not necessarily a good government. Technically excellent administrations may exist in detestable governments. We have known Latin American dictatorships that have had not only good but honest administrations (the corruption existed only at the highest levels), but this has not meant that the dictatorial government has been good. Nor will a good administration make an oligarchic government stop being oligarchic, that is, an obstacle to progress, a protector of injustice, and a corrupter of society, even if the servants of the administration accept no bribes and refuse to sell themselves to the highest bidder, as long as they persist in their loyalty to those who bought them first, the oligarchy.

The belief that there were democratic institutions and free governments in Latin America constituted the acceptance of a fiction, and to preserve this fiction, the unfree governments, complete with caste institutions, moved to take control of the Alliance where that was possible, and where it was not, to discredit, pervert, and castrate it.

The fact cannot be denied, even by the report on the Alliance which the Latin American governments had the effrontry to entrust to two politicians who, when they held power in their own countries, achieved no social reform whatsoever, Alberto Lleras Camargo and Juscelino Kubitschek. Lleras said:

> Certainly, as of today, the manner in which the Alliance has been administered by the United States is open to criticism, but it must be admitted that the countries of Latin America, despite the progress made recently, have made a very poor showing of their ability to organize administratively the coordination of the gigantic efforts to which they have committed themselves. . . .[5]

And another far from revolutionary politician, Raúl Sáez, a Chilean engineer and one of the "Nine Wise Men" who counsel the Alliance, maintained that "the Alliance created, installed, and activated largely by Latin America does not have the support of many governments."[6]

Carlos Lleras Restrepo, head of the Liberal Party of Colombia, was more explicit:

> We have been a little guilty of pessimism, because we have been quick to doubt the results of the Alliance, and, therefore, it ought not to surprise us that, in the United States, there has also been skepticism. . . . The Alliance must change the life of the great mass and not merely produce economic development without considering the way in which the benefits of that development are distributed. The Alliance has to become a popular cause.[7]

Here is an example of how the oligarchy takes advantage of the best intentions of the United States. During the initial stages of the Alliance for Progress, the Dominican Republic was governed by a Council of State made up of members of the oligarchy who had, for the most part, been in Trujillo's service but had not held positions of political power, due to the tight hold that Trujillo kept on them. This Council of State, which later on was to foment the military and political coup of 1963, organized a police force of more

---

[5] Lleras, *Report on the Alliance for Progress Presented to the OAS* (Washington, June 15, 1963), p. 25.
[6] Statement to *Excélsior*, July 28, 1962.
[7] Speech, September 23, 1964.

than 10,000 men, out of all proportion to the country's needs. These gendarmes carried clubs painted an elegant white. In Santo Domingo, these clubs were called *"alpros"*—people would say: "They gave him a good *alprorrazo";* or: "They broke up the demonstration with their *alpros"*—because rumor held that the clubs had been purchased with funds of the Alliance for Progress. It is possible that this was so, through some maneuver by the Council of State, and it is also possible that it was merely a rumor spread by enemies of the Alliance.

That the governments were bothered by what little degree of supranationality the Alliance had is amply demonstrated by what happened at the Rio de Janeiro meeting of the Inter-American Economic and Social Council in 1963:

> the Brazilians had a last card which they played to good effect two days before the end of the conference. They suggested in a "working paper" (that is, not a formal resolution), the creation of an inter-American fund for economic and social development (FIDES) into which financial aid, without strings, would be paid from the United States, from the Latin American countries themselves (in their precarious currencies), from western Europe and Japan and from "other governments." These funds would be disbursed to individual beneficiaries on the advice of a Latin American committee.[8]

That meant, in effect, that a committee of Latin American oligarchs (since they would be appointed by the governments, there could be no doubt that they would be oligarchs) would offer other oligarchs (the individual beneficiaries) the funds supplied by capitalist governments. Could anyone want a slicker sleight of hand?

Another oligarchic politician with democratic pretensions, Fernando Schwalb, Peru's Premier and Minister of Foreign Relations in the government of President Belaúnde Terry (himself a distinguished architect and a member of an old oligarchic family), said afterward:

> More than two years after the signing of the Charter of Punta del Este, the volume of aid obtained thus far has been insufficient to con-

[8] "In a Brazilian Teahouse," *The Economist* (London), November 23, 1963, p. 759.

vince one of the benefits attributed to this system of inter-American economic cooperation.

The aid itself, in some cases excessively burdened with conditions, is not turning out to be effective. It generates in the minds of its supposed beneficiaries, consciously or not, a feeling of threat or of unsuitable direction which the country involved is not inclined to accept.

We insist that the policy now in operation be revised in order to fit it to reality, bearing in mind that it is not likely to succeed under the present rigorous system. The rules have been devised by countries with a different social and economic organization, in the light of their own realities, and cannot function effectively in our environment. Aid with conditions—excessive conditions—cannot fail to be not only ineffective but unwelcome.[9]

Unwelcome, certainly, to the oligarchs, who would be made to give up some of their privileges as a condition for assistance to their respective countries. Is it not plain now why the oligarchs suddenly discovered their frantic nationalism? They wanted no conditions— as long as these conditions would favor the people and hurt the oligarchies.

To complete the chorus, here is one more ungrateful voice: that of the ex-President of Nicaragua, Luis Somoza, who asserted that the chief drawback of the Alliance for Progress is the slowness of the U.S. bureaucracy that passes on requests for assistance. Sometimes, he said, the remedy arrives when the patient is beyond help.[10] It is true that these mechanisms are slow-moving. But they can never be as slow as the Somozas themselves, who in two generations of rule in Nicaragua have done absolutely nothing for their people.

This catalogue would be incomplete without a beautiful example of cynicism on the part of Brazilian ex-President Kubitschek, who forgot entirely about agrarian reform while he was building Brasília and who, with an eye to a future candidacy, flirted with the Communist Prestes and the demagogue Goulart, later voting to depose this same Goulart. This paradigm of sensitivity, honesty, and sacrifice for the people was, no doubt, conscious of great moral authority when he wrote:

[9] Statement to Agence France-Presse (Lima), January 17, 1964.
[10] Statement in Tokyo, October 10, 1963.

Between the auspicious statements of the President of the United States and the execution of the program of the Alliance for Progress lies an almost frozen expanse. Between the words and intentions of President Kennedy and the timid and cumbersome course followed by the measures of the Alliance there is a discrepancy. . . . In lieu of a vital dialogue of the Americas, a sort of discouraging monologue has been going on.[11]

Alberto Lleras Camargo, who is in no way a revolutionary, had to confess in the report the OAS requested him to prepare, in which he also proposed the creation of the CIAP:

President Kennedy alone, in the entire hemisphere, defended the audacious plan to transform the lives of millions of human beings in the face of their own political opposition and the indifference of a major part of those whom it was to serve directly.

The reactionary right wing of the American world, therefore, was and is working against the objectives of Punta del Este. In the United States it was represented by the systematic enemies of all foreign aid, even more exalted now with the apparent initiation of a new program of expenditures; by those who maintain that loans and donations to governments only serve to encourage socialization in Latin America and weaken private enterprise; by the adversaries of the type of social-welfare investments recommended in the Charter of Punta del Este. In Latin America, by the system of the latifundia, which is always alert to any type of agrarian reform, entrenched in the governments and congresses; by a certain native capitalism, which accepts no restrictions upon its action but which defends itself with the same arguments as United States private enterprise, which is actually subject to strict competition and to anti-monopoly regulations; and, in general, by all the present beneficiaries of the social situation. . . .[12]

It cannot be said that no one knew of the existence of these enemies. A man who because of his position as U.S. Coordinator of the Alliance, could see matters not only at close range but also behind the scenes, and who knew all the disgusting maneuvering and was familiar with the unspeakable conditions that ministers

[11] Kubitschek, *Report on the Alliance for Progress Presented to the OAS* (Washington, June 15, 1963), p. vi.
[12] *Op. cit.*, p. vi.

and even Presidents put on acceptance of Alliance aid, Teodoro Moscoso, had to observe: "They are the great masses of Latin America—I call them the Voiceless Ones. They are the natural, and potentially the truest, friends of the Alliance. . . . Dilemma number one [for them] occurs in the area of reform." Another dilemma, he noted, is the opposition of the elites or dominant groups, who reap the riches of the country but spend their profits and their lives outside of it.[13]

Nor was the United States press unaware of these enemies. It quickly pointed them out—a thing that the Latin American press has only rarely done.

William Ryan, a correspondent who traveled with the Kennedy entourage during the President's visit to Colombia and Venezuela, wrote:

And for the most part, those who control the wealth continue to drag their feet, unwilling to sacrifice the privileges and advantages their class enjoys. . . . But if the rulers won't change voluntarily, those in Washington ask, what can be done except appeal to the people and hope that the pressure generated from below will move those on top?[14]

The newspapermen were not the only ones who saw this. Orville Freeman, U.S. Secretary of Agriculture, predicted "the redistribution of land will be bitterly opposed by many of the landlords" and pointed out that a key test for many South American governments will be their "courage and ability to cope with these pressures."[15]

The time is coming now when we must learn the lesson proved by the experience of other regions: The landowning oligarchy gives up nothing. Listen to Nasser on Egypt:

We believed in the beginning that it would be possible for us to turn over power to the old parties. We made only one condition: that they accept the six principles, above all, the most urgent at that time —agrarian reform. Our proposals were rejected. We realized then that we were asking the agrarian landowners who dominated one of

[13] *The New York Times Magazine,* August 12, 1962.
[14] William Ryan, in an Associated Press dispatch, July 2, 1962.
[15] Associated Press, July 20, 1962.

the parties that they themselves limit their own wealth and their own power.[16]

Do not think that this was all just words. The oligarchy acted quickly, sometimes through military coups (Peru, the Dominican Republic, Honduras), sometimes through an old procedure that shows how profound and sincere their nationalism is. In a single year, 1961, Latin American investment in the United States increased by $316 million, to reach a total of more than $4 billion.[17] That was the year in which the Alliance was launched, and the oligarchs were not sure of being able to hide their money. And these $4 billion represented only what was located in the United States, not to mention what was sent to Switzerland. Even so, it was four times the contribution of the United States in the first year of the Alliance. That is to say, if the Latin American oligarchs were as nationalistic as they claim (and as the Communists and Castroites who echo them like to believe), in one year, they could have invested sufficient capital to achieve four times what was realized through United States assistance.

But they preferred (they and their Castroite intellectuals) to accept the imperialists' money, to attack the United States for offering it, and to send four times as much to the United States and Switzerland—all in the name of the most pure and disinterested nationalism, of course.

When the Alliance was started, many people thought that it would be helped by fear, which would make the oligarchs give up some of their privileges. This thinking proved false, for three reasons:

1. The oligarchies knew "their" Communists and "their" revolutionaries better than anyone else did; they knew the degree of their moral corruption and their taste for public funds, and were convinced that they posed no danger as long as they could be provided with their jobs out of the public budget and their conscience-calming manifestoes to sign.

2. The oligarchies knew—or sensed—that their privileges could

[16] Interview with Gamal Abdel Nasser, by David Rousset, *Le Figaro* (Paris), March 30, 1964.
[17] Adolfo Figueroa E., "América Latina ante la urgencia," *Comercio Exterior,* April, 1963.

not be surrendered piecemeal; when the process starts it does not
end, and so they preferred not to surrender anything, thus hoping to
preserve everything.

3. For fear to have remained an instrument of pressure on the
oligarchy would have required, for example, that the Castroites
triumph in Venezuela, in Ecuador, and in Colombia, and that
Kennedy fail to face down Khrushchev over Cuba in October of
1962. This would have been a very high price. As soon as what
was called the Castro threat suffered its first setback, fear disappeared as an instrument of pressure.

And as fear ceased to be a factor, all sorts of "reasons" came
to light. For example, a Chilean economist declared that "to try to
modify overnight a class system that has existed for centuries is
playing with fire . . . it could lead to serious difficulties."[18]

The attitude of a substantial number of U.S. businessmen was
also harmful to the Alliance. They took advantage of it to demand
guarantees for their investments. For an investor to want guarantees
is natural, but it is not natural for him to suppose that a plan such
as the Alliance can provide them. To think that it can indicates that
he has absolutely no comprehension of the objectives of the Alliance, that he persists in a conception of Latin American society
that is at least thirty years behind the times. For there is no
guarantee possible beyond what can be provided by the structure
of the society in which he invests. The North American, French,
German, or British investor does not ask for guarantees when he
invests in his own country or in another industrialized nation. Not
even the prospect of socialist governments (in Great Britain or
Scandinavia) alarms foreign investors. However, they demand
guarantees when they invest in Latin America, without realizing
that the only meaningful guarantee lies in the industrialization
of Latin American society. To achieve this, it is necessary to renounce any investment guarantees under the present oligarchic system, since any such guarantee signifies a *de facto* alliance with the
oligarchy and thus an obstacle to the evolution of Latin American
society into a society that need give no guarantees because its own
structure serves as a guarantee. Great business enterprises are
capable of spending millions on exploration and study that either
return no profit at all or produce a profit only after several years.

[18] *Excélsior,* August 18, 1962.

But they appear to be incapable of understanding that the millions invested without guarantees in Latin America, if they expedited the transformation of Latin American society, would be much more productive and secure than the money spent on exploration and study.

An example of this sort of uneconomic attitude is the following statement made to a press conference by J. Peter Grace, head of a vast U.S. enterprise with investments in many Latin American countries:

> Latin American investments have never suffered from as unfavorable a climate as they do today, for the risks are very high and the return very small. . . . It would re-establish the confidence of private capital if the government of the United States gave tax concessions to private enterprise, such as, for example, a tax reduction in proportion to the devaluation of local currencies.[19]

Thus, the supporters of free enterprise ask for the protection of the state.

For their part, the Castroites and Communists opposed the Alliance on the pretext that it was "a new method of Yankee capitalist penetration." Once more, we see the concubinage between the most reactionary elements and those that pretend to be the most revolutionary.

However, this opposition was much more subtle than that of the Communists to the Marshall Plan (with the wave of political strikes it engendered in 1947–48). Shortly before the Punta del Este Conference, and for some time after it, Castroism appeared much less aggressive outside of Cuba. Havana wanted the oligarchies to conquer the fear that would make them accept reform; without fear, the oligarchies would feel free to sabotage any reforms that might be proposed. Havana knew that Castroism and Communism by themselves would not be enough to cause the failure of the Alliance. But Havana knew also that the oligarchies had many more weapons at their disposal with which to obstruct reform. And if reform were blocked, the Alliance would have failed and Havana could again adopt an aggressive posture and affirm that the only road to revolution is Castro's, the "Marxist-Leninist"

[19] *Comercio Exterior,* April, 1963.

road. The opposition of the oligarchies to all reform showed the validity of this tactic.

The Jacobin nationalists, in tune with the Communists, have even resorted to military coups. The noted expert on the Mexican revolution Manuel González Ramírez said not long ago:

> This Alliance for Progress explains, to my way of thinking, the militaristic avalanche which afflicts the hemisphere . . . because the traditional vested interests have taken the initiative to slow down the social change demanded by the hemisphere and promoted by the Alliance. . . . The objectives of the Alliance must have unnerved the vested interests and aroused their attempts to fight it in order to prevent social change. . . . [These objectives] simply are not welcomed by the vested interests; on the contrary, they are foreign and repellent to these interests . . . and they supply the incentive for attacks on the political system. . . .[20]

So the Alliance turns out to be more to blame than the militarists and oligarchs who incite military coups. In order to blacken the United States (since the Alliance appears to be a U.S. plan), the coup-makers are whitewashed.

It was logical that oligarchs, governments, investors, and politicians should sabotage the Alliance, should rape it when possible, and when it was not, that they should malign it. It was our mistake not to foresee this, to believe that fear and dollars would be enough to counteract these external enemies of the Alliance.

But no one could foresee that the popular movements, the authentic left (that is, the non-Communist left, since Communism is really on the extreme right), would turn their backs on the Alliance. And they did do this, however much they said in favor of the Alliance behind their backs. Some wanted to take advantage of the Alliance to secure better prices for exports of raw materials— raw materials produced by the oligarchy, remember—and others limited themselves to voicing their dismay and disillusionment when they saw that the Alliance did not prevent military coups. They had not understood that the Alliance was not an aspirin, but that it aimed to be a surgical operation (or rather, to provide the money for the operating room, the surgeons, and the convalescence). They

[20] Interview in *Novedades* (Mexico City), August 13, 1962.

could not comprehend that the Alliance was not designed to make prices rise or dictators fall, but rather to change a social structure thanks to which the people were dependent on raw-material prices and dictators were permitted to seize power.

The failure to anticipate that the left would defect shows that we did not see Latin American society as it was, but rather as it had been and as we wished it to continue, a society in which the middle class would represent an element of change and progress. Latin American society is no longer like this. Thus, our confidence in the middle class and its political movements deceived us, and even deceived many leaders of these very movements.

There is no doubt that the left should have taken the Alliance for Progress to its bosom. In its political campaigns, it could have said clearly: The Alliance offers us the opportunity to make reforms, because at this moment, it is to our interest and to the interest of the United States to do so, and for this reason, we should take advantage of the assistance of the United States and accelerate the rate of social change. If it had done this, the left could have exerted popular pressure on the oligarchy, and the Alliance would have won support. But instead, the left, afraid of being labeled an imperialist agent or a servant of United States interests, issued a few platonic declarations in favor of the Alliance, but it never adopted the Alliance, never made it a part of a fighting program, and so permitted the Alliance to fall into the hands of the oligarchs, the bureaucrats, and the technocrats. Perhaps there is still time for the leftist forces of the moment, such as they are, to realize this error, to try to recapture the Alliance and make it the base of their campaign. It is more likely, however, that this must be the task of a "new left," a left of the submerged masses that can incorporate much of the traditional left but which must necessarily be more than merely a product of it.

Even the labor movement failed. It asked to participate in the formulation of development planning and still has not succeeded in this. The Inter-American Regional Organization of Workers (ORIT) and the labor federations demanded this, and it was "granted" to them in 1963, in the highly touted "Declaration of Cundinamarca," drawn up by a group of experts and signed by the Labor Ministers of the oligarchic governments—the very governments that usurped or sabotaged the Alliance. Here is what the

CTV (Confederación de Trabajadores Venezolanos, or Confederation of Venezuelan Workers) said, in a country where the Alliance has come closest—and how far away it still is—to its original conception:

> We workers are interested in clarifying just what is meant by the Charter of Punta del Este and the Alliance for Progress, and we feel a sense of urgency in popularizing this program, but it is necessary also to let the directors of the Alliance for Progress and the governments know that the working class cannot be excluded from the direction and leadership of the agencies that hold in their hands the promulgation and control of these plans.[21]

Does this not prove that the Alliance has been abandoned, when the unions talk this way, when they must beg and sweet-talk, instead of organizing the peasants, the forgotten men, and mobilizing them to impose their participation in the Alliance.

What They Allowed to Be Done

We are used to hearing "If the United States had let this happen . . . If the United States did not oppose. . . ."

Well, since the Alliance started, the United States has opposed virtually nothing. No one can say that any plan presented to the Alliance was rejected due to pressure from the United States because it was too radical. The "Nine Wise Men," despite their timidity, had to reject plans from various nations because the plans were too timid. And it approved some that can only be described as idiotic, such as the Colombian plan based in large measure on intensifying the cultivation and exportation of coffee, at a time when all the coffee producers are complaining that prices are falling.

Actually, during the past few years—whatever the propaganda says—the situation has been just the reverse of what people believe. The nations of Latin America have not done what the Alliance has allowed them to do; rather, the Alliance has done what the governments have allowed it to do. And this has been very little and very far removed from the area of social change. In

[21] José González Navarro, quoted in *Jornada* (Caracas), August 7, 1963.

reality, what the Alliance has achieved is considerable in terms of assistance and is not inconsiderable in terms of what the governments should do themselves. But the Alliance was not created to solve individual problems or to make up for the negligence of the various governments, but rather to finance the temporary economic hardship resulting from changes in the social structure.

The United States built its own hospitals, highways, dams, and schools when it was underdeveloped. There is absolutely no reason for the United States to build hospitals and schools in Latin America. However, there is a very good reason why it should not; because to do so aids the oligarchy. The oligarchy should pay more taxes to provide for these services; if the United States provides them, it only means that the oligarchy has more money to send to Switzerland.

Between the time the Alliance was initiated and June, 1964, the United States helped build 326,000 homes and 36,400 classrooms, helped publish 11.2 million copies of technical books, helped extend 300,000 agricultural loans, helped supply 2,120 water-supply systems (benefiting 24.0 million persons), helped establish 624 health centers (treating 8.8 million persons), and helped improve the diet of more than 22.6 million persons.[22]

In 1962, more than 20 per cent of the foreign financial aid received by Latin America for development purposes was used for investment in health services, housing, community development, and education; in 1960, the proportion was 3 per cent, and in 1961, 15 per cent.[23]

In spite of this, today Argentina is still the only country that is self-sufficient in its school-lunch program. One out of every four Latin American children receives food from the Alliance.[24]

Should this not make the Latin American governments blush, as well as the parents who have not demanded meals for their children from "their" governments.

Do not believe for a minute that there is no limit to what the oligarchic governments will permit. Benefit the middle class, yes, because in this way its conformity is assured. But benefit the for-

[22] Associated Press, March 21, 1964.
[23] *The Alliance for Progress: Its Second Year, 1962–1963* (Washington, November, 1963).
[24] *Comercio Exterior*, August, 1963.

gotten men? Never. Here is one case: The Alliance builds homes in Colombia for $1,670, with a down payment of $780. In Cali, at the same time, peasant families arriving in the city without a place to live, pay $4.50 a month for a hut and consider this expensive. Nonetheless, $4.50 a month is what these ragged souls are willing to pay for a house. And it is for them that the Alliance should build houses, not for those who can pay $780 down, the parasites and the well-to-do who have already turned their backs on the people.

For the people of the Cali shantytowns—and of hundreds of Calis all over the continent—the government builds no homes, nor does it pressure the Alliance to do so. These people could find no one willing to sell them land, because they could not pay enough. And so they settled on abandoned and worn-out land (whose owners, nevertheless, would not sell it). And the government sent in the army to burn down the shacks built by these homeless people. Now let somebody try to talk about the Alliance to these 20,000 people of Cali.[25]

But yes, they will talk to them. They will say that the Alliance deceived them, that the United States favors only those who already live in comfort—when, in reality, the Alliance helps only those the government sees fit that it should help. Or is it conceivable that there would have been no Alliance funds for $2.25-a-month houses in Cali if the Colombian Government had demanded them? But did the government even ask? *No!*

Most of the housing credits have gone to savings and loan institutions, which re-lend the money but at an extravagant interest rate. Often money the bank received from the Alliance at a rate of 0.75 to 2 per cent interest costs a middle-class family that wants to build a house up to 12 per cent. In Peru, there was a national scandal over this sort of interest spiral. One expert says that "one of the unspoken reasons for ignoring the low-income families was that they were not as politically influential as the higher-income groups."[26]

[25] John P. Powelson, "The Land-Grabbers of Cali," *The New Leader* (New York), January 15, 1964.

[26] Charles Abrams, *Man's Struggle for Shelter in an Urbanizing World* (Cambridge, Mass., 1964), pp. 101–2.

All this has produced protest and warning from those still close to the people, such as the following from the Venezuelan unions:

The plans of the Alliance are being frittered away in projects of such small size that they could well be paid for by the interested parties themselves. The Alliance should concentrate on plans and activities of real scope. We workers want to help to assure that the plans of the Alliance for Progress are fully realized, and for this purpose, we are forming our own collective organizations to offer and solicit the co-operation necessary to accomplish projects that will contribute to the solution of our colossal problems.

We protest this perpetual round of conferences, where nothing planned and concrete is ever produced—only plans and projects that are far from the objective reality of our daily experience. These magic formulas, all of a uniform pattern, to remedy our people's ills, achieve nothing when demagogic governments try to present panoramas and settings that have no relation to reality. These offerings, based on unreality, are a type of deception that the people are not disposed to tolerate.[27]

Thus it turns out that the Alliance, having been structured as a plan to be achieved through the medium of the governments, is itself blamed and is the target of all the reproaches that properly should be directed against the governments.

The Balance Sheet

The experts never call bread "bread," much less wine "wine." The international experts do not even call rain "water." They dare to think about what they could perhaps suggest if they were on the staff of an independent and daring newspaper rather than working for an international agency, but the truth of the matter is that one should realize—not even by reading but simply by smelling the ink—that there is nothing between the lines of their reports. The experts of the Alliance have been much more daring than their colleagues. They dare, among other things, to suggest that it is necessary to accentuate, accelerate, amplify, expand, this or that program or activity, which is a way of saying, in their jargon, that what is urgent and essential has not yet been done.

[27] "Alianza para la libertad y la justicia," *Jornada,* August 7, 1963.

Thus it is instructive to review the balance sheet prepared by the experts of the Alliance itself of the Alliance's achievements to date.[28]

A common internal problem that persists in the region is the low production and productivity of agriculture. While some countries have experienced an expansion in agricultural production for export, this has been obtained in part at the expense of production for internal consumption, which in many cases has decreased in per-capita terms.

Has anything at all been done with an eye to the future in the most fundamental of all areas—agrarian reform?

the deficient, anachronistic structure of land tenure, and the political and institutional barriers to its change, constitute the principal obstacles to the more rapid development of agriculture and, in general, of the rural sector of the population of Latin America.

In compliance with the commitments . . . undertaken [in the Charter of Punta del Este and under the Alliance], eleven Latin American countries have enacted agrarian reform laws since 1961, while another four had already done so prior to that date. In addition, other countries have adopted various measures in connection with the agrarian problem, such as settlement and agricultural-credit programs. . . .

Despite the legislation passed since 1961, very little progress has been made to date insofar as concrete achievements are concerned, particularly in the field of redistribution of land, especially if we take into account the magnitude of the agrarian problem faced by Latin America. The laws enacted have not yet generated programs of sufficient scope and intensity to have a significant effect upon changing the region's agrarian structure.

In order for a program of agrarian reform to be successful (even when it is only a façade, the façade has to appear convincing), money is required, which must come from tax receipts.

Since July 1963 tax reform has continued at a relatively fast rate. It may be stated that, since establishment of the Alliance, all the coun-

[28] Except where otherwise specified, the material in this section is based on the Inter-American Economic and Social Council's provisional report, *The Alliance for Progress: Its Third Year, 1963/1964* (Washington, December 10, 1964).

tries have made efforts to adopt tax structure reforms and to improve tax revenue administration. . . . Notwithstanding the efforts made up to now by the different countries in the field of tax reform, the increase in current revenue has not been generally sufficient to make possible the volume of public savings required for the effective implementation of the investment programs needed to speed up the growth of Latin American economies.

That is, there have been true fiscal reforms in very few countries. In spite of this, the flight of capital continues, and still another study is to be made:

It is also recommended that CIAP make a comprehensive study of the flight and transfers of capital from the less developed to the more developed countries, determining:

a. The extent to which the principles of the Alliance for Progress are being weakened through:

1) using the psychological mechanism of investment security in the external sector, when the countries themselves are uncertain with regard to social emergencies;

2) absorbing the savings of high and medium income groups, and even of the lower income groups;

3) making use of confidential means of communication and contracts, which prevents the expression of public opinion regarding the matter concerned.

b. The extent to which this flow of capital could be controlled, for which purpose CIAP should propose pertinent measures to the governments.

This means that, until now, nothing has been done to stem the flight of capital belonging to the friends of the men at the top, and I can see no reason to think that the governments will be more receptive to a "comprehensive study" in 1965 than they were in 1961.

And in the countries where legislation on agrarian reform (so-called) has been promulgated, what has been done?

In general terms, it may be said that in the last few years, the preferred procedure has been to parcel out public lands and grant deeds to peasants who are *de facto* occupants of the land or to new colonizers, rather than to break up the big privately owned properties.[29]

[29] "Comisión especial del CIES sobre desarrollo agrícola y reforma agraria," *Boletín de la Revista Interamericana de Ciencias Sociales* (Washington), October, 1963.

Statistically, this has produced ridiculous figures: In Honduras, 10,375 acres were distributed in 1963 (and this seemed so excessive to the oligarchs that in 1963 there was a military coup). In Panama, it was planned to distribute 50,000 acres in 1963. In Peru, 4,225 acres were transferred in 1963, in addition to almost 75,000 acres—in the Amazon jungle. In Chile, 1,420 acres—yes, 1,420 acres. In Argentina, 246,250 acres.

On the other hand, in the countries where the revolution has occurred or continues, the situation is quite different. In Mexico, between 1958 and 1962, 26 million acres were transferred, or 21 per cent of all the land distributed since 1915. In Venezuela, in 1963, the Instituto Agrario Nacional (National Agrarian Institute) distributed 418,208 acres among 14,603 families, or about 25 per cent of the families benefited by this program between 1959 and 1962.

None of this should seem strange, considering that:

> The present programs of agricultural credit in most Latin American countries are inadequate and insufficient in respect to the kind and total value of the loans granted, with the result that the credit is not effective and not generally available to the sectors of agriculture that need it most.
>
> Unfortunately, credit to small farmers does not yet exist to any appreciable degree in Latin America. . . .[30]

Do these peasants who have no land or have land but no credit receive any assistance at all to allow them to live decently? Not even this is available. We find the Alliance experts still recommending that such efforts be launched *now:*

> Unfortunately, a large part of the Latin American citizenry, particularly urban and rural groups of workers, has not had an active part in promoting development through economic, political, and social means. . . .
>
> Such collective effort is of special urgency and complexity in the rural area of Latin America, where a more or less generally archaic economic and social structure constitutes the greatest impediment to active participation of the people in the life of the country. . . .

[30] *Ibid.*

To carry out this type of program, training courses should be established. . . .

In other words, at present the governments provide neither money nor staff to deal with the welfare of the peasants—or even to give them lip service.

The Alliance has exerted a great deal of pressure to be permitted to engage in a program of housing construction.

The seemingly important efforts which the countries have thus far made to solve the housing problem, such as structural and operational improvements, preparation of plans, establishment or strengthening of means of internal financing, etc., have not yet had as significant an impact as the magnitude and character of the situation require. Contrary to what had been hoped, the disproportion between the increasing number of families and housing construction continues to grow from year to year.

In Latin America, labor ministries have been in existence for decades. But after four years of the Alliance:

The deficiencies mentioned in connection with social policy and planning are especially acute as regards labor policy. It is imperative that the countries of Latin America adopt, without further delay, definite positions as regards labor policy, in view of the special impact that it has on social and economic development.

It would be reasonable to suppose that the governments would, at a minimum, have hastened to present at least skeleton plans to comply superficially with their commitments at Punta del Este. But by the end of 1964, only nine countries had made even this gesture. As for the nature of the plans that have been presented, let us listen to the Alliance experts again:

The very content of the plans should be improved in order to attain the following main objectives:
a. To avoid the usual excessively broad goals and projections and give greater importance to the sectoral analysis of programs, employing methods which permit the presentation of at least a first quantitative estimate of the correspondence between the expenditures and income planned for the main sectors. . . .

b. Considering that the private sector in Latin America generates a high percentage of the internal product, great importance should be given to defining and coordinating the policies that the government will have to follow in order to influence the action of private enterprise in accordance with the objectives chosen. . . .

e. The many defects still in the plans of the social sectors, especially in education and health, must be overcome. Moreover, in the preparation of general programs, greater attention should be given to income redistribution as one of the basic objectives of these programs.

f. . . . high priority should be assigned to the planning of agrarian policy in general, and to its coordination with agrarian reform programs.

In summary, from the Alliance report, we can see that the recently promulgated agrarian reform programs (except in Venezuela) have been pure sham, tricks of colonization and relocation, by which the poor Indians are sent to rot in the jungles. We can see that there have been fiscal reforms in the administrative mechanism, but not to achieve more equable distribution of taxes. We can see that the governments have made no effort even to create the administrative apparatus necessary to carry on programs initiated by the Alliance, such as community development and housing construction, in spite of the fact this would have allowed them to give jobs in the new bureaucracy to many of their political supporters. We can see that the governments have finally presented development plans worthy of amateurs, stupid in the best instances, and no more than a joke in the worst. Beyond this, they have not even concerned themselves seriously with setting up planning committees or agencies and even less with permitting popular or union participation in these phantom attempts at drafting plans.

If in four years the Latin American governments have done none of the things that they had promised to do and, in many cases, have not even bothered to try to save appearances, then what right do these governments have to ask for money, assistance, or respect from the United States, much less from their own people.

This leads us directly to the thorniest question, the question that the Alliance does not know how to resolve, the question of whether there can be what is called a "peaceful revolution."

Can There Be a "Peaceful Revolution"?

During his visit to Bogotá, President Kennedy stated that if a peaceful revolution did not take place in Latin America, it would be impossible to avoid a violent revolution.

President Johnson said in April, 1964: "If a peaceful revolution in these areas is impossible, a violent revolution is inevitable."[31]

I believe that everything said in this book and everything that one reads about and sees in Latin America proves conclusively that the "peaceful revolution" is unattainable at this point. We believed in it because we thought that the pressure of the middle class, American loans, and fear of Castro would force the oligarchy to give ground.

But the oligarchy has given up nothing, absolutely nothing really important. Latin America today retains as many characteristics of the oligarchic society as it did before the Alliance, and the masses live in even worse conditions than before it. Even the forces we thought would fight for social change have not done so.

It is time, therefore, that we question whether the concept of the peaceful revolution is valid in the Latin American context. We shall not consider here the philosophical and historical question of whether in any place and at any time a peaceful revolution can take place.

How is the Latin American revolution to be achieved? The answer to this immediately suggests other questions:

Can democracy be established by democratic methods?

Can there be a successful revolution that proclaims itself *in advance* to be peaceful?

In Latin America, I repeat, authentic democracy does not exist, not only because it is not true social or economic democracy, but also because as soon as it attempts to move a step forward, democracy ceases to function.

The transfer of power from the oligarchy to another social group has always been achieved through violence, at times long-lasting (Mexico), and at times short (Bolivia, Venezuela), but never by democratic routes.

An authentic democracy must be established, a democracy that fits Lincoln's definition. Certainly, this cannot be done overnight.

[31] *The New York Times,* April 22, 1964, p. 18.

But, whether quickly or slowly, can it be done by the democratic method? The answer seems clear. Not only our history, but logic as well, dictates that if there is no democracy, there are no democratic methods. Democratic methods can exist only where democracy exists, *ergo,* not in Latin America.

The United States had to resort to undemocratic methods (the Revolution, the Civil War), as did other nations, in order to establish its democracy and to advance it. There is no valid reason to deny this right to the peoples of Latin America.

But the present situation is such (by reason of very special—and, remember, transitory—circumstances) that perhaps it may be possible without great violence, without spectacular revolutions, without the risk of social cataclysms, to transfer power from the hands of the oligarchy to those of the people by undemocratic, but still relatively nonviolent, means. One of the fundamental objectives of the Alliance for Progress was to ease this transfer of power. If the Alliance fails, it is very probable that violence will be the only method left. It may come soon or late, but it will surely come, and with it, the moment in which the self-interest of the United States will support an outbreak of violence to eliminate the oligarchy and the dangers to Washington inherent in its continuance. It is, therefore, to the advantage of both Washington and the peoples of Latin America that the Alliance should not fail. And for this very reason, it is in the interest of the oligarchy, Soviet diplomacy, and the Communist movement to see that the Alliance does fail.

One example will clarify what I mean when I speak of methods that are undemocratic but nonviolent. When Juan Bosch was elected President of the Dominican Republic and took office, in February, 1963, he was faced with the problem of building democracy in a nation that had never really experienced it and that was emerging from thirty years of tyranny and two years of oligarchic provisional government. The oligarchy, servants of Trujillo but not his mentors, wished to retain power, and so, from the day of the elections, began to plan a military coup. Bosch could have done two things: either he could have persuaded himself that he could establish democracy by legal means, gradually, by persuasion and with the help of pressure from the United States (help which is not exactly a democratic method, but which must be solicited energetically), or else he could have taken the steps which were possible, which would not have been legal, but which would have been nonviolent, and which would have created the preconditions of a democracy and laid the foundations of an authentic democratic system. Two lines of action should have been followed (in outlining them, I am not making a post-mortem, because since I am a friend of Bosch, I was able to say it to him just as I write it here): He should have gotten all the top military leaders out of the country the first morning, without advance warning, by sending them as attachés to distant embassies; and he should have mobilized the peasants through the party that won the elections, the PRD. For these purposes, the PRD activists should have been used as temporary police to round up the military chiefs, while the peasants occupied the lands of the oligarchy (and not waste lands). The Congress would have given legal sanction to the whole procedure on the following day. But, for the moment, the army would have been decapitated, without bloodshed but at the same time without smiles, and the oligarchs would have found themselves with neither economic power nor military support at hand. Not violent—but not legal either. Legality could have come later—in a few hours, if necessary—at such time as it would have been possible to make it respected precisely because the obstacles to its firm establishment would have been eliminated by undemocratic means.

The illusion that democracy can be established by democratic means cost Bosch the Presidency after seven months, and what was more serious, it returned the country to the control of a dictatorship. It caused the United States to appear ridiculous and to be in the position of having to accept and recognize as the legitimate Dominican Government a handful of oligarchs and military leaders.

A year and a half later, the consequences of this illusion led the United States Government to land Marines in the Dominican Republic and to reverse its entire Latin American policy. If Bosch had carried out a genuine revolution that had established democracy, there would not have been any coup in 1963 and no pretext for landing Marines in 1965. To the many other reasons why the United States should support revolutions for democracy in Latin America, we can now add a major one: Revolutions in Latin America will protect the United States Government from the temptation to commit more dramatic blunders of the Santo Domingo type—and save the lives of some Marines.

Another example: Rómulo Betancourt had to construct an authentic democracy in Venezuela in the face of the opposition —often acting together—of reactionary militarists, enlightened Castroites, and terrorists. He did not always rely on democratic methods to overcome this resistance. I do not mean just the suspension of rights or imprisonments, which were perfectly legal. I mean the arming of peasants, who had been given land or knew they would be given it, and loosing them against the terrorists and rebellious soldiers.

To arm any particular social group is not a democratic procedure. But in this case, it allowed Betancourt to remain in power (to be the first elected Venezuelan President to finish his term and turn over power to his democratically elected successor) and to continue the labor of social transformation he had begun, which the alliance of militarists and Communists succeeded in slowing down but could not stop.

Castro's struggle against Batista was not carried on by democratic methods. What Castro did once in power is a separate and familiar story. But there is no doubt that when Castro went into the Sierra, he realized what the situation demanded. If the true democrats had done the same, instead of allowing themselves to accept the fiction that a dictatorship can be fought with democratic methods, Cuba would have rid itself of Batista without falling into the hands of Castro.

There are other dictatorships in Latin America. It is still possible to combat them by the methods Castro used (but did not invent) and other equally undemocratic (but prodemocratic) methods. And there is still time for the United States and any other democratic nation in the continent to decide to rid itself of myths and to encourage, assist, and sustain those who fight for democracy, however undemocratic their methods. This, of course, is not the task of the Alliance. But the Alliance should know that, if such a course of action were followed, once a dictatorship was overthrown, the Alliance would have to be prepared to repair the destruction of the battle rapidly, and the nations now suffering under dictatorship should know it, too, to remove some of their fear of the consequences of fighting their dictators.

When a democratic government employs force—not only military force, but the force of the people, as well—to defend the regime against Castroite guerrillas and Communist terrorists, the whole world approves. But if there were a military coup and the people went into the streets and fought bloody battles, during which lands were occupied and numbers of the oligarchy were killed, then approval would not be so widespread, although the attempt at a military coup would be as dangerous for democracy as the action of Communists or Castroites. More dangerous, really, because we all know that the Communists and Castroites could not seize power in Venezuela, while the military can seize power and have done so many times. The events in Santo Domingo in the spring of 1965 proved that this question is not purely academic, but at the same time, they furnished an extremely nasty and discouraging answer to the question.

It is necessary, therefore, to clarify the matter of the use of force in the defense of democracy. There must be no confusion about this, nor about the use of force to establish democracy.

How can democracy actually be established, a true social and economic democracy and not merely an electoral system, in countries dominated by oligarchies that enjoy the support of substantial elements of the military, if there are no opposing elements that can also resort to force? I do not want to say that they *should* resort to force, only that they should *be able* to do so. There is no dilemma here. It is not a matter of having to choose between the road of violence and that of nonviolence to establish democracy. There is only one road, which can be opened not with actual violence, but by the possibility of using violence. Outside of this, all other paths lead back to the very same point—a sham democracy dominated by the oligarchies. The only thing that would differ would be the names and the labels of the politicians serving the oligarchies, but the problems would remain and the oligarchies would go on ruling, exploiting, and oppressing the people.

If the revolution can be nonviolent, clearly there is no reason to seek violence for its own sake. By the same token, it is clear that if the expansion of the Soviet Union can be contained peacefully, there is no reason for us to wish to use force for this end. But it is also clear that the expansion of the Soviet Union cannot be contained, nor can the revolution in Latin America be achieved, if the willingness to act by peaceful means is not backed up by equal willingness to use sufficient force to crush any resistance. On the international level, this has been called deterrent force. On the national level in Latin America, the power to impose peaceful revolution means the power of the masses to exert such tremendous pressure that the oligarchies would deem it less costly to give up their privileges than to resist. This does not mean, of course, that this force must be exerted in the form of rifle shots, tanks, or barricades. It can be simply the force of elections, the threat to paralyze the country, or merely the enormous pressure that would be exerted by Latin American public opinion, if this category were expanded to include the great majority of the population of the continent—the submerged masses.

The United States should not forget that there are fundamental differences between it and Latin America. In the United States, it is a crime to seek to overthrow the government by force or by subversive means, but in the United States, there are democratic means of removing the government. In Latin America, there is actually no avenue that gives the people an opportunity to win an election or that guarantees a successful candidate that he will take office. In the United States, a democratic system, despite its imperfections, offers guarantees, whereas in Latin America there is no really democratic system and no system that offers any guarantees; it is a common error among North Americans who try to judge the Latin American situation to confuse democracy with a mere democratic façade.

There has never been any true democracy anywhere in Latin America. Even when the electoral mechanism is functioning, other mechanisms are present—those of class, pressure, coercion, and military threat—that rob democracy of its effectiveness. Thus the establishment of true democratic systems in Latin America must always be carried out by "illegal" means, assuming that what is "legal" is the prevailing *de facto* system which we desire to change, because no Latin American regime offers either guarantees or the means of its own democratic modification, nor could it offer them, since none is a democratic regime. One cannot, of course, apply the same criterion of what constitutes violence and illegality to both Latin America and the United States.

Ultimately, the talk of a peaceful revolution is only a device to calm public opinion in the United States. It would be more fitting to remind the United States that when any obstacle blocked its own evolution, U.S. public opinion was ready to use force to remove it. This was the means used in dealing with England, the Indians, the conquest of new lands in the West, and the Civil War.

There is no reason to ask the Latin Americans to give up the use of force as a lever. What we can ask, given the characteristics of our age, is that, if possible, this force be represented by something other than rifle shots. In any case, what is important is not to soothe public opinion in the United States, but rather to disturb the Latin American oligarchy, including that sector we call Latin American public opinion.

Only the frenetic supporters of unilateral disarmament would conceive of saying to Russia: "We believe in your good faith and we hope that our unilateral disarmament will induce you to disarm too." If Russia has not enveloped the whole world in war, it is simply because the United States has sufficient deterrent strength to spoil the Russians' taste for war and any advantage they might have as the aggressor. Now the Latin American people are the target of constant, daily aggression on the part of the oligarchy. The solution is not to tell the oligarchs that we renounce the use of violence in order to persuade them to renounce their monopoly of land ownership and political control; the solution is to create a deterrent force sufficient to make the oligarchy's aggression against the people and its exercise of a monopoly over political control both costly and disadvantageous.

For four years, the Alliance has offered the oligarchy (probably the only time this has ever happened) the opportunity of opening the way to peaceful social change. The oligarchy has not taken advantage of this opportunity and, by scorning it, has renounced automatically and for all time the rights it claims, whether they be real or fictitious.

The Alliance promulgated an amnesty for all the historic crimes of the oligarchy, on the condition that the guilty party change his ways. There has been no change. Now the period of the amnesty has passed. The criminal can now be taken, dead or alive. If the people capture the criminal (and they *should* do so, to end his exploitation and oppression), the reward they will receive will be political power, the right to decide their own destiny, at last.

The United States must make up its mind, and quickly, whether it is on the side of the criminal, whether it will help him to mock the law of history after having offered an opportunity for redemption which the criminal has rejected, or whether it is on the side of the people and will help them to capture the criminal. For the criminal, the oligarchy, the question now is not whether to continue committing his crime, but whether or not he will save his own life. In the not-too-distant future, he may have to decide quite literally.

Violence cannot be escaped by avoiding change. Perhaps it can be postponed for a few months, a few years. But its eventual coming cannot be prevented. Violence can be avoided only by making changes today, and the only way to make these changes is to impose them. For this, violent methods must be available, in other words, a force sufficient to dissuade the oligarchy from attacking or even resisting.

The most the Alliance and the forces of democratic change can do for the oligarchs is to save their lives, but not their power as well. And even if they could do anything else, they should not, for it would be unjust and impolitic, and would, in the long run, place the lives of the oligarchs in even greater danger. They made the choice that led them to the present situation. Why should the United States or the Latin American people have to pay to save the oligarchs from the consequences of their own free acts? Have they not suffered enough already—the people through their misery and the United States through hatred and loss of prestige?

The people never choose their own weapons. They do not seek violence for its own sake. The people employ the weapons that their enemies leave them or force upon them. In Latin America, they are always in a position of legitimate defense. In order that the legitimacy of this position be recognized, it should not be carried to excess. If the people are attacked with fists, they will respond with fists (if their hands have not been tied beforehand); if by shots, they will respond with shots (for which they can be forearmed).

The Alliance provided an opportunity for the people to triumph with words and money. The oligarchs kept the money and perverted the meaning of the words. It is now the duty of the Alliance to provide the people with the means of defending themselves and of overcoming their enemies. It depends in great measure on the Alliance whether or not the people go to excess in legitimate self-defense, but if they do, no one can hold it against them.

That this point of view is coming to be understood in the United States is evident from the comments on Latin America contained in Senator J. W. Fulbright's important foreign-policy speech, in March, 1964:

The historical odds are probably against the prospect of peaceful social revolution. There are places, of course, where it has occurred, and others where it seems likely to occur. In Latin America the chances for such basic change by peaceful means seem bright in Colombia and Venezuela and certain other countries; in Mexico many basic changes have been made by peaceful means, but these came in the wake of a violent revolution.

In other Latin American countries the power of ruling oligarchies is so solidly established and their ignorance so great that there seems little prospect of accomplishing economic growth or social reform by means short of the forceful overthrow of established authorities.

We must not, in our preference for the democratic procedures envisioned by the Charter of Punta del Este, close our minds to the possibility that democratic procedures may fail in certain countries and that where democracy does fail, violent social convulsions may occur.

We would do well, while continuing our efforts to promote peaceful change through the Alliance for Progress, to consider what our reactions might be in the event of the outbreak of genuine social revolution in one or more Latin American countries.

Such a revolution did occur in Bolivia, and we accepted it calmly and sensibly. But what if a violent social revolution were to break out in one of the larger Latin American countries? Would we feel certain that it was Cuban or Soviet inspired? Would we wish to intervene on the side of established authority? Or would we be willing to tolerate or even support a revolution if it was seen to be not Communist but similar in nature to the Mexican revolution or the Nasser revolution in Egypt?[32]

But in Latin America, no one dares speak out in this way. Of course, the fact that Fulbright cannot eliminate in one statement persistent habits of thought in the United States is evident in an example from Flora Lewis, one of the most intelligent North American journalists. In one of her reports on Zanzibar, a sentence ap-

[32] *The New York Times,* March 26, 1964.

peared that would seem strange, did it not represent so widely held a point of view:

> The American view also holds that though they are vanishing from sight in the present regime, there must be unidentified moderate elements in Zanzibar who may yet come forward. Then they could be supported.[33]

In other words, the fact that there was a revolution in Zanzibar that dissipated all the moderate elements demonstrates nothing, even to Flora Lewis. It does not demonstrate, for example, that the intelligent course of action, from the point of view of the national interest of the United States, would be to support the extremists and to attract them (for which there are means available that are superior to those of the U.S.S.R., including means other than material). But no; through a blindness as dogmatic as that of the Stalinists, the diplomats and journalists of the United States seem to believe that any regime that is not moderate must be bad. And what would happen if socially radical regimes allied themselves with Washington's foreign-policy positions? Do not forget that Washington has accepted the support of such socially and politically reactionary and fascist regimes as Spain, Portugal, and Saudi Arabia. Since the United States accepts the support of these radicals, why the obsession to look for moderates in countries where the moderates have failed—for if they had not failed, they would not have disappeared.

Let it be understood that I do not advocate that the United States encourage violence in order to establish democracy. This is something that the people of Latin American must do themselves through means within their own reach and of their own choice. What I do say is that the United States should not condemn in advance or veto (if any country actually can veto the actions of another, which I doubt) any method a Latin American people chooses to use to establish a true democracy in its country. It would be well for the United States to remember that the conditions of life in Latin America today are worse than any in the United States in those periods of history when the North Americans themselves resorted to violence as the only way out of what they considered an

[33] *The Washington Post,* April 4, 1964, p. 27.

intolerable situation—in 1776 and 1861. If this led to a strengthening of democracy in the United States, there is no reason why it should not have the same results in Latin America, for the North Americans, then or now, are not superior, or more democratic, or more politically able than any other people. And I insist that, in the present context, "violence" means not the substantive use of force, but the possibility of using it.

It is curious and depressingly illogical that when a *de facto* government is established under the pretext of maintaining order (to put an end to public violence or to block structural reform, as the case may be), sooner or later other governments will recognize and accept it. For Latin American governments, this would be natural, considering that, with rare exceptions, all of them consider their only function to be the maintenance of order to the advantage of the oligarchy, and whatever they do beyond this (political, social, educational, etc.), they do only as an indirect means of preserving order. But it is incomprehensible that a government such as that of the United States, whose national interest consists in strengthening the capitalistic system, should be so myopic as to believe that the maintenance of order is reason enough to accept a dictatorial or oligarchic regime. For the interests of the United States would best be served if there were disorder in Latin America, if the existing anachronistic anticapitalist order should change and be replaced by a capitalistic order.

The United States should begin to look for and to accept in advance the existence of *de facto* governments in Latin America, not to maintain the old order (which after so many years has become disorder) but to establish a new order, for the very simple reason, as we have just seen, that there can be no new order without *de facto* governments. Not conservative governments, but reform or—even though the word has lost much of its value—revolutionary governments.

Dictatorships seek to maintain the disorder (disguised as the old order) that makes dictatorships necessary. The revolutionary governments wish to create an order that would not make dictatorial illegality a necessity. As José Carlos Mariátegui, a Marxist, said some years ago: "The revolutionary is a man of order."[34]

[34] Mariátegui, *Siete ensayos de interpretación de la realidad peruana* (Lima, 1928).

Moreover, whatever anti-Yankee propaganda may say and whatever U.S. commentators may believe, neither the United States nor any other world power can halt events in another country, however small it may be. Albania laughs at the U.S.S.R. and Haiti at the United States. If the Latin Americans want revolutions, they will have revolutions sooner or later. Accordingly, the intelligent thing to do would be to line up with the coming popular movement rather than oppose it, knowing that opposition will be fruitless.

But, apparently, one of the strange characteristics of what is called, with great exaggeration, United States diplomacy, has been to do the opposite of what diplomacy has historically always done. The diplomat is like a woman; he never says yes or no, and never shuts doors or windows. But as soon as an event takes place, the U.S. diplomat, on the other hand, feels an irresistible urge to adopt a clear position. He shuts his doors and windows, and when he would like to move out of one position, he finds that he himself has blocked all the exits; and when he wants to move into another, he finds that he himself has barred all the entrances.

Whatever the United States or any other world power does cannot, I repeat, change Latin America's course; it cannot prevent a violent revolution. It can, of course, speed up the revolution or delay it and can orient it toward the democratic or antidemocratic camp. Sufficient proof of all this can be found in the out-of-tune concerto played in unhappy harmony by the blind-and-deaf intelligence services, military, and diplomatic corps of the United States in the Santo Domingo performance of things-that-ought-to-be-avoided.

But if the United States persists in talking about the peaceful revolution and in giving the impression that it will tolerate only this sort of revolution, what will happen is that the potentially revolutionary elements—the people, the forgotten, submerged masses—who are not anti-Yankee, since they do not share the frustrations of the middle class, will become anti-Yankee because they will see in the United States an obstacle to the revolution they need.

To insist on a peaceful revolution means no revolution at all. No revolution means opening the gates to technocratic militarism, which will, in turn, open the gates to Communism. It also means driving social forces that were not previously anti-Yankee into anti-Yankeeism. In the world today, anti-Yankeeism is equivalent to pro-Sovietism and, indirectly, to the adoption of measures leading rapidly to totalitarianism.

These could be the consequences of the blind, irrational, cowardly, and bureaucratic attachment on the part of U.S. diplomats to the idea that there can be peaceful revolutions in Latin America.

What worries me is not whether the United States has more friends or fewer, but that its attitude may push potentially democratic elements into the arms of the Soviets and thus frustrate the forces of revolution and cause them to become counterrevolutionary, like all those who accept Soviet methods of development.

If this blindness on the part of the United States were to persist, everything that is blamed on the United States now—both what is deserved and what is hung on it as a scapegoat—would be nothing compared to what would be blamed on it in the future, and rightly so, for having slowed down social change in Latin America with the excuse that it should come about by peaceful means.

Under these circumstances, the popular movements would be even more culpable if they were to wait for an O.K. from the United States to do things the United States could not prevent. That is, if the popular movements, in fear of alarming the United States, were to renounce violence (not so much its use as the ability to use it), they would be as responsible as the United States for the abandonment of the Latin American people to the actual armed violence of the oligarchy.

The Alliance for Progress of 1961 would have been absolutely unthinkable in 1945, at a time when it would have been necessary and effective. But even so, the concept was in formation. What forward-looking Latin Americans were thinking fifty years ago is today commonplace in both the United States and Latin America. In the same manner, what some of us Latin Americans are thinking today—and because of it being labeled mad "Communist" dreamers—will be commonplace tomorrow. But we must be sure that "tomorrow" really means tomorrow and not in the next generation, when today's ideas will be as out of date as those of the Alliance are now.

In many areas—international relations, the war against poverty, desegregation, the Alliance for Progress, space flights, military strategy—concepts are accepted and defended today that only yesterday were thought to have been devised by the enemy and which Senator

McCarthy would have considered proofs of Communism. The idea that Latin America needs a true and unadulterated revolution to establish social, economic, and political democracy, and that this can be achieved with democratic objectives only if the forgotten masses participate in it together with the United States and the popular movements, will tomorrow appear to be so obvious that we shall wonder why it was not immediately accepted when it was first stated.

The people, who have been patient thus far, are beginning to show signs of impatience. At the same time—perhaps out of fear of this impatience—the middle class and the intellectuals, who were impatient in the past, show signs of an angelic patience in the face of the oligarchy.

We are probably about to witness a reversal in roles. Those who in the past urged progress will now be the brakes on it, and those who were a dead weight in the past will be the dynamic force.

Thus we have arrived at the moment of choice: whether to be surgeons or faith healers. Either we operate to cut out a cancer or we deceive the patient with aspirin or, even worse, with magic potions.

The Revolution from Below

What is called the peaceful revolution should have been carried out—when there was still time, if there ever was—by the governments, that is, as a revolution from above.

The governments and what used to be called the upper class did not make this revolution and thus destroyed whatever possibility of a peaceful revolution there might have been.

The nonpeaceful revolution (for it need not necessarily be violent) can only be a revolution from below. Who is it that wants this or is in a position to achieve it?

Every day we watch the governments of Latin America accepting the aid of the Alliance while at the same time scoffing openly at their commitments, siphoning off Alliance funds, refusing to implement the reforms they have promised, or else making sham reforms. This shows that it is not yet possible merely by the pressure of loans, diplomacy, and the threat of Castro to force the oligarchic governments to kill off the social group which they represent and whose interests they administer.

In order to effect the necessary changes, pressure must be brought to bear from within the country itself; and it must be so overwhelming that opposition to it would be more dangerous and costly than giving way. In short, there must be new forces to take up the reins of power.

What forces?

The middle class, some years ago, felt the desire for change and had the power to bring it about, but at that time, there was no instrument such as the Alliance (due to the shortsightedness of the United States' Latin American policy), and without such a cushioning instrument, the middle class became uneasy about the consequences of change. Today, the middle class has lost its dynamism; it is still in the ascendant but in a different context, for it has taken on bourgeois characteristics. Having failed to make the revolution years ago, when it had the will, it compromised, to a certain point, with the oligarchy, a compromise that made its situation much easier and automatically paralyzed its ability to force social change. Moreover, the tendency toward technocracy (toward a technocratic militarism, probably) means that the middle class (whose members would benefit, but, in no event, would be willing to produce capital for development out of their own labor, by lengthening their working day or cutting their real income) feels more inclined toward methods of social coercion than to democratic methods of development. This feeling is present in at least an important segment of the middle class, if not in all of it, especially in the segment that because of its youth is the most dynamic and has no nostalgia for the struggle for democracy still retained by the older sector.

But there is today one part of Latin American society, the most numerous and, until now, the most passive, that has much to lose from technocratic militarism and much to gain from the Alliance, if there were a way to awaken their interest and combativeness on behalf of the Alliance, and to show them how to use it. This is the part that we have called the submerged mass.

The fundamental problem, for the Alliance, lies in mobilizing these submerged levels of society, in finding the means of arousing them from their passivity and making them press for changes in the structure of society. This pressure would shake the middle class out of its flirtation with the technocratic militarists and would return it to its position of old—in the vanguard of the fight for social change. At the same time, if this pressure were sufficiently powerful, it could force the oligarchies to give ground, or where they refused, it could throw them out of power. The latter course would not be easy, certainly, nor could it always be done peacefully. But, in any event, violent pressure for democracy is preferable to violent pressure for totalitarian systems.

We already know in advance that as the popular movement gains strength, it will be called Communist or pro-Communist (especially if a demagogue as servile to the wishes of the oligarchy as Goulart can be called a Communist).

It is possible that many ill-informed commentators will echo these accusations, as they did in labeling Rómulo Betancourt a Communist. This would not matter. The enemies of the popular movement will oppose it not because the movement is Communistic, but solely because it is popular, and the accusations of Communist affiliation are hurled (by the very people who always marched right along with the Communists) only to cover the decapitation of the movement, justify it, and make it tolerable.

Every popular movement must know beforehand that it will be accused of being Communistic, and it should be determined to maintain its anti-Communist stand in spite of this fact. For the anti-Communism of the popular movements is not intended to please the United States, the military, or anyone else, but rather to take account of the simple fact that the Communists are the allies of the oligarchs, that they have served the United States whenever it suited the U.S.S.R., and that they oppose authentic popular demands. In this sense, the appropriate line of conduct would be to follow the admonition of the poet Juan Ramón Jiménez: "Don't do it just because they say to, and don't refuse to do it just because they do not say to."

I can hear some self-styled democrats objecting: "But if we awaken the people, how can we be sure that the Communists won't take them over?"

We cannot. Luckily these things cannot be guaranteed. Listening to talk like this, we can almost be glad that there is such a thing as Communism to scare these "democrats" just a little, for without it, they would be worse than they are.

What sort of democrats can they be, if they are afraid that under equal conditions, the Communists, rather than the democrats, would win the people? They are the same ones who, a generation ago, said: "Better that the people don't know how to read. They are less unhappy and less ambitious this way."

If we must fear that the Communists will take the people away from us—the people we have been able to awaken—we had better try to join the Party right now.

"And suppose we unleash terrorism by awakening the masses?" other fools inquire in a strangled voice. Let us see. . . .

A handful of fanatics using terroristic methods can keep an entire nation on tenterhooks, if they have the intelligence, discipline, and explosives. In Venezuela, there must be no more than two hundred hard-core terrorists. One man, armed with low-power bombs, led the New York police around by the nose for months a few years ago. And the activists of the Secret Army Organization, which produced such a sensation in France during the final period of the war in Algeria, numbered only a few dozen. Just as a maniac can kill the President of the United States, a hundred dedicated men can keep a whole country in a state of nerves, provoke flights of capital, discredit the army, and even cause a government to fall. The example of Fidel Castro and his student allies in Havana proves this.

The same can be said of guerrilla groups. Neither Castro nor the FLN in Algeria ever had a large number of effective troops, nor does the Viet Cong, nor in the resistance movements of World War II was the number of guerrillas and terrorists ever in proportion (given the number of German troops mobilized against them) to the havoc they wrought.

To disturb social order, fan popular anxiety, to produce the disintegration of a regime and its allies, to isolate and topple it—all this is not impossible. The difficult part is to find the necessary fanatics and an organization to direct them that has a political, not merely a terrorist, mentality. This combination of political and adventurist spirit has been found and can be found again any time and anywhere in Latin America. Sometimes they were liberal, at other times merely ambitious or anti-imperialistic, and now they generally are Castroites.

Why did this combination succeed in Cuba and fail in Venezuela?

The answer seems obvious: because in Cuba they were fought with strictly technical (military) weapons, whereas in Venezuela they were fought with political methods.

Up to now, Communism has never exerted any attraction over the mass of the people. Its influence is limited to intellectuals, students, and technical and middle-class elements who wish for overnight development at the expense of the people and to their own benefit, for they see in Communism the means of making themselves into a governing caste. On the other hand, the struggle against dictatorship, without the Communist label, always enjoys popular sympathy.

In Cuba, Batista's actions in the political area were doomed to failure, because they were based on an attempt to assure the transfer of power to an accomplice of the dictatorship. Thus the dictator found it necessary to rely on the army, and a corrupt army, used to military coups and dirty business, is never an effective fighting force. Even if it had been, it could not have been successful, just as the unmilitaristic army of the United States is not successful in Vietnam.

On the other hand, in Venezuela, Betancourt waged the struggle in the political field. Although the army and the police took part and were supported by harsh judicial measures, they were never more than auxiliaries of the political activity. No one ever says (perhaps not to humiliate the Venezuelan officers who are not yet cured of the virus of militarism) that the ones who really fought the guerrillas were the peasants, rather than the military. Why? I have explained this in a previous chapter: because some had already received land from the government, others hoped to receive it, and they all knew that if the guerrillas won, they would take the land back in the name of a supposed collectivist revolution. Betancourt triumphed over Castroism because he knew how to organize the peasants (through his party and the labor unions) and how to make them realize the danger the guerrillas represented to their ownership of the land. It was political action that isolated the guerrillas and terrorists, not the army or the police.

The oligarchies cannot mount this sort of political action precisely because they are oligarchies, because they cannot give the peasant land (and with it, the security and satisfaction of knowing that the old oligarchic owner no longer controls his life, which is perhaps as important as the land itself), and furthermore because under an oligarchic regime, labor unions are suppressed and timid and lack the combativeness they showed in Venezuela. And because at this point, no one believes the promises, or even the acts, of the oligarchic politicians, whether they present themselves as conservatives, liberals, or revolutionaries. We have examples of this in Colombia, where the violence in the countryside continues (which the Castroites have exploited only in the last few years), and where neither an agrarian-reform law that is a joke nor all the liberal rhetoric can stop it, as well as in Argentina, where guerrillas have now begun to appear.

The oligarchy, then, is the Communists' greatest ally, because it creates the conditions for terrorism and does not permit the development of conditions under which terrorism can be combated and isolated by political methods, the only methods that can be successful. This is apart from the tacit alliance between the oligarchy and the Communists, which I have mentioned earlier, in speaking of the concubinage between the Communists and the militarists. Do not forget that in Venezuela, Castroites and military friends of Pérez Jiménez acted together and that some of the latter were with the guerrillas.

To want to keep the oligarchy in power, under the pretexts that property is sacred and that violence and disorder must be avoided, is the equivalent of inviting the Castroites and Communists to repeat the Venezuelan experience under conditions that would not permit answering their challenge with the popular political weapons that made them fail in Venezuela. Choosing Venezuela as his battleground was an error on Castro's part. But in any other country, he would be sure to find more favorable conditions (except in Mexico, for the same reasons as in Venezuela).

Latin America is in the position of a man who is forbidden to marry and who is surrounded by syphilitic prostitutes. If he then contracts syphilis, who can blame him?

Is it necessary to point out that in this simile (which is closer to reality than it may seem), the prostitutes are the oligarchies and the syphilis is Castroism? The logical solution would be to allow Latin America to have a normal marriage with the democratic revolution. But to do this, the prostitutes must be cleared out of the way. If not, we will achieve only a confusion from which we shall all emerge infected.

To think that terrorism and guerrilla activity can be curtailed by preventing the circulation of Che Guevara's (or any other author's) book on the subject is an example of an ingenuousness that can be found only among the police or diplomats of the old school. What makes terrorism and guerrilla activity impossible or fruitless is not a lack of "technical education" on how to make Molotov cocktails, but rather the creation of a climate in which those who want to become guerrillas find themselves isolated or considered reactionary. And this, the oligarchs, the military, or the democrats without social feeling are incapable of doing. Only really popular movements can achieve it, because isolation and condemnation are effective only if they come from the people. Condemnation from the press, the radio, or in official speeches makes no impression on terrorists, but a good beating administered by a group of workers really does.

Very well, how can the submerged masses be mobilized?

The Mexican revolution was successful in this area, and there are two more recent examples to prove that it is possible. In Bolivia, after the revolution in 1952, the miners became a privileged caste, within the general level of misery, by rendering the bill for their struggle with dynamite charges against the military forces. Then a time came when the miners sought to impose their program and candidate on the whole country, and the government was able to isolate them and overcome their resistance thanks to the fact that agrarian reform had politicized and organized the peasants, and that the middle class, instead of being won over by Communist propaganda, as in other countries, had been incorporated within the MNR. Thus in Bolivia the masses, despite their low degree of political education, knew how to act in defense of their interests and of the democratic system—however imperfect it was—which the revolution had established.

Subsequently, the leaders of the miners allied themselves with the remnants of the old oligarchy, the "new" generals, and the Communists, and overthrew the MNR government. When the miners saw that this alliance would destroy them, they fought, but they were defeated by the army because they had isolated themselves. Bolivia, therefore, may appear to be a poor example of what I have been saying. In fact, it is the best example, because it proves that a real revolution, even if it suffers setbacks and failures, achieves some basic things that are there to stay: in Bolivia, the nationalization of the mines, the dignity of the peasants. Generals and leaders, as usual, will kill, steal, and vanish. And then, will the Marines be sent to La Paz also? For the Santo Domingo situation will most certainly be duplicated in the *altiplano.*

Those who are afraid to awaken and mobilize the masses, because they fear this will open up a Pandora's box (and their rhetoric is generally as tasteless as that image), can soothe themselves by looking at the case of Bolivia and calm themselves completely with the case of Venezuela.

Under the leadership of Betancourt and Acción Democrática, which organized and mobilized them, the masses acted in defense of democracy and of the social reforms that had already been achieved. The ones who were ensnared by Castroite propaganda were those who are most likely to succumb in the future to the technocratic mentality.

This double lesson should convince the existing populist movements and those that arise in the future that they should put their trust in the submerged masses and orient all their activities toward awakening and mobilizing the masses. If these movements do so, they can undoubtedly succeed in forcing the middle class, the intellectuals, the students, and perhaps even the technocratic military men—who always tend to follow the ideological fashions that seem most likely to triumph—toward democratic solutions.

It is clear that methods must be found to reach the submerged masses, to employ those elements which until now have been politically marginal, to invent new systems of popular organization, and above all, to abandon rhetoric and discover what the goals of the masses really are. There will be the great surprise when it becomes apparent that these goals are much more democratic, much less extremist, and much more solidly national (but certainly less nationalistic) than those expressed heretofore by public opinion.

Someone has said that France was always one war behind: In 1870, it fought Prussia with Napoleonic tactics; in 1914, with the techniques of 1870; and in 1939, with the strategy of 1914. It can also be said of Latin American that we are behind the times in the area of social change—all of us: politicians (especially politicians), sociologists, economists, diplomats, and intellectuals. In 1945, we worried about dictatorships without seeing the social problems that were coming to the surface just as in 1927, for example, we were concerned with anti-imperialism without foreseeing the semitotalitarian dictatorships that even then were imminent.

I must point out that the Alliance for Progress is not behind the times as far as the social changes of the moment are concerned. And this is the cause of the phenomenon, logical but not, therefore, any less depressing, that the Alliance for Progress, precisely because it is in accord with the facts, is not in accord with the people who should welcome it, for these people are still thinking in terms of an earlier social change. Today they think about the development of the middle class, when they should be thinking about the rise of the masses, the slow ascent of the submerged peoples.

This, in short, is the problem of the Alliance; this explains its isolation, its loss of identity, its perversion, its failure in terms of the middle class, and its lack of success in terms of the masses.

The problem, thus, is one of the instrument and the hand that must wield it. The Alliance is an instrument for the people, but it is operated by the people's enemy or, at best, those who are indifferent to the people or parasites on them.

It is necessary to go to the people, before the military and the technocrats do, not as protectors, as well-intentioned patresfamilias, but rather to become integrated with the people and to assure that the people seize their destiny in their own hands and stop acting through go-betweens. This does not mean trying to make them participate. It means recognizing their role as protagonists, ceasing to think of them as a chorus at times for their oppressors and at times for their protectors. There is no need to protect or defend the people; they must protect and defend themselves.

In most Western countries, the governments are better than the people. In Latin America, the people are better, much better, than their governments. Within the governments and the limited strata that comprise public opinion, policy is determined more often by prejudices, irrational reactions, and unadmitted interests than by principles, continental or national interests, and good sense. But within the masses, there is more common sense, more political intuition, more sincerity and fewer prejudices than among their so-called leaders, those guardians who never render accounts. But the truth is that the people have come of age, that they no longer need guardians; the only thing they need is to be taught how to sign their names.

Who will teach them? The technocratic militarists who by demagogic suggestion would make them sign a renunciation of their own liberty just as they come of age, or the democrats who, recognizing the causes of their own past failures, would teach them to sign their first true emancipation?

Don't tell me that the people are not ready. If they are not, it is the fault of the democrats, for the democrats' *raison d'être* is precisely to make them ready. And if they are not, the urgent, immediate, and unavoidable duty of the democrats is to throw themselves into making them ready, without worrying about sacrifices or risks.

And don't say that there are no means to do this. If the Alliance for Progress, the Inter-American Development Bank, and the attempts at continental unity have any meaning, it is precisely that of being able to supply the material means to achieve this accelerated preparation of the people. It is not the houses, the hospitals, the land distributed, the schools or highways built that is important. What is important—what we have forgotten up to now —are the families who must live in these houses, the sick who must be treated in these hospitals, the children who must learn in these schools, the truckers who must drive over these roads, the peasants who must own these lands. . . . Now is the time for us to remember them. Now is the time, above all, when we must not put ourselves, or allow anyone else to put himself, between them and the houses, the hospitals, the schools, the highways, and the lands.

Going to the People

The capacity for violence—or, one might say, the possibility of fire—is the only thing that can possibly prevent true widespread and unchecked violence. The middle class has lost this capacity. Only the people, the submerged masses, can be expected to retain it in the future.

But the submerged masses are submerged. We must make them conscious of their interests and of the possibility of satisfying them,

and make them understand that their interests coincide with those
of society. The amorphous masses must be converted into organiz-
able masses. Conditions should be created that enable the masses
to produce their own leaders and theorists.

In short, it is necessary to go to the people.

So far, all this is nothing but a lot of words. It is easy to talk
about going to the people. It is less easy to accept the idea, because it entails inconveniences and risks. But progressing from the
idea to the act, actually going to the people, that is truly difficult.
How can it be done in the concrete case of Latin America? How
can we bring the submerged masses to the surface of society? How
can we make them listen and understand so that tomorrow they will
no longer need to listen to us, it will be we who will need to understand them?

In the end, it comes down to this: The unsubmerged elements
must give the initial impetus to the masses, who will ultimately
submerge them. Nonetheless, it is the least difficult way to do what
must be done. Such elements exist today, as they always have. They
were the ones who created the labor movement, which was originally an effort, remember, not so much of the proletariat as of
the *petite bourgeoisie,* who were disgusted with the conduct of the
bourgeoisie and the oligarchy. There have been such people in the
past and there are some today, even within the oligarchy itself.
And today there are people who are disgusted with the new passivity of the middle class, among them the most sincere of the young
Castroites.

Consequently, it is essential to invent new means of approaching
the people, of speaking to them, and above all, of making sure that
they gain the opportunity to speak for themselves.

I believe that whatever method is proposed will have to re-
semble, in its general form, something along the lines of a Peace
Corps. But it must be a Peace Corps whose fundamental (but not
exclusive) mission is not to instruct the people how to live without
germs, but to teach them how to fight to create such a life. A Battle
Corps, in a manner of speaking, free of any connection with governments, parties, or official agencies.

This naturally poses a primary question: that of developing leaders and activists for the movement "to the people." But if the movement is to be effective, this question will resolve itself. The first

leaders must come from the student sector, from the unions, from the cooperatives, and from similar organizations. As contact is established with the people, leaders will come from the people themselves, as well as from the groups I have just mentioned, once they are reintegrated with the people.

This process can be aided, and should be, by publications, courses of study, improvised schools, meetings, and travel. But that is not the essential factor. What is essential is that these impatient, dissatisfied young people, eagerly waiting for an opportunity, dare to take the step forward. The day when they are told: "If you step forward, you will be backed up—now, in the period of preparation, and later, during the long struggle itself—by the full weight of the Alliance," that day the leaders will appear.

A French expert's remarks on technical assistance can be applied to this search for methods of going to the people:

> Contrary to a widely held opinion, the problems of development are simple. If they are complicated to solve, if great effort is expended in discovering subtleties and refinements in the structures of underdeveloped nations that do not actually exist there, it is because people stubbornly insist on using more and more complex analytical and laboratory methods for elementary diagnoses. The abuse of mathematics in the human sciences and the delight in esoteric discoveries has led to the development of a real logomachy of development. Clear thoughts, we might almost say commonplaces, can now be expressed only in interminable equations.[35]

Development plans have their own generals and even their own shock troops—their experts—and money and equipment to execute their experts' projects. But the infantry is lacking. The people are the infantry. The infantry cannot be mobilized by force alone; it must have a certain morale. This morale is represented by the desire for progress and the desire for freedom. This is what the Alliance for Progress should have given the Latin American people, this is what an alliance can still give the people if it goes to the people directly.

All the Latin American writers on political law talk excitedly about municipal autonomy. In fact, the municipalities live a lan-

[35] *Le Monde* (Paris; weekly ed.), January 23–29, 1964.

guid existence without any degree of autonomy and the municipal agencies are simple instruments of political bossism, that is, means of impairing what little democracy we enjoy. The people live in municipalities, and it is possible that, if these municipalities are offered the means to do things for the benefit of the people, and if these offers reach the municipalities, the people themselves will demand more action from the municipalities and will fight to transform autonomy from a paper reality into a flesh-and-blood reality, and will put leaders at the head of these municipalities who enjoy the confidence of the people.

It is easier for the people to wage a peaceful fight for change within the municipalities than to engage in an unorganized struggle on the national level, and it is easier to organize the people, or to begin to organize them, on the municipal level than on the national. Moreover, the field of municipal activity can be the breeding ground for future leaders of the people. Until now, except in a few countries, the municipality has been only a name. The Alliance could convert it into a fact, a fact with considerable influence on Latin American life.

Except for the Communist, Castroite, and some Christian Democratic movements, most of the political parties and labor unions in Latin America have no active young membership. This separation of generations is perhaps one of the most telling proofs of the inability thus far of the movements of the democratic left to adjust to the new demands of Latin American society. If the parties that proclaim themselves the supporters of social reform cannot attract the youth, then the parties lack something. What is it? I believe it is communication with the people. The young are more absolute, more uncompromising, and more emotional than the adult militants and they tend to relate to the people. If the parties do not bring them to the people, they are attracted to the groups or movements that give them at least the illusion of fighting for the masses. From this derive the nuclei of youth who engage in terrorism and guerrilla activity, convinced that this is the way to serve the people. This conviction is sincere and has nothing to do with the objectives fixed by the adult promoters of terrorism and guerrilla agitation.

The young are not equipped with the means of comparison. They have never known anything but an oligarchic regime. For this reason, when they become aware that there are other realities more attuned to their aspirations and their dreams, they become impatient.

It has been said that universities must sometimes provide not what the society wants but what it needs. In Latin America, one of those times is now. The society doubtless desires technicians but what it needs is revolutionaries. Unfortunately, our universities provide neither. They are too mediocre to develop technicians and too conformist to produce revolutionaries.

But that is where the students are. And they, in their first years of study, want to be with the people.

One of the ways in which Communists and Castroites succeed in attracting Latin American students is by giving them a sense of usefulness and of mission. One must have a very low opinion of the students to think that they follow the Castroites and Communists simply because they provide an excuse for skipping classes, running wild in the streets, and amusing themselves by harassing the police. The Alliance could give them this same sense of mission and make use of their intransigence. For this, two things are necessary: first, not to fear the action of the students, to be convinced that the Alliance can be more seductive than Communist propagandists; in other words, to have complete faith in the objectives of the Alliance. This means restoring the original meaning of the Alliance. The other condition is to attract the cooperation of the groups that need the students—the cooperatives, peasant organizations, unions, etc.

In other generations, Latin American students cooperated with the labor movement, as, for example, in the people's universities that were established in Peru around 1920 right after a textile workers' strike which became a general strike in Lima. Even today, there are certain activities of a practical sort that we could call "going to the people." For instance, in Chile, in Bolivia, and even in Brazil, students assist in literacy campaigns. In Ecuador, they established clinics and worked on the solution of community problems, until the present dictatorship, because of the suspicion that every dictatorship feels toward students, put an end to these activities.

There are many areas in which students can work and at the same time satisfy their desire for a sense of mission. One example: Migration from the country to the cities is constant and heavy; the peasants arrive in the cities in search of better living conditions and a pleasanter existence, but in general, they lack any skill by which to earn their living in the cities; they fall into the hands of labor contractors who pay them indecent wages, and they thereby constitute a threat to the efforts of the unions; they live crowded together in houses hardly worthy of the name, and around the city, they create great belts of misery, whose social instability makes them centers of political delinquency. This process encourages alcoholism and, in some countries, the use of narcotics (such as coca and marijuana), and provokes psychological dislocations that have telling effects on the personality of the semi-urbanized peasant. Up to now, the unions have not concerned themselves at all with orienting these peasants, organizing them, helping them to find work, and assisting in their vocational training. The peasants, by virtue of the very fact of having moved from the country to the city, are receptive to all kinds of influences and have great curiosity. If the unions, in cooperation with the students, would attend to these peasants, prepare them politically as well as professionally, organize them, and give them a democratic concept of their requirements and the means of satisfying them, these rural masses in the process of urbanization could constitute a magnificent pressure group against the oligarchy. To the masses, the objectives of the Alliance are familiar and understandable, simply because its objectives would satisfy their needs. I believe that Alliance funds must be used for such activities—not to build hospitals, not to provide water systems, but to make the masses aware of the fact that they need hospitals and schools and water, and that they can get them and much more if they fight for them, and to show them how they can fight with methods that lead to democracy. This is a practical case that outlines clearly what the Alliance could do in its initial stage.

Students, cooperatives, and unions can collaborate in many other activities; for example, among the Indians, among peasants who are ready to be organized or those already organized who may need assistance in creating cooperatives and managing them during the early stages; naturally, they can operate also in the solution of problems of community development.

In some matters, the Alliance has dealt directly with the people, but in few so far. And at times, it appears that obsession with "principle" is more burdensome than political convenience. For example, in 1957, two North American companies closed their large meat-packing plants in Montevideo. The workers acquired them and put them back in operation, and they have now been running for several years without a boss and without state control. I am speaking of the Establecimientos Frigoríficos del Cerro, S.A. (EFCSA, or Associated Slaughterhouses of Cerro, Inc.), which has been fought all along by the Communists and the most regressive elements of the extreme right. They seek state ownership of deficit operations and private ownership of those that make money. The one we have mentioned has been completely successful, but EFCSA lacks working and reserve capital, and the Uruguayan banks place their money at 18 to 24 per cent annual interest. EFCSA is the largest exporter in the country and the only anti-Communist bastion of the Uruguayan proletariat. Nevertheless, this germ of true "direct democracy," capable by itself of opening up a new road, does not have the necessary support of the "free world."

In contrast, the U.S.S.R. bought 20,000 tons of meat from the Nacional and Castro meat-packing plants in Uruguay. And in spite of the fact that EFCSA received an A-1 rating from the United States Army inspector, the U.S. armed forces have not purchased a single pound of meat from this workers' plant.[36]

Danton said that three things are needed to win a war: *"De l'audace, encore de l'audace, et toujours de l'audace."* For the Alliance to triumph, three things are essential also: politics, yet more politics, and always politics.

By this I mean that the fundamental prerequisite, from which all others derive, consists in placing the problems of the Alliance on a political level, in conceiving of the Alliance not as only an administrative, technical, economic, or social plan, but rather as an essentially political one.

Politics as a concept of plans for the future can guide the Alliance to proper fulfillment. The millions of dollars, the experts, the good intentions are not enough. What is needed is a sane, effective, well-thought-out political concept. Basically, this means deciding what we want Latin America to be tomorrow and using the Alliance to make the picture a reality. The technicians, experts, economists, and administrators can help in the search for the best and least costly ways to arrive at the goal. But the goal is something

36 Riera, *loc. cit.*

that only politics can determine. This does not exclude the free play of group interests and the pressures these interests exert. On the contrary, just because this play of interests is necessary and reasonable, it must be politics (which alone can make this play of interests into something constructive and useful) that marks the road and fixes the goal.

In practice, this means that popular organizations and unions must assume direction of planning for the Alliance and must take the lead in efforts to prevent the failure of the Alliance and its perversion into a series of Potemkin reforms. They must demand and secure full participation (not as observers or consultants, who serve only to sugar-coat the pill) in national planning agencies. For this, the unions must know what they want to discuss and must develop their own ideas about how any plans they approve are going to affect not only the labor sector but the whole nation.

To achieve this objective, the unions must know how to attract —not in the distant future, but right now—two social groups without whose support the unions' field of action will remain limited: the intellectuals and the peasants.

Despite the fact that they often adopt radical positions—but always platonically—Latin American intellectuals have seldom cooperated with the unions. The mutual distrust that exists between the two groups must end, and a new era of cooperation must begin. The unions must have recourse to technicians, experts, and men of culture who share their outlook and hopes. This should not be difficult since it would be the best way of giving the intellectuals and experts a feeling of usefulness and effectiveness, of action, which the existing society cannot provide. Of course, it requires subtlety and, most of all, an understanding of the fact that unions are something more than just negotiators of work rules.

The unions should try to attract the peasants, who are organized in only a few countries. In the rest, they are dispersed and ignored. If agrarian reform is to succeed, it must have the active collaboration of the peasants. The collaboration can be achieved more readily through union action than by any other means.

All this represents a minimum program: The labor federations should organize the peasants, where it has not been done already; they should establish social study centers, training schools for their activists, people's universities, in which intellectuals, experts, and students would work together. The federations should also urge the popular movements, cooperatives, peasants' organizations (where they exist), and organizations of democratic intellectuals and students, to set up centers or groups for the study of national problems. They could then proceed without delay to formulate joint points of view concerning what the Alliance program should be in each country, and could then establish a common line of action to force the governments to accept these plans.

This minimum program of union action must also be carried out by the popular political movements in their own ways; they, too, must formulate solutions and press for their acceptance.

Here is an example of why this must be the course and why it is fruitless to rely on the governments to take action. In June, 1963, an Inter-American Conference of Labor Ministers met in Bogotá. It recommended many things. Most of them could have been put into actual practice by the action of the very ministers who had recommended them.

None of these recommendations has become fact. The most important was for a study of means of providing the unions with a voice in planning. Another was for a study of the possibility of establishing workers' banks in Latin America. So far, not one workers' bank has been created. And it is easy to foresee that when and if such banks are in fact created, legislative hocus-pocus will put them under the government's thumb. Thus, they will never be instruments of pressure for social change.

In the face of cynical jokes like that of the Conference of Labor Ministers who recommend things that they themselves can accomplish and then do not, it is time to ask ourselves whether Latin America does not face the choice between studies without reforms and reforms without studies. Certainly reforms preceded by study are preferable; but thus far, the studies have served to recommend reforms but not to bring them to pass. Thus, we must conclude that one of the missions of the Alliance should be to deal with the economic disequilibrium or other economic consequences resulting from reforms that lack the basis of previous study.

No one fights for hospitals or gets excited about them. What the Alliance needs is enthusiasm and a fighting spirit. Without these, it is just one more aid program.

Mobilize the people? Yes, but for what?

Create a Battle Corps? Yes, and better that it should create itself. But, for what purpose?

The answer can be found in the questions themselves, if we remember that what truly matters is not how far we have advanced, but how many people we have left behind. And in Latin America, only a handful have advanced, while legions are left behind.

Giving and Taking Away

The Communists and demagogues offer a goal. Democracy, on the other hand, can offer only a means, because it is no more than a system of good political education, not a solution to the problems at hand. Democracy is limited to creating the conditions in which solutions can be sought. This disadvantage can become an advantage, in the long run, if the democrats understand that in order for democracy to have success in the face of demagoguery, it should do more than offer a means; it should also give material things, tangible things—things such as land.

The population of Latin America is constantly increasing without a parallel rise in agricultural and livestock production, which results in a lower and lower standard of living. [In 1959,] Latin America imported 8 per cent more foodstuffs than in 1956, which is patently absurd if one considers that only 30 per cent of the arable land is cultivated and that it has the lowest crop-yield rate in the world.

Whereas in the United States and Canada, land is worked in medium-sized agricultural units, in which a single family works and administers the farm with excellent productive returns, in the nations of Latin America, the land is abandoned or suffers from two evils endemic to the landholding system: excessively large holdings in a few hands (the latifundia) and holdings that are too small to be operated economically (the minifundia). Six things are essential in order for Latin America to develop its agricultural units: (1) deeds of title or legalization of rural-property ownership; (2) nearby schools for the education of peasant children; (3) good communications from the farms to commercial centers; (4) good and efficient public-health and welfare services, which are also accessible; (5) extension of agriculture under technical direction; and (6) sufficient credit.[37]

[37] "Un seminario latinoamericano sobre problemas de la tierra," *Mundo del trabajo libre* (Mexico City), March, 1960.

These observations sum up the political, moral, economic, and social motives of agrarian reform. If a system of property does not succeed in satisfying the minimum needs of those who depend on it, if after a century and a half under this system, agricultural productivity remains at the lowest level in the world, then it is clear that the system is inefficient and, by virtue of its consequences—misery, ignorance, oppression of the peasants—immoral.

Agrarian reform does not mean merely breaking up large properties and distributing parcels of them to the peasants. The land must be divided up where it is economically beneficial to do so. Where economic reasons dictate them, new forms of land utilization must be adopted, such as communal, cooperative, or medium-sized holdings and mechanized planting. But the decision to reform the existing system of land tenure must always take into account that higher productivity should not be the sole objective of such reform, but rather that higher productivity should be cause and effect, at the same time, of greater justice and freedom for the peasant and for society as a whole. Agrarian reform must benefit not only the peasants, but the rest of society, as well.

In this sense, a fundamental objective of agrarian reform must be the creation of conditions whereby the peasant will very soon enjoy the same protection, well-being, and legal guarantees as the worker and the member of the urban middle class. The proletariat and the middle class have fought for decades to gain these conditions. The peasant, because of the very circumstances of his existence, can fight only by surprise attack and during moments of great political fervor. It remains to the people of the cities and primarily to the middle class to share with the peasant the benefits their fight has brought them—and to do this because of strict justice, for ethical reasons, as well as because of practical, economic, and political considerations.

Without agrarian reform (that is, without real justice and freedom in the rural sector), all objectives of planning and programing are brought to nothing, because the oligarchic groups can make these methods a mere instrument of their own rule. And without planning and programing, industrialization becomes parasitic, producing only suffering for those whom it benefits least.

Urbanization—a widespread phenomenon in our America—increases the demand for agricultural products. If, as at present, they must be imported, the availability of currency and foreign exchange for the purchase of capital goods decreases, and industrialization suffers. To avoid this, the dietary standard of the urban masses is reduced. In short, industrialization, without a program of agrarian reform to increase agricultural productivity, must be forced either to slow its pace or to maintain its pace at the cost of general hardship.

The absence of an agrarian reform—which gives peasants a sense of their own social function, and enables them to live in the country without feeling they are making a sacrifice and without being tempted to seek industrial employment—is a threat to the living standard of the industrial workers.

A system of agrarian reform (whatever its form: association of minifundia, distribution of state or fallow lands, division of latifundia, cooperative exploitation according to local needs; and whatever its method: taxation, expropriation, sale, credit) which would be concomitant with a program of agricultural reform (mechanization, technical modernization, rationalization of credit, diversification of production, international distribution of product, technical training, construction of communications, improvement of methods, increase in educational facilities, agricultural extension) would have as its consequence the creation of a rural middle class that would invest its savings in agriculture and whose stability and solvency would encourage urban investment in rural projects. This, in turn, would increase national capital available for investment and, by the same token, true national participation in industrialization.

The problem of investment continues to be acute in the area of industrialization. Although the countries of Latin America prefer investment from national sources, and when, as is customary, this is not forthcoming, investment from international public sources, the fact is that most industrial investment is private in character and from foreign sources. For a weak national economy with little internal capital, foreign investments always offer dangers, although these may not be as great today as they were in the past. However, if the national economy is strong (and more than that, if it is part of a coherent and coordinated continental economy), such investments are harmless and can even be genuinely beneficial. Great Britain, France, even the United States, Switzerland, and the

Scandinavian countries, receive a large volume of foreign investments that pose no danger. The economy of Latin America can feel safe from the danger of foreign investment—even without becoming as highly industrialized as these countries—if it can succeed in becoming stable and balanced, with increasing investment from domestic sources and a steady rate of development in excess of the rate of population increase; these conditions can be met only through an agrarian structure at least as advanced as the new industrial structure, and this can be achieved only through agrarian reform.

Solidly based and self-sufficient industrialization can never be achieved unless there is an expanding domestic market, which can be provided only by the rural masses. And such a rural market for manufactured products can come to be only through the development of a rural middle class. Finally, a rural middle class cannot be formed without changes in the existing system of landholding and modernization of agricultural methods. Ergo . . .

The appearance of a rural middle class as a result of agrarian reform would consolidate democracy, not only because it would signify the solution of a problem that has always been the cause of antidemocratic pronouncements and attitudes, but also for the same reason that the process of democratization has been accelerated by the urban middle class, which was spawned by expanding industrialization. Moreover, this rural middle class would serve as a counterweight to the urban sector and as a safeguard against any tendency to orient development along totalitarian or antihuman lines; thus, it would direct economic development toward greater freedom and greater social justice. In addition, the rural middle class could ensure against certain dangers inherent in development that, without being political in themselves, have obvious political consequences: the tendency toward mushrooming cities growing in disordered and uncontrolled proportions. And in a continent where, because of religious beliefs and a low cultural level, it is not yet possible to adopt methods of combating the demographic explosion, the increase of agricultural production would contribute very importantly to a general improvement in living standards to an extent that industrial development, however much it advances, could never equal.

In its zeal to industrialize, Latin America has engulfed itself in debt. This would not represent any danger if it were certain that this credit would produce sufficient capital for its own liquidation. In 1950, the public foreign debt of Latin America was $1.74 billion; by 1955, it had risen to $3.61 billion; and in 1963, it totaled $9.10 billion.[38] Industrialization such as we are now seeing has its limits, imposed by the size of its domestic and foreign markets. There is no certainty that industry can expand perpetually or in sufficient measure for the debtor nations to cover their indebtedness, especially since, on the pretext of promoting industrial development, these nations persist in an anachronistic and unjust fiscal system and tolerate the perpetuation of the old ways of the financial oligarchy, which in many Latin American countries holds the whiphand over the landowners. Agrarian reform, on the other hand, would permit the industrial expansion indispensable to meet the debts already contracted.

In short, without agrarian reform, there can be no stable democracy, no general social justice, no healthy development. Industrialization without agrarian reform must, of necessity, be parasitic; social justice without agrarian reform must be only partial; democracy without agrarian reform must perforce be incomplete.

Gradual agrarian reform is dangerous because it invites those it harms to encourage the military toward *coups d'état* that will frustrate the process of reform; because it allows the financial oligarchy to take over the reform machinery, to convert it into a source of income and power, and thus pervert it. Also such agrarian reform would not exert the influence that it should on the process of industrialization, since the resulting market would emerge so slowly that its effects on the development of industry would hardly be felt.

Agrarian reform should be rapid; its results should be felt immediately in the economy. This would deprive its enemies of time to marshal their opposition or to take over its machinery, and it would, moreover, spark an immediate effort to end the inhuman conditions under which the Sub-Americans—the peasants and Indians—live.

What are the obstacles to agrarian reform? On the one hand, the threat that the attempt to achieve it will trigger military coups. On the other, the fear of provoking active objections from those whose

[38] Figures released by the Inter-American Development Bank, March 26, 1964.

property is expropriated. No system of national agrarian reform has succeeded, thus far, in overcoming these obstacles entirely. The military threat has been avoided in some cases, but the question of indemnifications has never found a solution that has not aroused vociferous protests.

But if a Latin American plan of agrarian reform could be established that took into account differing national realities and the variations in the degree of agricultural development from country to country, a plan that coordinated production and made use of specific methods of reform suited to local conditions, then there would be no need to consider the possibility of a continent-wide military movement against the reform. The first obstacle would be eliminated without the need to make concessions or dilute the strength of the reforms.

If this plan were financed with international public funds, by loans from some international institution, then the problem of indemnifications would be solved. They could be paid with such international public funds on condition that the payments be reinvested in the country where the lands were expropriated; thus, industrialization would receive an enormous injection of fresh local investments; the landowning oligarchy, dispersed and divided, would find itself just one more element of the capitalist industrial structure, and the oligarchs would, of necessity, have to change their mentality. The agrarian-reform process (since it must certainly be accompanied by a program of agricultural reform), in combination with the effects of the industrial development it would promote, would be sufficient not only to cover the interest on International loans, but to repay them as well. And this would be much more useful and productive in terms of development than moneys spent on technical assistance out of private international credits.

There are many voices—some well intentioned, others not—clamoring that there can be no agrarian reform until the peasants are prepared for it, and maintaining that illiterates should not be given the vote. But history contradicts them, by showing us first that it is never possible to prepare anyone to succeed his rulers because the rulers never allow it. The only such preparation history has permitted is what is achieved by the very action of taking power—committing errors in the process, perhaps, but learning by doing. The Alliance was conceived precisely to compensate for the effect of such errors. History shows further that, in Europe and the United States, the peasants had not been "prepared" when they were given land—neither were the slaves "prepared" to be free men when they were liberated, nor could most of the voters of Europe or the United States read and write when democracy was consolidated in their countries. Why should it be different for Latin America?

The example of Mexico has been cited many times as an argument against hasty agrarian reform. It is said that agrarian reform has failed in Mexico. But Mexico has achieved the greatest democratic political stability of any country in Latin America and has also progressed furthest in the process of industrialization; at this point, Mexico can talk about reforming its agrarian-reform system and assert that the rural problem is the most important problem it faces, without such statements bringing the nation to the brink of a coup or creating insoluble political problems. All this has been possible precisely because Mexico achieved an agrarian reform that, although chaotic, violent, and disorganized, created a peasant middle class and gave humane support to democracy, at the same time as it was destroying the foundations of oligarchic power. These are the very objectives that agrarian reform must attain in the rest of Latin America; the purely technical and economic objectives will come later through adaptations and reforms of the reform. The fundamental need is to create those preconditions that make possible not only the first stage of agrarian reform, but also all the reforms of the reforms that may be necessary in the future. Moreover, this capacity for self-reform—derived from the revolution—is not limited to agrarian questions. In 1961, Mexico modified its fiscal system. In 1964, a further reform was announced, since "at present, revenue from taxation of the proceeds of labor, particularly salaries, provides a greater portion of Treasury income than revenue produced by taxation of the returns on capital investment."[39]

Nowhere in all modern history (nor, I believe, in all history, for that matter) is there a single instance of an agrarian reform that was not brought about under pressure. The European agrarian reforms that followed World War I, although moderate in scope, were possible because of the disintegration of society in the coun-

[39] *Excélsior,* May 24, 1964.

tries that had lost the war; agrarian reform in India was possible, to the small extent to which it has been achieved, because the maharajahs and great landholders, who owed their existence to the system of tribute established by the British, found themselves without any support once India had won her independence; in Mexico and Bolivia, agrarian reform was attained after violent revolutions that left the forces of the oligarchies without power or the capacity to resist; in Venezuela, it came after the violent overthrow of Pérez Jiménez, when those who supported him, among them the oligarchs, became confused and lacked the courage and opportunity to defend themselves; in Japan and Taiwan, where the two most complete and effective examples of modern agrarian reform have been produced, the change was imposed by an occupying power, the United States. An outstanding expert on these reforms has observed:

Clearly, the key to successful reform in Asia is the degree to which the controlling political forces of a country are willing to support reform and their readiness to use *all* instruments of government to attain their goals. Those against whom the reforms are directed will not divest themselves of their property and of political and economic power simply because a government wrote out a decree. Besides, despite the threat of Communism, the great fears generated by the French Revolution or by the Bolshevik Revolution in 1917 are not immediately in evidence in Asia. The conclusion is inescapable: if the peasantry is to get what is promised, peaceful and democratically managed reforms are not going to fill the bill. Government coercion, whether practiced or clearly threatened, is virtually unavoidable.

It is generally supposed that the Japanese and Taiwanese reforms and the abolition of the zamindari system in India were peaceful affairs. A closer look will reveal that they were peaceful because the landlords in the first two countries knew that overt opposition would have met with drastic punishment. In India, the zamindars knew that public opinion was overwhelmingly against them; and as the British went, they went. The Taiwanese reform took place under the aegis of a military-authoritarian government.[40]

The latifundia must be viewed in their political role, as well as from the economic and social points of view. The dangerous lati-

[40] Wolf Ladejinsky, "Agrarian Reform in Asia," *Foreign Affairs* (New York), April, 1964, p. 459.

fundium is the one that is in the hands of those with an oligarchic mentality and oligarchic interests, because their possession of these lands allows them to control the entire economy of their country and paralyze its progress. These latifundia must be taken out of the hands of the oligarchs. But there do exist in Latin America, although they are few, latifundia that we could call capitalistic; that is, they are mechanized and are worked with modern business methods—and produce a high yield. These latifundia should not be broken up, for their economic efficiency justifies their continued existence and they are not elements of oligarchic power. The *latifundista* who exploits his land with capitalistic methods, has a capitalistic, not oligarchic, point of view, and in the present context of Latin America, he represents an element of progress. This characteristic of some property owners has not been particularly evident in the past, because willingly or not, they have been allied to the oligarchy. The moment that the economic power of the oligarchy is destroyed and the latifundia are taken out of the hands of the oligarchs, the capitalistic *latifundistas* will stop lending their support to the oligarchy and will reveal their true progressive character. This, of course, will not relieve the laborers on these capitalistic latifundia of the need to wage an organized fight to improve their living standards, as must those of any other capitalistic enterprise.

The name "agrarian reform" has come to be given to what heretofore was known by the less explosive term of "colonization." We see thousands of Indians sent into the jungle to cut timber and die of exhaustion, for the purpose of putting front-page headlines in the newspapers about agrarian reforms in countries whose governments we know are in the hands of the oligarchy. We must not be deceived. This sort of thing would not be true agrarian reform even if great tracts of land were distributed to the peasants. The oligarchy would retain its power and the peasants who received the land would still be controlled by the oligarchs.

In Paraguay, which has always been ruled by dictatorship, except for two or three brief intervals, twenty-five families own territory greater than the combined area of Denmark, Belgium, and Holland.[41] This alone obviates the need to explain why giving land without taking it away is not true agrarian reform.

[41]"Silent Birthday," *The Economist,* May 10, 1964.

Neither in Latin America nor in any place else where there is an attempt to reform the structure of society would anything be called reform that is limited to giving without taking. In other words, it is important to give land to the peasants, but it is more important to take land away from the oligarchs, in order to take away the political power that over the course of a century and a half has transformed Latin America from a series of viceroyalties, richer by far than the Thirteen Colonies of North America, into a series of countries that require assistance from the North to continue their development. For the only valid explanation for this regression is the political power of the landowning oligarchy.

Agrarian reform must be given priority. Without it, industrialization will be no more than a means of accentuating the divergencies between the privileged group and the submerged masses who pay for its privileges. The opinion is widely held in Latin America that whoever is progressive, of the left, and socially advanced in his thinking is an unconditional partisan of industrialization. Much more good is imputed to industrialization than actually is possible. Industrialization is only what we make of it, and until now, we have succeeded only in making it a new social parasite.

Industrialization at all costs, without parallel social reforms in other areas, only stimulates and accelerates the transformation of the agrarian oligarchy into an industrial oligarchy, and the "oligarchization" of a considerable portion of the new middle class. From this derives the emergence of dictatorial technocratic tendencies, with the possibility that methods of development will be adopted that deny liberty and frustrate justice.

Planning appears indispensable to any meaningful economic development. But planning is no panacea, as the Marxists believed for some time, and as most educated Latin Americans seem to believe today. Planning provides no immunization against the risks implicit in the sort of industrialization currently being carried out.

Until now, planning has used production as its point of departure. The result has been a growing trend toward piecework, production incentives, and increases in productivity without parallel increases in the income of the producers. It is unnecessary to dwell on the political and social perils inherent in planning based primarily on this consideration. To avoid these dangers, planning must be carried out from the point of view of consumption. Planning systems based on production have been the rule in the U.S.S.R. and its satellites with catastrophic results; they tend more and more to plan and program in terms of production.

Planning, moreover, is not per se either good or bad. Whether it is good or bad depends on who carries it out, who does the planning and programing. If the job is left to the oligarchs, it will be terrible, for it will inevitably tend to satisfy only oligarchic interests, as has been the case until now with national budgets and customs tariffs. If the planning is done by technicians, it will doubtless conduce to great efficiency, but it will also contain the seeds of anti-democratic factors. If planning is to contribute to the general well-being of society, it must be carried out on the political level—with the help of technicians, certainly, but following a political course set by the electorate. This requires a delicately balanced negotiation, an interplay of give and take, which is the fundamental element of democratic society in any of its forms.

Of course, many nations became industrialized during the nineteenth century, as did Russia in the twentieth (although the process of industrialization was well advanced in Russia by 1897, when Lenin wrote his book on *The Development of Capitalism in Russia*). Although these examples of industrialization were not well balanced, they achieved general economic progress; in a sense, by exerting pressure on one point, they exerted pressure on all the points of the economic reality of their society. Unbalanced development is still development. If one insisted on waiting for all the ideal prerequisites to develop, one might just as well wait for the Greek calends.

But this unbalanced development has been successful only in societies that possessed a democratic tradition and a large middle class. Moreover, the development was achieved in conjunction with a new technology, the invention of new machines. And even so, it imposed its share of suffering, injustice, waste of effort and even life, and did not avoid—very much to the contrary—the crises and the wars that only added to this waste. No one can prove that a balanced development process would have prevented the hardships, but one can safely say that the hardships would have been fewer and the injustice they brought much less.

As far as development is concerned, economists in general do not worry about costs that cannot be measured, the imponderables.

But politicians—at least, democratic politicians—must always have these costs uppermost in their minds. They must have sufficient faith in their own ideology to be certain that it can provide solutions that avoid suffering and prevent injustice. To achieve development on the same basis of suffering and injustice brought about by the mechanization and industrialization of the nineteenth century, one need not be democratic and revolutionary; one need merely be a comfort-loving and unimaginative conservative and limit oneself to accepting the fundamental economic "laws" as they are expounded in any college textbook, or a Communist concerned more with dogma than with human beings. But the true revolutionary (and I insist on the word "true") must know how to achieve the same, or even better, results at a much lower cost in suffering and injustice, and above all, he must be able to assure that the result is not in itself unjust, as it was in the cases of the nineteenth-century Industrial Revolution or the Soviet societies.

This conviction, then, is not enough, but it is fundamental. It is possible to develop the economy without it, but the price of the development will not be justified.

The objective is to be able one day to speak of all Latin America as Mexico's Gustavo Díaz Ordaz spoke shortly before his election to the Presidency:

Capitalization, rather than being based on the reduction of the essential consumption of the lower-income classes, should be based on the elimination of superfluous spending by the higher-income classes. Social justice is not only an objective of our economic development, but is also a means of securing it. Without a market, there can be no industry; without purchasing power among the great mass of the population, there can be no market. The greatest stimulus to investment is the maintenance of a constantly growing and expanding market.

The objective of our planning should be abundance and well-being, not restriction and poverty. We should plan with freedom for greater freedom; this can be achieved when the need prevails.

Waste and ill-advised investments must be eliminated. The scarcity of our financial resources imposes upon us the obligation of rigorous planning of public and private investments; both are resources [of the country]. Those resources left over after the basic needs of consumption have been satisfied should not end up in the hands of those who by hoarding or conspicuous consumption will not put them to productive use.[42]

This seems so elementary, so obvious, so clear and simple! But in order to be able to enunciate such a policy, Mexico had to undergo a revolution. And outside of those few Latin American countries that have had their revolution, these phrases would be utopian or subversive.

The desire to be able to speak phrases like these and *to make them become reality*—something so modest and so simple—can move the masses.

This is what we have forgotten.

[42] Speech by Gustavo Díaz Ordaz, *Excélsior,* March 2, 1964.

IV

MEMORANDUM FOR AMNESIACS

Recapitulation

IT WOULD appear unnecessary to add anything to what has already been said. But self-induced amnesia is so widespread, in both the United States and Latin America, that it will pay to drive the nail home once more.

Let us recapitulate: Latin America is retarded, far from being industrialized, with a submerged mass of inhabitants whose life becomes worse by the day, because Latin American society is an oligarchic society in which the great landowners retain a *de facto* grip on political power and the economy. The middle class and the more urbanized sector of the working class wanted a change a generation ago, but the dictatorships then blocked them, and the United States did not accept the idea of social change. Twenty or thirty years ago, the Alliance could have counted on the middle class to transform Latin American society. Today, the Alliance has not succeeded in attracting the active, sincere support of the middle class, while the working class's living conditions have already improved so much that it gives the Alliance only halfhearted support. Both these social groups are afraid to meddle with the structure of society. The middle class today tends to seek efficiency and development by methods it considers the most expeditious—capitalization through overexploitation and even further reduction in consumption by the masses. In this process, the middle class is supported by the technocrats and the young military men, because none of these three groups will be overexploited in the process, nor will their rate of consumption be reduced. Rather, they hope to form a part of the new oligarchy.

This hope separates the middle class and its allies from the land-owning oligarchy and, at the same time, separates them also from the working class, who see their present position threatened by the desire for Soviet-type capitalization.

In order to distract the attention of the intermediate social groups from their anxiety and frustration, the oligarchy becomes more and more "nationalistic," more anti-Yankee, in its behavior, and, by so doing, attracts the support of Castroites and Communists. These two movements are confident that if the middle class, the young military men, and the technocrats gain power and initiate paternal-istic reforms from above, they will have to seek Communist sup-port to organize the masses and to force them to accept, and even to approve, the overexploitation that would follow.

We conclude from all this that the interests of the submerged masses of Latin America and the national interests of the United States coincide. There is no one else with whom either of the two can make common cause. One other sector is now vacillating on the side of the middle class—i.e., the organized working class. But as soon as the organized workers realize that the middle class pro-poses a system of capitalization at their expense, they will see that their true interests are the same as those of the submerged masses.

When this happens, we will be confronted with the seeming para-dox of the most capitalistic and most democratic nation of the world allying itself, through self-interest, with the laborers, the peas-ants, and the most abandoned and miserable groups in Latin Amer-ica. And we will be faced with the further paradox that their common interest is to make a revolution that will destroy the land-holding oligarchy as such, will wrest its political power from the oligarchy (which is why it is essential to take away its lands), and will create the conditions out of which can be built a stable democ-racy, a modern, open capitalistic system, and a society free of sub-merged masses.

An alliance of this sort—between the United States, on the one hand, and the working class and submerged masses of Latin Amer-ica, on the other—not only could destroy the power of the landowning oligarchy, but also would remove the temptation to promote development by "efficient" methods (that is, Soviet and totalitarian methods) and would force the middle class and even the technocrats to adopt democratic solutions, as the only means of gaining a position in the society that would replace the oligarchic society. The young military men would, in this context, exercise a moderating effect within the armed forces, for their interests would be more attuned to a capitalistic society based on reform than to the old creaking and obtuse ruling cadres.

We can see that, on the one hand, the dangers are grave and imminent, while on the other, the solutions are obvious and free of great risk. For who would consider it risky to appeal to the masses to create a capitalistic society? Do not forget that all capitalistic societies now in existence were created by the masses, and by masses that were just as submerged as those of Latin America today.

Who will mobilize these masses? The organized sector of the working class, part of the middle class, even groups of students, intellectuals, and professionals, if we know how to rouse them to a consciousness of their interests and an understanding of the fact that these coincide with the interests of the submerged masses.

From all this, we can derive one policy, for North Americans and Latin Americans alike.

The existence of the United States (apart from whatever its policy may be) represents a revolutionary force for change in Latin America, which explains, to some degree, the phenomenon of anti-Yankeeism. Since the United States has, at times unconsciously and in spite of itself, this function of being a revolutionary catalyst, it makes sense to talk about the country and to try to talk to it.

Since it is by no means certain that self-induced amnesia will not blur the outlines of the reasoning expressed in these pages, I am going to set down a few conclusions, for the use of Latin American coffee-table strategists and North American cocktail-party pundits, among whom, I am sure, there are a few diplomats, economists, union leaders, students, intellectuals, and politicians.

Of course, I am not terribly optimistic. In the process of noting down my conclusions, I am reminded of the proverb that says: "Don't give me advice—I know how to make my own mistakes."

Conclusions for North Americans

North Americans find themselves caught between the oligarchs and the people. They must choose sides. They should reconcile themselves to playing in Latin America the revolutionary role already indicated. And not even if such keen minds as those of Barry Goldwater, the head of the United Fruit Company, and the Grand Dragon of the Ku Klux Klan joined in drafting Washington's Latin American policy could they possibly change the fact that the mere existence of the United States functions as a revolutionary force in Latin America.

If this is so, the logical and sensible course for Washington is to see that the revolution is not made *against* the United States, or with the United States as a bystander, but takes place *with* the United States.

For this reason, the United States should adopt a policy in opposition to the interests of the landowning oligarchy, the conventional armed services, and those U.S. elements who support either. To do so, it should first deprive Fidel Castro of his role as the principal force in determining Washington's Latin American policy.

The national security and prosperity of the United States—which, logically, must be the guideposts of its international policy—does not gain anything from the maintenance of the social and political *status quo* in Latin America. On the contrary, much can be lost. They can benefit only from a popular revolution that establishes democratic regimes, creates a rural middle class, develops a modern capitalistic system, and makes the great mass of the people bourgeois.

It is not the Latin Americans' job to see that this point of view is adopted in the United States. This is up to the North Americans themselves. The most that we in Latin America can do is to point out the present reality, free of myths and prejudices, and to indicate a few ways by which the United States can help change this reality.

The United States should put an end, radically and finally, to all assistance to Latin America that is channeled through the various governments and governmental agencies, and should continue, and even increase, only the assistance that goes directly to the people or their organizations (cooperatives, unions, universities, etc.).

In the course of the polemic between high-level officials in the United States and Great Britain over trade with the Communist bloc, the British have said that a fat, satisfied Communist is less aggressive than a lean and hungry one. To this Secretary of State Rusk replied:

> The principal problem we see is that we cannot guarantee that the Communists will use the resources that are available to them to make themselves comfortable and fat. They may keep themselves lean and use the resources available to them for armaments, and for the support of subversive activities in other countries. . . .[1]

But even if there is no way to be certain that the Communists eat what is served them, there are ways to be certain that the oligarchs of Latin America do *not* use what they are given to fatten their people, but rather use it to strengthen their regimes and to pay lower taxes. The problem of the Alliance is the same as that of those who want to trade with the Communists—how to assure that it will be used to make the people fat? In both cases, everything indicates that the people are not getting any fatter. But while this fact militates against trade with the Communists, it does not work equally to prevent Alliance aid from going to the oligarchic governments of Latin America. There is no reason to suppose that the consequences in the case of Latin America will be any different from those that the United States seeks to avoid in the case of Communist trade.

Someone may say at this point that the United States, at the time in its history when it felt it necessary to have recourse to force in order to remove the obstacles to its development, did not constantly ask for money from other countries, as the Latin Americans do today. That is true, and precisely for that reason, one of the objectives of this book is to point out the need for the United States to end all aid to Latin American governments, or at the very least, all aid whose purpose is not to maintain a minimum of economic stability, which coincides with the United States' own economic interests, but rather to assist the social development of Latin America. Out of the total of the funds earmarked for social assistance, the people actually share in only a minimal portion. The exact amount is im-

[1] *The Washington Post,* March 22, 1964, p. E4.

possible to calculate, but it can be no more than 20 to 25 per cent of the total. The rest stays with the oligarchs. Only one who is quite ignorant of history could believe that the oligarchs can be forced to effect necessary reforms by a simple warning that all such aid will be cut off if they do not. Until twenty or twenty-five years ago, the Latin American oligarchy had not received any aid at all and still did not renounce its privileges. Today the oligarchy would raise a deafening howl if aid were taken away, it would become still more rabidly and negatively nationalistic, possibly it would even nationalize some foreign companies, but it would not on this account renounce any of its privileges.

Cutting off or blocking aid can work against democratic governments, which must bear in mind the movements of public opinion. But these tactics have not worked, and there is no reason to suppose that they will in the future, against oligarchic governments which could not care less about the people's welfare.

These methods are impossible to utilize because there are too many vested interests, too many imaginative bureaucrats, too much fear of what might happen, and above all, fear that the oligarchic governments might seek aid from the U.S.S.R. (which to me personally would appear excellent and commendable and, ultimately, beneficial to both Washington and the Latin American people). But since such a radical switch is not in the offing, the United States should at least try to reduce government-to-government aid as much as possible and to increase direct aid to the people quickly and substantially.

By the same token, all assistance to Latin American armies should be cut off, and the U.S. military missions should return to Washington immediately.

This will not happen either, and probably no one will come any closer to a realization of the need for it. Nonetheless, need there is, urgent need, and for that reason we must talk about it.

The armies of Latin America serve absolutely no function. As they exist today, they could not offer the slightest reassurance in the case of aggression from outside the continent. During the Cuban crisis of 1962, in all of Latin America there was not one single plan for the evacuation of one single capital. Neither are the armies of any use for police operations—as was evident in Venezuela and Colombia and in Argentina in June, 1964. They serve only to reinforce the occupation of their own countries by the oligarchies and to flatter the United States military missions into thinking that they are more powerful than the White House and the Department of State combined. Since no prospect exists that the White House and the Department of State will be able to override the U.S. military men detached to Latin America (as was proved again in Santo Domingo in the spring of 1965), the United States will have to expect that when the Latin Americans recognize this fact, they will compensate for this inconvenience by the speed of their action against it. Washington and North American public opinion should, therefore, approve the actions of a really democratic government (or one with sincere intentions of establishing a democracy) that, when it takes power, distributes land to the peasants within twenty-four or forty-eight hours and dismisses all the generals or else sends them off as military attachés to Iceland, Thailand, and Mauritania. Moreover, Washington should feel relief at such speedy action, for it will spare the United States from the embarrassment (which would also, at times, be dangerous and would, in all cases, be damaging to U.S. prestige) of seeing its military mission devote itself systematically (and often, I suspect, without orders, through a sort of Pavlovian reaction by the members of the mission) to undermining what the Embassy and the technical-aid mission are trying to do in support of a democratic government.

In fact, to prevent such a situation from arising—since the complexities of domestic politics prevent Washington itself from scotching such a development—the United States Government should offer all the facilities at its disposal to expedite the travels of high Latin American military officers to polar or desert areas. Simultaneously, it should take steps to provide credits, machinery, fertilizer, seeds, etc., within a few hours, to any democratic government starting to distribute land.

By suspending assistance to governments and armies and by recalling its technicians and military advisers, the United States would create the optimum conditions for the successful and effective functioning of the Alliance for Progress. But these optimum conditions will not be created, for the simple reason that, in the United States, there is neither an awareness of the need for them, nor, probably, the objective possibility of creating them.

Consequently, we must realize that the Alliance will have to face up to the bureaucrats and certain U.S. military men, as well as to the Latin American oligarchies. If it succeeds, the Alliance will have contributed not only to progress in Latin America, but also, indirectly, to the development of the United States.

From now on, we must realize (and the North Americans must realize it, too) that, by a political paradox, the United States is compelled to aid at the same time, but by differing methods, the oligarchies and their armies, as well as the forces which seek to destroy the oligarchies and to return the armies to their barracks.

There is a plus factor here, for until a short while ago—until Kennedy—only the oligarchies and the armies were receiving assistance. Now the people are being helped also, and they will have to be helped much more.

I do not know if this nonsense of spending with both hands in order not to wound the sensibilities of some high officials and generals, or not to demand a bit of imagination from them, is the product of the "affluent society" or of the "waste-makers." Probably, it is a combination of both. Be this as it may, it is fundamentally a problem for the United States, since it must pay for its own waste and for the consequences of its own mistakes.

For us in Latin America, the matter reduces itself to the knowledge that the oligarchy will be a little richer and the armies a little more corrupt and that, correspondingly, our work will be made easier because of this corruption and more difficult because of this wealth.

Such is life. Our consolation is that, for once, the money is not coming from our pockets.

No one should think that, whatever Washington does, the feeling of distrust on the part of Latin Americans toward the United States will disappear. It is based not on anything concrete and recent, but on recollections, general attitudes, differences in ways of life, and old wounds. The change will come, along with the basic transformation of Latin American society, when this changed society—and precisely because it *has* changed—no longer needs to take refuge in the past nor to have recourse to scapegoats.

Furthermore, the United States should realize that it will always be the scapegoat for Latin America, at least until a substitute scapegoat is found. Such a substitute is readily at hand: the oligarchy, which has the advantage of being a real goat, evil-smelling and rest in history books. And by abandoning its policy of "selling" itself, the United States will have achieved the objective that it has never been able to reach before: to leave the past in the past.

What does it mean to be a friend of the United States, supposing that it does mean something? Is it to support the international policy of the United States, for example, while at the same time expropriating U.S. businesses that do not obey the law? Or does it mean allowing these businesses to flout the law, while, at the same time, flirting with Castro and the neutralists? Or does Washington want to have its cake and eat it too: support for its foreign policy and a hands-off policy toward U.S. business? Then, what will happen to a democratic government that supports Washington in the United Nations, does not expropriate anything, and finds itself faced with a great and powerful U.S. business enterprise which prefers to negotiate with Communist-dominated labor unions (because they are less demanding) rather than with free unions, and which thus strengthens the Communists' power? The question is not hypothetical; it reflects a reality all too well known at various times and in various countries during the last twenty years.

The United States' anti-Communist policy in Latin America seems like that of a physician who injects a patient with a serum in the hope of stimulating the production of antibodies in the secondary fluids—the saliva and the gastric juices—rather than in the blood. What can it matter that the activists, the *bourgeoisie,* even the labor leaders, are anti-Communists? It is the people who should be immunized against Communist propaganda, because the people would be the first victims of a Communist system, and because the people are the only social force that can give the Communists a real victory. However, the oligarchy has so scorned and forgotten the people that its scorn has infected the myopic anti-Communists, who are more worried about three Communist professors in a university than about fifty Communist organizers among the peasants.

Venezuela, the country that has achieved the most radical social transformation in all of Latin America, has an "image" outside its borders of being a reactionary country, simply because its government adopts energetic measures (applied more by the people than by the so-called forces of public order) against Castroites and Communists and because it assumes, in its foreign policy, its own position of defense against Castroite Cuba. This image is the product

dirty, and with much to atone for. For reasons of its pre
no other, the United States should support the moveme
the oligarchy.

The irrationality and, at the same time, the depth
Yankee feeling can be seen in a personal anecdote:

Scene: A class in a political-education school in Santo I
I am explaining the method whereby, through the techi
emulation, norms of production are increased.

The students agree, and one comments: "The same thii
pened in Trujillo's sugar mills."

I add: "And it also happened in Soviet factories under the
regime." My statement produces a sudden silence. This is tl
portune moment to get to the bottom of the prejudices of the

"Why is it that what you condemn in the case of Trujillo y
not condemn in the case of Stalin?" I ask. "If the system of en
tion is bad in the Dominican Republic, it is just as bad in the S
Union. But whenever the Soviet Union is criticized, even tho
you are not Communists, you become impervious to reason
deny the facts. Why?"

One student—whom I know personally and who has fought
Communists with his fists on several occasions in defense of I
democratic party—explains: "Because the United States helpe
Trujillo."

"So, if your girl deceives you, will you ask to be castrated?"

The image had the desired shock effect, and the discussion became a more generally political one, in which we could analyze
their prejudices and the elements of truth that had given rise to
them—since the United States did, in fact, aid Trujillo.

To me, this anecdote seems useful to explain the constant and
inexorable reactions of politically oriented Latin Americans toward
the United States, including those with the most demagogic intentions. And at the root of these reactions there is always an undeniable truth: the past policy of the United States in Latin America.

If the Alliance—or any other U.S. plan—attempts to "sell" the
United States to the Latin Americans, it will succeed only in ag-
gravating resentments and reviving old memories. Not until the
Alliance becomes a multilateral (or, preferably, supranational)
plan will it cease to awaken distrust and resentment. The past relations of the United States with Latin America will then be laid to

not only of the campaign of Castro and the Communists in Latin America, but also of the inability of journalists and commentators to believe that, in the social area, an anti-Castro government can be as radical as Castro, albeit by other means. The false equation *anti-Castroite = conservative* has damaged Venezuela and damages all true anti-Communists, that is, all the enemies of the oligarchy. The European and U.S. journalists who after the rise of Castro became experts overnight on Latin American affairs are as much responsible—or more so—for this mental confusion as is Communist propaganda.

And, for example, they are also responsible for the sympathy felt toward Goulart (before he fled his country without a fight) because they referred to him as a "leftist," a term that has prestige in Latin America. It would be well for these writers to realize that by applying the term "leftist" to Communists, Castroites, and demagogues, they are doing them a great favor, and distorting the truth into the bargain. The leftists seek more freedom and greater social justice; the Communists, Castroites, and demagogues neither want nor give these things.

To soothe U.S. public opinion, accustomed as it is to thinking of "leftists" as Communists, U.S. writers dwell on anti-Yankeeism in Latin America.

When U.S. politicians and commentators discuss internal, and even world policy, they always have their feet firmly on the ground; they know that they are dealing fundamentally with questions of power. But when they start talking about Latin America, they turn to a sort of rosy sentimentalism, and instead of thinking in terms of power, employ phrases fit for novice missionaries. I do not know if it is a guilty conscience about the past or an excessive fondness for the picturesque that causes this amnesia about fundamental concepts. Whatever its cause, when one talks about Latin America with a North American, it is necessary to remind him of basic principles before a sensible discussion can begin.

As far as feelings of guilt are concerned, certainly the United States has cause for them (one can invoke Texas, California, Veracruz, Nicaragua, Panama, Santo Domingo, etc.) but Latin America has even greater cause; one can invoke the names of almost all the political parties and almost all the Presidents of the twenty Latin American countries, who over a century and a half have done more harm to their own people than all the depredations of the United States combined.

The United States seized Texas—that is true and it is not commendable. But consider what Santa Anna was doing there at the same time. The United States has occupied Santo Domingo—most recently with deplorable results. But what about General Melgarejo's occupation of Bolivia in 1864? And if the wetbacks have been treated badly on U.S. farms, how are the Ecuadorian plantation workers treated by their bosses? In the last analysis, it has been the Latin Americans who have done the most harm to Latin Americans.

If one were to give advice to the United States, it would be to stop feeling guilty about its relations with Latin America, because this creates a false basis, and also because the Latin Americans, very prudently, do not put much faith in the practical effects of this guilt feeling. But the North Americans—and, consequently, their politics, too—are as they are; no one can change their puritanism except themselves. It is not my job, nor is it the job of any other Latin American, however much we may wonder at the fact that in the one country in the world where it is possible to be an epicurean, there is less epicureanism than anywhere else. Let them have their puritanism. If we wish to deal with the United States, we Latin Americans must realize that we shall encounter a mixture of the healthy cynicism which must regulate all international relations—as long as nations remain—and of the morbid sense of guilt which characterizes North American policy. If we realize this, we can stop being surprised by a good many perfectly predictable phenomena and can end our hypocritical complaints that the North Americans are as they are.

The feeling of guilt has a disastrous effect in two respects: On the one hand, it makes North Americans paternalistic, so they do a job the Latin Americans should do for themselves—North Americans build hospitals, provide milk for children, etc., all good things, but Latin Americans should do them on their own. On the other hand—and this is more serious—the feeling of guilt makes it difficult to examine clearly whether the cynicism of U.S. foreign policy is well founded. In the case of Latin America, this cynicism has been, until now (because of shortsightedness, prejudice, acceptance of clichés, and an ignorance of the facts), a source of catastrophic errors. At best, the cynics have identified the interests of the United

States with the myth of the peaceful revolution. But this supposed harmony of interests has always worked to the disadvantage of the United States. These interests would have been much better served if the cynics had been clear-eyed enough to see that, in Latin America, the national interest (and even the interests of North American businessmen and the military) coincides, in reality, not with the interests of the oligarchs, the military, and the guardians of public order, but with the interests of the submerged masses.

I was once asked what the United States could do in Latin America to encourage democracy. The United States finds itself at a disadvantage vis-à-vis Moscow, for the Soviets have at their service the forces of the several Communist parties, whereas Washington has nothing but the USIA, which is worse than nothing; it is, in fact, a negative element, whose only effect is to make the Yankees hated because of its never-ending praise of life in the United States.

The Communists offer a theory—Communism—with its dreams and illusions, and they play on the people's prejudices. What can the United States offer?

The answer, which should not be surprising, even coming from one who considers himself a socialist, is:

The United States should offer what it has—its capitalism. It should make capitalist propaganda. Not free-enterprise, United-Fruit-Company, Standard-Oil propaganda, but capitalist propaganda. And this program would be successful, because what Latin America wants, what anyone wants who lives under a feudal system, is capitalism. People in the United States act as though they are ashamed of living under capitalism, in a world in which there are nothing but capitalist systems—of which the United States version is the least onerous and the most susceptible of being changed and replaced.

The Alliance, as I have already said, was the means of painlessly effecting the transition from Latin American feudalism to capitalism. The capitalists of Latin America, rude, cowardly, brutalized by their alliance with the oligarchy, did not know enough to see that. But the transition remains necessary and inevitable. We are moving either toward a democratic capitalism or a totalitarian capitalism. If the capitalists do not see that (and U.S. capitalists are as blind in this respect as their Latin American colleagues), the people do. It is logical, therefore, for the capitalists to be helped and help in making the transition.

Conclusions for Latin Americans

The Latin American who is not a member of the oligarchy or one of its servants finds himself caught between his prejudices (that is, disguised forms of fear) and the revolution. His situation is paradoxical, for the fear of change will lead to the actualization of all the evils that produce the fear. And the need for revolution, which also terrifies him, can lead to the avoidance of the things that make him afraid. But the word "can" is conditional. The condition arises from the fact that only by choosing the revolution will the Latin American be freed from his fears and prejudices.

The Latin Americans have already achieved the first part of this liberation, or rather, it has been achieved for them.

We must accept this as unquestionable, albeit humiliating: It was the United States, and more specifically the Kennedy Administration, that destroyed the taboo that protected the oligarchy. No Latin American popular leader, leftist or socialist, ever dared to talk about the oligarchy, or about the need for agrarian reform and revolution in the energetic terms employed by Kennedy and his colleagues of the Alliance.

Only by recognizing this fact can we understand that the destruction of a taboo is not enough, that it is necessary to go on to the destruction of the very thing the taboo protected—in this case, the oligarchy.

And if we remember that the first part of the task—perhaps the most difficult part, since it entails a change in ways of thought—was offered to us on a silver platter by "Yankee imperialism," then, if only out of pride, we may perhaps make up our minds to begin the second stage—to undermine, chip away at, and finally overthrow the oligarchy.

The Latin American is very realistic as far as his interests are concerned and very sentimental about the interests of others (through a sentimentalism which is another way of being realistic, since it is intended as a means of blunting the effect of these alien interests). This game must end, for it leads only up blind alleys filled with fogs of rhetoric that make it impossible to be sure what are principles, what are sentiments dressed up as principles, what is pragmatism disguised as idealism, and what is simple and direct realism.

The Latin American who wants to alter his society must be a realist. This means that he must be willing for other countries— especially the United States—to treat him with the same realism with which he should treat the United States. He must know that sentimental reproaches and grand pronouncements about principles mean nothing in international politics, and that these principles mean nothing on any plane of politics if they are not supported by interests, that is, by force.

Instead of complaining every time a U.S. company tries to secure advantages and privileges, instead of blaming U.S. military missions for *coups d'état,* the reform-minded Latin American should realistically anticipate that the military missions will try to undermine anti-oligarchic democracy, that foreign business enterprises will try to secure advantages, and realistically supporting his principles, must be willing to prevent the granting of special advantages and the success of military revolt. And if to accomplish this, he must pragmatically advise a U.S. official to take an extended vacation in the United States or remind a foreign company that there are laws in effect in his country, he should do so as a matter of course, as simple facts of daily life, for such they are, and not opportunities to show off in the parliament.

Francisco Miró Quesada, a Peruvian philosopher of that group of oligarchs which produces technical experts, has dared to write:

> Because man was thought of as a theoretical concept, he now arises as a threatening reality. We find ourselves with the man of the community and the man of conflict, with the man of the city slum and the man of the peasant's hovel, with men who demand and threaten, here, there, beside us, and face to face.[2]

To me, this passage reveals the enormous effrontery that allows Latin American intellectuals the luxury of thinking of man as a theoretical idea—even as an idea that serves to earn them their bread, their fame, and the rostrum from which they employ it as a subject for their books and lectures—and nothing more than an

[2] Francisco Miró Quesada, *La ideología de Acción Popular* (Lima, 1963).

idea. And suddenly, when the idea assumes human form and flesh-and-blood force, then they find that it is a "threatening reality."

But it appears to me an entirely just reality and this is, to a certain extent, a consolation. We should learn to think of this forgotten man, this brutalized creature of the slums, this untutored peasant, not as a threatening reality but rather as a hope, as the only hope remaining by which Latin America society can become a modern functioning society, a society not of angels, not of perfect beings, but a nation of common men, just as disagreeable as all men, but with full stomachs and a certain ability to select their own leaders.

It will not be easy to accustom ourselves to this—to viewing as a hope those we have usually regarded as a threat. But unless we do, there would be no purpose in going to the people, to the "threat," unless we did so as one approaches a bomb to remove its fuse or detonator. And if we do not remove it in this case, we will not be able to alter our society before the explosion comes.

Apart from prejudices and propaganda, there is something else that justifies and explains the Latin Americans' distrust of free enterprise. By definition, free enterprise should not be able to be adapted or subjected to any regime not economically libertarian. Very well, the oligarchic regime is, as a matter of fact (although the fact is disguised) a controlled regime, and yet free enterprise has always gotten along with it and defended it as an ally. If free enterprise had a mission which could have justified and established it in Latin America, it was that of supplanting the oligarchy, of fighting this uneconomic group and replacing it with a system of economic freedom. Now that free enterprise has failed even to attempt this task, there is no reason to trust in its virtues nor to regard it with special respect.

Very well, let us be frank and ask: If Latin American capitalists do not fulfill their mission, why should foreigners do it for them? Why should we expect foreign investors not to follow the example of the oligarchies of the countries in which they invest? Of course, mass exportation of profits is not good. But why should foreign investors exhibit more patriotism than the oligarchs, who always export their profits, and who often do not even bring them into their own country, but instead remit them to their Swiss bank accounts directly from the foreign market where they are earned?

If the governments do not know how to force the oligarchs to respect the law, why should they so harass the foreigners? In part—it is painful to say it—for the same reasons that the Jews were persecuted in the Middle Ages: envy, a sense of inferiority, and in order to take advantage of the relative vulnerability of the foreigner —and in part also because obsessive Communist propaganda and cheap nationalism point to the foreign investor as the principal enemy.

In this sense, Communist propaganda favors the oligarchy, which is also interested in having a steady barrage of Communist and Castroite propaganda against the United States. The only people who have not realized this fact are the businessmen themselves and the Washington diplomats.

Clichés and easy ideas have often contributed to the paralysis of Latin America, to the detours from paths of progress. For example —and experience shows this to be true, however much we may close our eyes to it of loyalty to our preconceived notions—when foreign capital is invested in our countries in accordance with their laws, it is a factor for the liberalization of society. But both what is called the extreme left and the extreme right have attacked foreign investment, not for the danger it might offer, but rather for its possible effects as a liberalizing force to create the conditions that make reform possible and necessary. Neither the extreme left nor the extreme right wants social reforms; foreign capital that respects local law is a force for progress and, thus, leads the way to social reforms. Therefore, foreign capital must be attacked. And since the real motives for the attack cannot be revealed, it is decked out in the trappings of nationalism, of anti-imperialism, or of any other cause, while in reality the attack represents only another attempt to continue to keep Latin America immobilized within the strait jacket of the anachronistic social systems still prevailing among us. The United States, Germany, Italy, Scandinavia, Canada, were industrialized with foreign as well as domestic capital. And none of them lost their independence. But in none of them were the forces of immobility stronger—as they are in our case—than the forces of change. And in none of these countries were the slogans, watchwords, and the fear of labels more powerful than the desire for progress.

But the people will never forgive the foreign investors for one thing—for continuing to be friends of the oligarchy. In this respect, they consider the foreigners more to blame than their own countrymen. Let the foreigners then take exquisite care not to appear to be friendly to the oligarchy, not to intervene in politics, to engage in business and *nothing else*. Because if they do anything else and that something else favors the oligarchy, a day will come when they will have to pay, and probably a disproportionate price. Then they will want to be defended by the government, which to do so must oppose social change, and, if it opposes that, it will harm its own national interests. . . . It would be well for foreign investors to foresee this chain of consequences and to be able to realize what risk they are running.

I know that the businessman understands less of economics than the most uneducated of his employees, and that, for this reason, he does not realize that agrarian reform, a change in social structures, and the destruction of the oligarchical society are all in his best interests. If he does not understand, so much the worse for him. It is not our job to teach him. We will have enough of a job teaching our own people; we are not tutors for foreign investors. But from now on, they should recognize that it is the law of all the nations of Latin America (an unwritten law and by that token all the more severe) that the foreign investor should not in any way assist the oligarchies. Whether the law is just or unjust is of no importance. That the investor feels it should not be so is of no importance. What is important—what will be most important for the investor—is that the people of Latin America are beginning to look on the friends of the oligarchies as their enemies. This must be well understood.

For decades, it seemed easy for us to be apocalyptical and to point out the catastrophes to follow if our proposals were not followed. They were not followed and there was no catastrophe.

It has been said that the middle classes must initiate substantial reforms lest the Russians come and do it for them, and also that, unless they reform, dollar aid will come to an end. Very few, however, seem to believe that these reforms are intrinsically good and that they are justified on the grounds of social justice or even of economic efficiency. The incentives which appeal to these middle groups appear to be much more pragmatic. But unfortunately for the Alliance, fear does not seem to be a very effective spur to action. To the people of

Latin America the cold war, in spite of Cuba, is still a remote affair between distant nations, whereas the land owned in Argentina, Colombia, or Chile is an overwhelmingly concrete reality. The future well-being of a just and efficient society is very much an affair of the future whereas tax-evasion pays immediate dividends and social prestige is something enjoyed at first hand. . . . There are many who maintain that the northern neighbour cannot afford not to give aid to her southern allies. Once this cynical thesis is accepted, noisy inaction becomes the most reasonable course and the much publicized reforms recede further into the future.[3]

We must change our ways of speech, or better, our ways of seeing and feeling things as they are. Because if we think that we can move people through fear and greed, we have a very poor notion of our compatriots. If we really look around us, we shall see that it is easier to mobilize people with justice than with greed, with freedom rather than fear. I refer to mobilization for battle, not to create a permanent collective tension as is done by totalitarian regimes.

Neither greed nor freedom, neither fear nor justice will make the oligarchs and their allies give way. It is a matter of knowing what will mobilize the people against the oligarchs. We tried to move them by greed and fear and they stayed at home. Let us try something more realistic than this puerile game of cynical amateurs manipulating the "vulgar passions." Let us try, for example, something very real, something that is often effective but seldom used in Latin America—idealism. And let us remember that true idealism makes a virtue out of necessity.

Reforms cannot be carried out at long distance. The land cannot be redistributed, the way of life of the peasants and the slum dwellers cannot be changed by remote control, through laws and administrative methods; these are all very well to assist in the process, but they are only auxiliary. Reforms must be made by flesh-and-blood men, on the land itself, in the midst of the very men whose lives are going to change and who will then be willing to risk their new life against Castroism, the militarists, and the Communists.

No one should think that he can stay at a safe distance, once the process of reform has begun. Nor should it be so, because nothing that made these reforms necessary should be safe from their

[3] Véliz, *op. cit.*, p. 22.

reach. Has anyone stopped to consider that reforms would not be
needed, that it would not be imperative to fight, to sacrifice, to risk
life, or to write books such as this, if Latin American society had
not become choked up, if something had not stopped its advance?
These reforms are not the caprices of resentful radicals or solutions
thought up by dreamers. They are intended only to allow Latin
American society to kick off the brakes, to march forward more
energetically and, in a few years, to make the advance that was
blocked for decades, even centuries. It is not the reformers who are
to blame for reforms, but rather those who made them necessary.

We must put an end, once and for all, to the complacency that
causes us constantly to feel sorry for ourselves and our situation and
to look for someone on whom to heap the blame.

A perfect example of this state of mind is found in a quotation
from the Argentine writer Ernesto Sábato: "The artist's lot is hard
to endure anywhere in the world, but here it is doubly hard, for we
must also endure the painful lot of Latin American man."[4]

What would Sábato say if he were Asian, African, or just simply
Albanian?

There is no need for exaggeration. Being Latin American is no
harder and no worse than being anything else. And the only thing
that makes the lot of Latin American man painful is the fact that
he is the perhaps only human creature who in the middle of the
twentieth century still finds himself with an opportunity of choosing
what his lot is to be. There is no doubt that this pains him, and he
puts all his energy into his pain.

Let us try to be pained less and to act more. And let us leave
the pain for a time when we have refrigerators and we can put it
inside to cool off. In the meantime, let us get going after both the
refrigerator and universal suffrage. And let us remember that one
cannot be achieved without the other.

We know what the oligarchs are like: intractable, twisted, canny,
hypocritical. Knowing this, we must shun any political dealings with
them. With the oligarchs, the same thing will happen to us as with
the Communists; we will think that we are using them while all the
time it is we ourselves who are being used.

We know what the military are like: hypocritical, capable of
swearing allegiance as they plot the "salvation of the fatherland,"

---

[4] Ernesto Sábato, *El escritor y sus fantasmas* (Buenos Aires, 1963), p. 8.

puerile in their vanity and parvenu business dealings. Let us not expect them to grab our chestnuts out of the fire. When the military turn against a dictator they once supported, they do so out of fear that the people will get to the presidential palace before them and, instead of letting the dictator leave the country with his suitcases stuffed with dollars, will throw him out the window. One must not deal with the military, for if they agree to give their help one day, it is certain that they are already thinking about who will ask their help tomorrow.

We know that the United States Government will not stop giving aid to the oligarchic governments nor will it break off its relations with their armies. We know that the U.S. diplomats and military men will never share the same objectives. Just as in Latin America, the people are the foundation of the future, so in the United States, the people can help us much more than any official agency.

Let us give up here and now the thought that, if we fail, we can blame our failure on the oligarchs, the military, or the United States. These three are facts of life, just like the fact that women become pregnant, that tobacco causes cancer, and that alcohol makes one drunk. If we wish to ignore these things, we do not belong in politics.

I believe that if one point stands out in this book, it is that the middle class has nothing to gain from its surrender to the oligarchy, because the privileges the oligarchy allows it to enjoy are only transitory and if the revolution comes—and it will come—and if it finds the middle class at the side of the oligarchy, the revolutionaries will deny that class any share in the political power it did not help to win, and its frustrations will persist.

The organized working class, or the sector of the proletariat that makes up union membership, should put an end to its acceptance of the *status quo*. The day when the technocrats and the military decide to make the revolution from above, the workers will pay the price of these experiments in paternalism, and the unions will be emasculated by the technocrats and delivered into the hands of the Communists.

The peasants, the unorganized sector of the proletariat, the forgotten urban masses, cannot take action by themselves. They can develop neither a program nor an organization unless someone organizes them and points their own needs out to them.

Who is this "someone" to be? No special group, since all social groups, as such, have turned their backs on the popular masses. But within each of these groups, there are nuclei and individuals who understand the situation, who wish to make their voices heard, who are willing to mobilize themselves in order to mobilize the people. These individuals and the masses share many interests in common—and the whole future.

That is enough talk about the people. Let us start to *make* a people.

The Alliance Is Dead . . .

The Alliance, as originally conceived, did not succeed. What is left is a bureaucratic structure, mountains of mimeographed paper, a sarcastic smile on the lips of the oligarchs, and pangs of guilt on the part of the politicians of the left who did not take advantage of the Alliance and make it theirs.

What is now called the Alliance is just another plan of assistance —no one knows to whom or why.

The Alliance for Progress is dead.

But though many battles are lost, the war may be won. The Alliance for Progress was a battle lost—not the first or the last.

Lost battles are valuable if they teach us how to win. The first Alliance, the one that is dead, will not have been useless and its hundreds of millions of dollars will not have been wasted, if from it we have learned how to win the next battle.

We know who killed the Alliance: the oligarchic governments of Latin America. We know who allowed them to kill it: the democratic left. We know who supplied the poison: the bureaucrats and technicians. And we know who would have defended it if anyone had bothered to let them know that it existed and needed defenders: the people.

Those who do not learn from history are condemned to repeat it, said Santayana. And Marx had completed this sentence in advance; when history is repeated, he said, what was a tragedy the first time will be a comedy the second time.

We cannot allow ourselves, then, the luxury of failing to draw the proper lessons from the death of the Alliance.

A great deal was said about how the Alliance was going to be what the Marshall Plan had been for Europe. Three years after the Alliance had been launched, this was carried even to the point of trying to create an organ, the CIAP, patterned distantly on the Marshall Plan's organs. Perhaps it was thought that copying the bureaucratic pattern would produce the same result. But a fundamental difference was overlooked: The European governments were capitalistic and socialistic, not oligarchic. They were vitally interested in the progress of their countries, and even the most obtuse European capitalists knew that, without progress for the whole nation, there would be no progress for themselves. The governments of Latin America want progress for their countries only so far as it can prove useful to the oligarchies, and in their actions, they seek only to benefit the oligarchies. The mechanisms of the Marshall Plan, based on cooperation between governments with a national spirit or an inter-European spirit, cannot be carried over to a plan like the Alliance, which has to take into account the existence of governments animated solely by a spirit of caste. In Europe, the Marshall Plan could operate with the governments. In Latin America, if the Alliance is to be what it was designed to be, it must operate, not merely without the governments, but against them.

I say "against" because the objective of the Alliance is to assist in the transfer of power to new hands, for without such a transfer, there can be no social change, and without social change, there can be no progress, and without progress, there can be no allies that amount to anything, nor can there be tranquillity, prosperity, markets, or valid anti-Communist action. And since the governments and the oligarchies that they represent are opposed to all genuine change, it is essential to combat these oligarchic governments to achieve the goals of the Alliance.

The old structure will inexorably topple, and there are two architects aspiring to raise a new structure. One, the Communist (technocrat-demagogue-militarist) has the plans but not the materials; the other, the democrat, has the materials through the Alliance and several models to follow, but he has not drawn up his plans. The work force, for both architects, is to be found in the people. It remains for the democrat to expedite the drafting of his plans and to attract the work force before the Communist contracts for them to construct an edifice in which this work force will be given only the cellar.

If we have learned this lesson, if Latin Americans as well as North Americans have learned it, then the dead Alliance will have left a fine legacy. And then we shall be able to shout:

. . . Long Live the Alliance!

The concept and the objectives were fine. The methods failed. The experience of this failure should prompt us to find proper methods by which to reach the objectives which failure has made no less fine.

We must form a new alliance.

The name that we give it matters little. Perhaps it does not even need a name. But it must be an alliance for the revolution which was talked about at Punta del Este, and which, at the same Punta del Este meeting, the governments of Latin America took it upon themselves to abort.

The Alliance, by putting certain goals within our reach, should have had the effect of making our final objectives more modest, and at the same time of making us more radical in our choice of methods to achieve these objectives. But by not bringing us any nearer to our goals, the Alliance had the opposite effect; it made the objectives of many people more radical, while moderating their methods. Out of this has come a widespread conformity among the social groups that were looked to as potential forces for change. We must now once more radicalize our methods and bring our goals within reach.

The Alliance was designed to achieve in a relatively short time what will come about sooner or later in any event; it tried to achieve its goals by means that did not favor the enemies of democracy.

Now it rests with us to achieve, what otherwise will come during our sons' lifetime by who knows what methods and to whose advantage we cannot foresee.

The Alliance was a defensive alliance, designed to defend us against Communism, Castroism, and dictatorships, including the dictatorship of want.

The new alliance should be offensive. It is time now for us to take the initiative. Against Communism, against dictatorship, against misery of every kind, against the essential cause of all this—the oligarchic society.

The United States Army has counterinsurgency schools. We should learn from these schools. We should learn that in South Vietnam counterinsurgency has achieved nothing. It would have been much more worthwhile to teach the South Vietnamese to organize insurrections, guerrilla operations, and terrorism in North Vietnam. By the same token, we should have learned that fighting by traditional military methods against guerrillas in Colombia, Argentina, or anywhere else is a long, tedious, costly, and often ineffective process. Castroite guerrillas in Latin America represent a reactionary insurrection. Against such a force, it is revolutionary insurrection, not counterinsurrection, that is effective. And what better insurrection could there be (an orderly, legal insurrection, but insurrection against the Establishment, all the same) than effective agrarian reform. This is what the oligarchs fear much more than Castroite guerrillas, many of whom, I suspect, the oligarchies assist financially.

Latin America has never had a utopia. It has substituted myths instead.

In order for the new alliance to be successful and, especially, in order for Latin America to change in the ways that it needs to change, it is essential that we draft a program for the future, that we decide what we want Latin America to be, that we offer a utopia. The fact that utopias are utopian is unimportant; this only increases their attractiveness and their power to move men to action.

We are not trying here to construct utopia. This is not a matter for one man or one group. It must come from the masses. For the Latin American people, perhaps the greatest utopia—and no small utopia, at that—is to be able to eat their fill and feel themselves the masters of the land they walk on.

The new alliance certainly will not provide a utopia. But it can very well—and it should—make it possible for the utopia to cease being only that and to become reality. This is its proper mission.

Please, I beg in the name of everything you most desire, no more new official agencies. No more bureaucracy. No more technicians. No more experts. No more studies. No more seminars. No more round tables. No more reports, ordinary or special. No more study trips. No more evaluations. No more inquiries. No more training of trainees to train trainees. No more symposiums. No more panels. No more regional conferences. No more investigating committees and subcommittees. No more specialists. No more tourism at the expense of the Indians or salaries paid for by the peasants, or millions of mimeographed pages (full of errors and errata), which cannot be used even to paper the shacks of the slums because when they reach them, they are already garbage.

Let the new alliance be what it wants to be or can be—modest, improvised, phantasmagoric, picturesque, devised by raving lunatics, anything, it does not matter as long as it is not a new cesspool of technicians, experts, and bureaucrats whose livers constantly require three medicines in order to function: a secretary with a discreet voice, a carpeted office, and a first-class airplane ticket.

There are a good many reasons to wish that the new alliance be poor. (We have already seen that the millions and hundreds of millions of dollars never reach the people, anyway.)

If we are to attract members of the middle class, students, intellectuals, union leaders and activists, professional people to make up the first cadres of the alliance—only the first; after that, the cadres must come from the people themselves—we must attract them for the beauty and passion of their action itself and without any other inducement.

The corruption of the oligarchic society is such that even its idealists cannot be trusted if there is money in question. They probably will not steal it, but their idealism will begin to fade, their actions will become less contagious and the people will smell the old aroma of greed and lose confidence.

In a manner of speaking—and by saying this, I know that I am exposing myself to ridicule—the new alliance should begin with a movement of puritans toward purification. The political air of Latin America is so dirty, so full of every sort of filth, that the first task is to learn to breathe clean air.

Whoever passes this first test of the poverty of the new alliance will gain in pride and faith an effectiveness that nothing else could give him. There will be plenty of time left to him, as to any other, to become corrupt, to rise or to fall, once the fundamental objectives are achieved.

All great movements have begun in this way. I doubt that the new alliance can be a great movement if we do not initiate it with purity and poverty. Let us not, however, allow ourselves the illusion that we shall thus have done with the inevitable, and even humanizing, intrigue, envy, maneuvers, and cynicism.

But there is one principal and overriding reason for the poverty of the new alliance. The alliance must be hard, and it cannot be both hard and rich. The dead alliance proves this.

The new alliance must travel on horseback or by bicycle; it must have as its secretaries students who have not yet learned spelling or schoolteachers who have forgotten it by now; it must hold its meetings in dusty local union halls, among sacks of corn in co-operative stores, in the back rooms of drugstores, in the doorways of peasants' huts.

The new alliance must not only think of the people. It must operate in the midst of the people and with the people. It must be the people.

Reports should be verbal and, if possible, short. Studies must consist of experience accumulated over long hours of work. Seminars should be held around glasses of tequila or pisco.

This does not mean Franciscanism or "ennobling" poverty. On the contrary, it means an escape from poverty. And only one who is in a situation can escape from it.

The people, who have seen so many apostles in Cadillacs, so many saviors in first-class hotels, so many protectors with bodyguards, must start to regard the people of the new alliance as their own kind. This has to be done without tricks and deceit. The new alliance must be of the people.

I am not trying to preach a romantic attitude. I do not want anyone accustomed to living well to start living poorly (or to pretend to) in order to serve the alliance. This would be demagoguery. But there are many who cannot enjoy their comforts wholeheartedly while others are suffering. They must be the yeast for the new alliance.

The ideal, an attainable ideal, would be for the new alliance, in its first preparatory stages, to depend on funds to be supplied by the people themselves. These funds would have to be spent very sparingly. Travel would have to be in third-class carriages or on muleback. It would be necessary to sleep in peasant homes and to eat what there was, for every penny spent would mean a penny's worth less of food for those who contributed it.

If all this were achieved, after the first great push—a costly process, no doubt, to be assisted by the United States and by individual and organized Latin Americans—we could justifiably feel that the alliance was taking root and was becoming something of the people.

The alliance will be a true alliance the day that the people are willing to pay for it, when they find it sufficiently useful for them to sacrifice for it a few cigarettes, a few drinks, an evening at the movies, or a ribbon for the girl friend.

Allies Without an Alliance

We have had one well-organized Alliance, with a constitution, administrators, high- and middle-level officers, technicians and experts, a surplus of studies, and a deficit of popular confidence. This Alliance found no allies.

Perhaps the time has arrived for us to try—without attempt at paradox—for allies without an alliance, for the people to collaborate, to work together to achieve common goals of mutual interest, without creating great organizations and administrative apparatuses and free of the dead weight of bureaucrats and technicians.

Out of our mistaken belief that we could force the oligarchy to make reforms, another error was born, which we still have time to correct. This consisted of wanting the Alliance to produce tangible results immediately—highways, hospitals, etc. Actually, what the Alliance should have done was dedicate one, two, or three years to giving the masses a consciousness of their potential, organizing them, and bringing them up to the surface of society—all of this through the people and popular movements of the countries involved. This initial task of giving the people the power to exert pressure was essential if the Alliance was then to enter into the area of actual achievement—once the people began to exert pressure on their governments.

If the concept of the alliance is to mean anything in the future,

I believe that we should again begin the labor of organizing the submerged masses. When these masses are raised from the depths, when they make themselves heard and their pressure felt, the new alliance will be able to offer material assistance in other activities, always on the condition that these new activities are carried out in accordance with the desires and with the participation of the no longer submerged masses. The creation of the cadres by which the masses must be mobilized, of the leaders, of the organizations of these masses is the first step. Without this first step, anything that is accomplished will benefit only the oligarchy, and although the masses may grab off a few crumbs, the oligarchy will be the ones who profit.

One result (indirect but not unimportant) of the success of the new alliance, would be a logical solution of the Cuban problem. For any really popularly based Latin American government able to say that it had achieved agrarian reform, that it had raised the masses up from the depths, that it had nothing to fear from military coups, for such a government, Castro would be only a petty tyrant off on his island. Then the Latin Americans themselves would find a way to finish off this tyranny, without the vacillation, conniving, and weakness of the oligarchic governments, who have used Castro to appease their own Castroites and to buy their complicity in the perpetuation of oligarchic society.

But we must not try to seek this result other than marginally, for if we fix it as an objective, we shall be deflected from the real purpose of our action.

On the other hand, there are results that form part of the objective itself: to keep other Latin American people from being dragged by their oligarchies to the fate suffered by the Cubans at the hands of Castro; to create the conditions by which Latin America can acquire all the vices of modern societies—and all the advantages as well—and can tackle the problems common to all twentieth-century societies and resolve them, for better or worse, by democratic means; to make it unnecessary for us to continue screaming for things—democracy, liberty, social justice—which should be as common as going to the movies. And above all, to put an end forever to colonialism in Latin America, to the system that has converted the Latin American countries into colonies of their oligarchies, occupied by the armies of these oligarchic powers.

Because with so much talk of colonialism and imperialism, it seems that we have had no time to look at how the colonies of the European powers in America have turned themselves into nations, while the people of Latin America continue under the colonialism of the great landowners.

All this probably sounds very rhetorical to those accustomed to the concreteness of diplomatic threats and extortion. But go to the country, to the poor slums, talk to the people, and you will see that for them, these phrases have real meaning.

I feel confident that these pages have made it clear that the interests of the people of the United States and those of Latin America are one and the same. Or at least, they have been for some time. It has been clearly demonstrated also that this common interest demands that it be proved in Latin America for the first time that an authentic democracy serves the cause of development better than any other method. To do so, it is necessary to overcome a number of obstacles: the power of the oligarchy, the blackmail of the ideological terrorism of Castroites and Communists, the virtual alliance of the "leftists" and the oligarchs, and the danger of a technocratic militarism which becomes more clearcut every day.

To achieve this, there is only one tool—the people, the only means no one has used so far, the only means which thus has not failed or disappointed us.

But to mobilize the people is not an easy task. There are no formulas for it. In each country, each province, each village the proper method must be found. And those to be mobilized are as numerous in the cities as in the villages.

One thing is sure; this is a task in which governments should not intervene under any circumstances. Let them continue, if they desire, with the fiction of the Alliance, while the people make this new alliance, an alliance of allies without treaties or committees.

In the United States, why has there been no effort by the labor unions, the cooperatives, the Democratic Party and even certain groups within the Republican Party, other parties (however subversive and small they may seem), or certain churches, to help the Latin Americans bring their submerged masses to the surface? And why should the same thing not be expected of certain parties in Latin America, especially from their younger members, from labor unions and various other organizations?

How can we say in advance what form this action should take? If we tried to dictate the form in advance, the movement would fail. In one case, it will be a student who will organize the peasants of his town during vacations, with the peasants then organizing others in their district. In another, it will be three schoolteachers who will establish a center to attract the youth of the region. In still another, a lawyer and two bricklayers will hold a series of meetings to denounce exploitation of tenants. In other areas, an engineer will be able to advise the peasants on how they should one day divide up this or that badly managed great hacienda in order to increase its production. And a cooperative will be able to organize short courses to train union leaders in one area, while a union in another city tries to train organizers for the cooperatives. Housewives can be organized, and students and fishermen, too, if they wish, each in the manner he chooses. What is important is that they be organized and that, out of their organization, they find the conscience and the will to govern themselves democratically.

The rest, the road that will have to be followed (sometimes calmly, sometimes with impatience, sometimes without patience) to reach this goal of democratic self-government will be something that the future will soon make clear to us and that present subjects and those aspiring to be future citizens will have to decide on as they can. What is important is that, when they decide, they find that those who taught them to organize are disposed to support them and that the people of the United States, and of the few Latin American countries that are already half-democratic, are disposed to bring effective pressure on their governments to support them.

We can be sure that, whatever method they adopt to further their struggle, it will be better than the brutal militarism, the deaf oligarchic corruption, or the nationalistic demagoguery of Castroites and Communists, who are incapable of mobilizing the people but capable of paralyzing them. Whatever the people do—however bad it may be—will always be better, much better, than the present, with its blatant corruption, its cowardly and boastful conformism, and the prospects of an alliance between capitalist technocrats and Communist organizers.

Besides, there is no reason to assume that the people must act badly. Whenever we speak of the people, we see a man with a knife in his teeth. Actually, it is our ability to form, educate, organize, and orient the people speedily, by forced marches, that will determine what they do. And what they do, even if it is worse than we hoped, will be better, I repeat, than the best that we have today. For the tomorrow that the people create can be improved, whereas the present, created by the oligarchy, can only become worse.

To separate ourselves from the rottenness of present-day Latin American society should in itself be a reason for taking action and a source of pleasure in this action.

Let us move to concrete examples.

In the initial period of our action, the entire effort should be devoted to preparing mobilizers and organizers of peasants, workers, and students, and afterward to supplying them with essential tools, such as material for political education, libraries, study and discussion centers, propaganda material, perhaps means of transportation for organizers. During this stage, popular assistance from the United States will be indispensable.

As soon as these first cadres begin to perform and to organize, it will be the Latin Americans themselves who will contribute their own aid. This is possible precisely because until now they have never done so before, and now it is time for the man in the street to be permitted the pride of doing things for himself.

All these people of the masses discovering for the first time that politics can be something for them and something clean, because they all at once made it clean (although in time they will learn how to dirty it), all these people organized with the vision, the enthusiasm, the dynamism of something new, such as what it is like to form part of a group and to decide, to talk, to have to think, to study problems, and to propose solutions, and to become emotional and impassioned and to come to blows—all these people with these new experiences will provide a tremendous force for change that will endure over a period of years. This force will be able to rejuvenate the populist movements and the unions and impose on them a degree of radicalization of method, of renewal of leadership groups, or else they will create new action groups where none exist or where they are thoroughly fossilized.

Of course, in a few years, these masses will acquire the conformism, the subterfuges, and the dirtiness of those who preceded them in the illusion of being able to change society. But in those years— if the concept of the Kennedy Alliance has in fact created some real possibilities of change—the masses can work miracles, can give the first push to the process of transformation by destroying the fundamental obstacle to change. Only a few years, I repeat. Years that we must utilize, unless we wish to become the scapegoats for our own incompetence. If we do not take advantage of these years, demagogues will appear who will know how to take advantage of them and who will end up, they and their techniques, in the arms of the Communists. And then, while the oligarchs are in Europe, enjoying their Swiss bank accounts, what will we be able to do for our people? Nothing. Nor for ourselves. Not even blush when we look at ourselves in a mirror.

In the second stage, when outside aid would be unnecessary, or at least not indispensable, our U.S. allies will have another task: to exert pressure on their government while at the same time convincing public opinion that the Pentagon should keep quiet when it sees popular pressure replacing the oligarchy in the seat of political power, taking the oligarchy's land and distributing it to the peasants, and sending the oligarchy's generals on extended vacations. Then at once ships will begin to arrive in Latin American ports loaded with tractors, seeds, fertilizers, and even a technician or two as ballast.

And when you say ships, say also credits and food and all the things that now are squandered under the "administration" of the oligarchic governments. The popular forces must know that their U.S. allies can assure them that when they take power, they will have the means available of making social reforms that will be as radical as they are truly democratic. In other words, that they then revive the multinational, supranational, continental, political agency that Kennedy originally conceived the Alliance for Progress would be.

Technicians will be needed then, of course. But they must be a special kind, capable of viewing their action, their counsel, their evaluations in a political light, as a political rather than a technical function. These experts will have to be trained, for very few exist today. While Latin America is training organizers, agitators, propagandists, political educators—the seedbed of leadership for the near future—the United States will have to begin training politicized experts—the only kind that can be really useful to the Latin American revolution. The universities can help in this, in both North and South America, the former preparing politicized technicians (including no less politicized Latin American technicians) and the latter providing facilities for the organization of people's universities in unions, cooperatives, and country towns.

I do not know if all this can be done without some kind of coordination. I fear that it will be essential, but an effort should be made to keep it to the barest minimum of bureaucracy and administrative ramifications.

This should be done, in any case, without pay, with the people contributing their time. The Peace Corps uses this system to remedy local faults. Perhaps volunteers could be found—even for administrative coordination, alas—to apply large-scale remedies to large-scale faults.

But do not think that a few unions or one democratic committee or one university is going to advance this task by sending a few representatives who know nothing of Latin America and will meet the peasants in the lobby of the local Hilton Hotel and begin to talk in terms of hundreds of thousands of dollars.

What is involved is a very personal labor, begun by a few Latin Americans and North Americans who know each other and have much in common. It must be enlarged and rapidly put out roots without, in the process, losing its personal tone, the feeling of achievement each participant has. In a way, this labor will help give meaning to the lives of those engaged in it, as did the workers' movements in Europe and the United States over several generations.

Basically, this alliance of allies without a treaty will develop not only leaders, organizers, future governors, and above all, the future governed, but also the developers themselves—and perhaps also a few future diplomats and policy-makers who will shape United States policy toward Latin America and Latin American policy toward the United States—on both sides, a policy as necessary as it is now nonexistent.

Is it madness to believe that all this is possible? Whoever knows the forgotten people of Latin America knows that they have been waiting for decades for someone to speak to them and that until now they have heard only what has been said to distinguished Latin Americans. But in any case, madness or not, it is all that is left to try.

Every policy that has been proposed has, as far as I know, had more or less catastrophic results. It is senseless, therefore, to say that all this is vague, utopian, and unrealistic. On the contrary, to go to the people and to fight alongside them is a very concrete act, and certainly feasible; it has been done successfully elsewhere and in Latin America, as well. When every other alternative has been tried without success, to adopt the only one remaining is realism itself.

But the shameful fact remains that we have decided—if we do decide—to go to the people only as a last resort, when there is nothing else left to be tried.

But I suspect that all the steps that history takes forward it takes in order to leave behind just such shame as this.

Let us only hope that it disturbs us sufficiently to make us hasten to free ourselves from our shame.

INDEX